D1505340

THE
POWER
OF
BELIEVING

STERLING W. SILL

THE POWER OF BELIEVING

STERLING W. SILL

BOOKCRAFT
Salt Lake City, Utah
1968

First Printing, 1968

Lithographed by
Publishers Press

Salt Lake City, Utah
United States of America

Foreword

In accepting the 1968 Republican Presidential nomination, Richard Nixon said that the one who was elected President this year would face greater challenges than those which confronted Washington or Lincoln. At no time in our history have more vital considerations been hanging in the balance than now, yet we may not be doing very well in solving our problems. Among other things, our nation now faces the herculean task of maintaining peace abroad and restoring order and Christian righteousness at home.

Every individual citizen is involved in the general problems. No one lives unto himself alone. No one can sing an oratorio by himself, and no one can have some one else live his life for him. Like the President, each of us must carry his own share of the general responsibility. America and Americans have a divine appointment to maintain our particular section of the world as a citadel of freedom, the home base of righteousness, and the seat of world progress and leadership. We must do whatever is necessary to keep human dignity, understanding and fairness alive in the world. The best way to accomplish our goals is to make the best and the most of our own lives, maintaining a strong hold on our Christian faith with a firm belief in, and an effective practice of, the doctrines of the Christian religion.

Shakespeare could have been describing our day when he wrote, "The times are out of joint." And we were born to set them right. As Thomas Paine was feeling the pressures of our earlier American difficulties he said, "These are times that try men's souls." And he described those who shrink from performing their duty in their particular crisis as "summer soldiers" and "sunshine patriots." But now as well as then those who stand for right and honor are entitled to the love and appreciation of every person in the world. Our task is not an easy one. Mr. Paine said, "Tyranny, like Hell, is not easily conquered." Yet we may win the greatest satisfaction, because the harder the conflict the more glorious will be the triumph. Mr. Paine said, "That

v

which we obtain too cheap, we esteem too lightly." Our country was built upon the solid foundation of Christian principles, and though we may sometimes find them difficult to live, these principles are still the only basis on which the traditional benefits of freedom, righteousness and human dignity can ever be obtained.

In his book, *Modern Man in Search of a Soul*, Carl Jung, the Swiss psychologist, wrote: "Among all of my patients living in the second half of life there has not been one whose problem in the last resort was not that of finding a religious outlook on life." Mr. Jung said that the problems of all of the "troubled people" with whom he worked came because they lacked the vitality that real religion bestows upon its devotees. And he gave it as his opinion that no one can ever really be healed of his trouble without gaining or regaining a healthy religious outlook.

There can be no question but that a real return to living the right religious principles would solve all of the problems of our present world no matter which side of age thirty-five we may happen to be living on. Individually and collectively all of us are seeking the great blessings of health and happiness, and life grants us these benefits only as we conform our lives to the divine laws of order. The key to every success is found in our ability to follow the teachings of the life of Christ which were given to us to follow. Dr. Henry C. Link once said, "Nothing puts so much order into human life as to live by a set of sound principles." And the most sound principles are the principles of the gospel.

The two primary essentials of the Christian religion are faith and works — they involve our "believing as well as our behaving." These two important success ingredients still give the meaning to everything that we do. When Abraham Lincoln was once asked for a definition of religion he quoted a faithful old soul from Indiana who said, "When I do good I feel good, and when I do bad I feel bad." This natural law of consequences is a significant part of everyone's success.

God is not merely a great law-giver. He is also a great life-giver as well as a great life-saver, and his direction to us as found in the holy scriptures is our greatest world resource. Billy Sunday once recommended a Bible exercise that would be very appropriate for our day. He said:

"Twenty-nine years ago with the Holy Spirit as my guide, I entered at the Portico of Genesis, walked down the corridor of the Old Testament art galleries, where pictures of Noah, Abraham, Moses, Joseph, Isaac, Jacob and Daniel hung on the walls. I passed into the music room of the Psalms, where the spirit sweeps the keyboard of nature until it seems that every reed and pipe in God's great organ responds to the harp of David, the sweet singer of Israel. I entered the chamber of Ecclesiastes where the voice of the preacher is heard, and continued into the conservatory of Sharon and the lily of the valley, where sweet spices filled and perfumed my life. I entered the business office of the Proverbs and went on into the observatory of the prophets where I saw telescopes of various sizes pointing to far-off events. Some were concentrated upon the bright and morning star which was to eventually rise for our salvation and redemption above the moonlit hills of Judea, and some were focused upon the last days and were illuminated by his glorious second coming to the earth. I entered the audience room of the King of kings and caught the visions written down by Matthew, Mark, Luke and John. Thence into the correspondence room where Paul and Peter, John and James were writing their epistles. I stepped into the vision room of Revelation, where tower the glittering peaks of promise and where the King of kings is sitting upon the throne of his glory with the healing of the nations in his hands."

The great principles contained in the "Book of books," though penned so many centuries ago, are as much in point today as they were when first written. They contain the answers to the problems challenging us in these latter days. There is a story told about an East Indian prince who, while visiting Queen Victoria on business of state, asked her to tell him the secret of England's greatness and glory. The queen simply handed him a copy of the Bible and said, "This is the secret of England's greatness."

To understand and live the word of the Lord will continue to be the secret of all greatness and all glory, both collective and individual. It is hoped that the following fifty-two discussions of these moving gospel principles, given over the radio during the fifty-two Sundays of the past year, will be of help to the reader in meeting the challenge of this greatest of all our enterprises, which is the building of our own eternal life and happiness for both here and hereafter.

CONTENTS

The Power of Believing

FROM EVERY DESIRABLE point of view man needs to believe. A child has a profitable feeling of security, health and happiness, when he has an adequate belief in his parents. One of the most profound influences shaping youthful minds, characters, personalities and spirits is the strong firm democratic hand of parental authority directing them toward proper goals. We get stability and balance from knowing that our leaders can distinguish clearly between right and wrong. And we are strengthened when we feel in them a courage matching their convictions. To believe in our leaders inspires in us the confidence that we are a part of a world of order where our own progress is reasonably certain.

A child receives a damaging shock when he discovers that his parents have lied to him, or that their convictions are based on misinformation. Or that the parents are too weak to demand success. A child needs to feel that his parents have superior wisdom and that they are able to protect him against any evil including that which he may bring upon himself. If one can properly safeguard his faith it becomes very difficult for anything else to spoil his success. But when one can no longer believe, and he lacks a secure objective to tie to, then his fortifications are all destroyed and he becomes like a ship without a rudder or a compass without a North Star.

A young person who has a firm belief in his parents, in himself, and in God has a much better chance of becoming a stable, happy, successful, useful adult. A strong basic faith is the foundation for every success. This includes a determined purpose to achieve, and a well organized way of life. But when one has little or nothing to believe in he is likely to become frustrated, rebellious, neurotic and mentally disturbed.

In about the same way adults find security and success as they are able to relate themselves to some higher authority in which they can have an unlimited confidence. Like a child an adult may be seriously disturbed and lose his balance when his belief is badly shaken.

Just before Joan of Arc was burned at the stake at age 19, she said, "Every man gives his life for what he believes. Every woman gives her life for what she believes. Sometimes people believe in little or nothing and yet they give their lives to that little or nothing. One life is all we have and we live it as we believe in living it, and then it's gone. But to surrender what you are and to live without belief is more terrible than dying, even more terrible than dying young." More than most other things in life a man needs to believe in what he himself is doing. He needs to know that his daily activities are worthwhile. If he cannot believe in the goodness of his company and the excellence of his own merchandise a serious conflict of interest starts generating his own failure. And this counter force can soon destroy his sense of morality and his accomplishment is reduced to the level of his belief. We should carefully nurture that natural "upward reach" which someone has called a "God instinct." That is the divine influence urging everyone upward and onward toward perfection in every field of activity. When this inborn trait is distorted or loses its power then ideals are forsaken and the confusion that results pulls him down.

Demosthenes once said, "No man can have a high and noble character while engaged in petty or mean employment, for whatever the pursuits of men are, their characters will be similar." And no one can rise higher than his faith and his ability to get it into operation. A man recently recommended a certain business proposition to several of his friends while believing that they would be greatly benefited thereby. When he discovered that his faith had been founded on falsehood causing him to mislead his friends and waste their money, he felt that life was no longer desirable and so he shot himself. One of the great truths of our world is that "Man does not live by bread alone." We live by our faith, our faith in God, our faith in ourselves, and our faith in the work that life has given us to do.

In 1835 a French visitor Alexis DeTocqueville made a study of the United States. In writing the report he said, "America is great because she is good and if America ever ceases to be good she will cease to be great." To reach a maximum of effectiveness every American should believe in America. And every American should feel his own individual responsibility for keeping America great by keeping her good. As we pledge our allegiance to "one nation under God with liberty and justice for all" we should understand our own specific part in bringing that mission about. And when we subscribe to our national motto "In God We Trust," we should know something about the kind of being in whom our trust is being placed and what our relationships with him should be. We are better citizens and better human beings when we can actually say "We believe in God;" meaning that we trust him, that we believe he lives, that we understand the kind of being he is, and that we believe he knows his business.

The founding fathers believed that they were acting under God's directions in setting up this great democracy to foster freedom, righteousness and human dignity. George Washington said, "The singular interpositions of divine providence in our behalf have been such as could scarcely escape the attention of the most unobserving." In his inaugural address of April 30, 1789, he said, "Every step by which we have advanced to the character of an independent nation seems to have been distinguished by some token of providential agency." And then, in drawing up their Declaration of Independence, the founding fathers said, "Therefore we, the representatives of the United States of America in General Congress assembled, appealing to the Supreme Judge of the world for the rectitude of our intentions do in the name and by the authority of the good people of these colonies, solemnly publish and declare that these United Colonies are and of a right ought to be free." Immediately above their signatures they wrote this great line, "And for the support of this declaration with a firm reliance on the protection of divine providence, we mutually pledge to each other our lives, our fortunes, and our sacred honor." It would give us far greater strength if we added our own personal endorsement to theirs and then, as they did, put up everything that we have including our lives as our personal guarantee to make it good. Governments were instituted by God for the benefit of men and we are obligated to search out good men to make good laws. We are better men when we fully understand that God will hold us personally responsible for how well these laws are obeyed.

But man must also believe in himself. One of our greatest human concepts is that we are the children of God and that we were personally created in his image. We were also endowed with a set of his attributes and potentialities. The full development of these abilities is one of the purposes for which we live.

The poet said:

> Trust in thine own untried capacity
> As thou wouldst trust in God himself.
> Thy soul is but an emanation from the whole:
> Thou dost not dream what forces lie in thee
> Vast and unfathomed as the grandest sea.
>
> No man can place a limit in thy strength.
> Such triumphs as no mortal ever dreamed
> May yet be thine if thou wilst but believe —
> In thy creator and thyself.
> At length some feet shall stand on heights now unattained,
> Why not thine own, press on — achieve! Achieve!

We get greater personal power when we believe in God and in our country and in our own worthwhileness. God did not go to all of the trouble he did in placing us here upon this earth for us to waste our lives in failure.

One of the biggest problems of our lives comes in our believing in ourselves. We often make unfavorable comparisons against ourselves. We know more about our own weaknesses than anyone else does. And sometimes when we are not strong enough to properly handle our temptations, fears, bad habits or sins, we develop damaging inferiority complexes and destructive feelings of guilt. These belittling attitudes may seriously injure our own self-confidence and initiative. We should also be able to handle the criticism of others without allowing it to destroy our faith in ourselves. Sometimes while trying to learn, a child may make an error as a result of which a thoughtless parent may over-impress upon his immature mind the thought that he is fundamentally bad. Such damaging over-condemnations have often placed scars upon delicate human souls which forever prevent them from functioning effectively. And certainly most of us need more, rather than less, belief in ourselves.

Of course the greatest power in the world is the power of God. And according to our own faith, repentance, and self-discipline he has offered to make some of this power available to us. The Apostle John said about God that all things were made by him and without him was not anything made that was made. (John 1:3) We feel this power in such scriptures as those that say "And God said, let there be light and there was light." He said, "Let there be a firmament in the midst of the waters . . . and it was so." (Gen. 1:6-7) One of the titles describing God is "Omnipotent." He is "all-powerful." God is in the sun and the light of the sun and the power thereof by which it was made. (D&C 88:7) He furnishes the light for our eyes as well as for our understandings. (D&C 88:11) And just before his ascension Jesus said to the apostles, "All power is given unto me in heaven and in earth." And then he gave those of his own day a share in his omnipotence by saying, "Tarry ye in Jerusalem until ye be endowed with power from on high." There is power in God's Spirit. And there is also power in our righteousness, and there is power in our believing.

In a stimulating lecture to the Hebrews the Apostle Paul pointed out that God's power is made manifest through faith. He said, "Through faith we understand that the worlds were framed by the word of God. By faith Abel offered unto God a more excellent sacrifice than Cain. By faith Enoch was translated." By faith the walls of Jericho fell down. Faith is the first principle of revealed religion. It is the moving cause of all action and the foundation of all righteousness. Paul says that without faith it is impossible to please God, for he that cometh to God must believe that he is and that he is the rewarder of them that diligently seek him. (Heb. 11:6) But faith is also the first principle of science. It is the first principle of physical and mental healing. On one occasion Jesus was talking to a father about healing his son, who had an evil spirit. Jesus said to him, "All things are possible to him that believeth." (Mark 9:23) He didn't say that just a few things were possible. He said that all things were possible. Then through his tears the father of the stricken child cried out, "Lord, I believe. Help thou mine unbelief." (Mark 9:22-24) And that should be our own prayer. We can greatly increase our success when our unbelief can be changed into faith and we are able to firmly say, "Lord, I believe."

More than anything else as we say our prayers, we ask for strength. We want the strength to grow, the power to overcome our problems. And much of this power comes from our expertness in believing. The dictionary describes "power" as the ability to bring about physical, mental, moral or spiritual accomplishment. It is the strength that guarantees our success in performance. We sometimes refer to the leading nations as "the great powers." That means that they can do greater things than the lesser powers. But as individuals God has also made us the custodians of some great powers. He has given us the powers of reason, the powers of straight thinking, the powers of repentance, the powers of faith, and the power to take action on all of these. We have mental powers, spiritual powers and motive powers. We have a power in our influence, and Lord Bacon said that "Knowledge is power."

In physics, power is described as the rate of energy transfer by which an engine does its work. Someone has invented the term "horsepower" to measure the work done by a machine. We attempt to measure the destructive power of an atomic bomb by calculating its equivalent in millions of tons of TNT. But the power that made the world is greater than TNT. And in order to get his power into us we need to understand the being who created and controls it. Correct ideas of the character and nature of God are necessary if we are going to exercise intelligent faith in him. We need to believe that he is a real person. That he lives and that we will become like him as we have a strong ambition to follow him. If we keep all of God's commandments we can increase the TNT in ourselves.

Isn't it interesting that usually the hardest thing we have to do is to handle ourselves. When we are able to get the same kind of control over our brains, our tongues, our emotions, our ambitions and our faith that we now have over machines, then we will be well on our way toward becoming one of "the great powers." When Socrates said, "Know thyself," he may have had in mind one of his own techniques for discipline and motivation. While he was in the army, he learned to deal with himself as two people. One was General Socrates and the other was Private Socrates. The responsibility of the one was to command and the duty of the other was to obey. These are both great skills. To get power into ourselves we must know how to reduce evil and get the greatest motivation into our faith and our righteous ambitions.

We never become intellectual, or cultural, or spiritual, or righteous unless some stimulus is promoting and pushing the particular idea involved. The great eternal goals and everlasting satisfactions established by our eternal Heavenly Father help us to increase our strength. We need to get as much TNT as possible into our faith so that we may say, "All things are possible to him that believeth."

Adjustments

S OMETIME AGO a doctor took some X-ray pictures of my spinal column. The pictures showed a couple of places where some of my vertebrae had assumed incorrect positions. This was important not only because it weakened my back itself, but also because the dislocated vertebrae were impinging upon delicate nerves and preventing them from doing their own jobs effectively. The backbone is the center and main support of the entire physical body; but it also houses the spinal cord that runs from the top to the bottom of the body's trunk. This great cable of nerves is indispensable to the body's welfare as it controls, vitalizes and regulates all of the body functions. Without a backbone there would be much less to identify us as human beings. Without a backbone one might more resemble a jellyfish or some lesser creation. Next to the brain which it supports, the backbone may be about the most useful device ever invented.

A school boy once wrote an interesting essay about the backbone. Among other things he said, "Your head sets on one end and you sit on the other." But in between these two points some wonderful things are supposed to take place. This magnificent wonder called the brain serves as the presiding officer for the entire personality. It is held in its high place by the backbone, and then by means of this great spinal cable it sends down its messages to control the welfare of every other member of the body. The backbone is made up of 24 individual bony sections called vertebrae, and each vertebrae is individually constructed with a spinal opening so that the nerves from the central cable may have an entrance and an exit highway over which they may serve the various body organs. Each vertebra is identified by a name or a number. The first one immediately under the head is called Atlas, the second is called Axis, the seven vertebrae in the neck are given a kind of family name called Cervical. The twelve in the rib cage are called Thoracic and the five located at the base of this wonder operation are known as the Lumbar vertebrae. The nerves that make their exit through Thoracic number 2 serve the heart, those going through number 6 serve the stomach, and those through number 10 provide for the kidneys.

Men familiar with the body have drawn out the details of this great human nervous system so that we may understand how it serves every area of the body. So closely knit is this fantastic network that it is impossible to stick the finest pin into the body at any point without striking a nerve. When one has a break-down in his nervous system the whole body tends to collapse. But with all of the jolts, jars, strains and whiplashes that most of our bodies get as we make our way through life, we sometimes get a slipped disc, or one of these important vertebrae gets so knocked out of place that it pinches down on the nerves it con-trols and the individual involved has a kind of partial nervous breakdown at that point. That is, a dislocation of one vertebra may cause those particular organs controlled by it to seriously malfunction.

As the doctor was explaining to me the reasons why the various members of my body should work together harmoniously, I thought of the parable on body teamwork given by the Apostle Paul when he pointed out to the Corinthians that "The eye can-not say unto the hand, I have no need of thee, nor again the head to the feet, I have no need of you." Paul said, "God hath temp-ered the body together . . . that there should be no schism in the body, . . . but that the members should have the same care one for another." He said that if one member suffers, all members suffer with it. (I Cor. 12:21-26)

When one of my vertebrae blocks off the nerve exits from my spinal cord it is actually saying to another important part of my body system," I have no need of thee." This particular lack of harmony in my backbone was causing distress in my voice box and in my hands. And in an attempt to get me back in shape, the doctor laid me out on his table and with some rather sharp jabs up and down my spine, attempted to persuade the offending sections of my backbone to get back into line so that the proper team functioning mentioned by Paul could be carried on effectively. After a series of adjustments extending over a few weeks, some other photographs were taken indicating that the vertebrae causing the disturbance were yielding to the pressure. As they cooperated to improve their position the oppressed parts of my anatomy were able to reassume a more normal functioning.

But while I was lying there on the table with the doctor punching my backbone, it occurred to me that maybe I could use some "adjustments" in some other places. Unfortunately my backbone is not the only member of my team that occasionally gets out of line. Sometimes my faith, my spirit and my attitudes could also profit from some good vigorous adjustments. And judging from what other people tell me about their own problems, I assume that the need for adjustments in various areas makes up a big share of our common complaint. Everyone also has a religious backbone, a moral backbone, and an occupational backbone that are likely to get out of joint occasionally. Recently I heard someone being discussed who had a few kinks in his moral backbone and they referred to him as being crooked. Or when a worker slips a disc in his attitude about his employment things may begin to go wrong which can only be corrected by making some adjustments and getting things back in their proper working order. The reason that Americans spend billions of dollars for occupational supervision is to have someone available to give workers an adjustment when some labor problem begins pinching off their industry, or shutting down their courage, or making them unhappy and complaining.

We also have a lot of troubles with our religious nervous systems. Even those members of the twelve apostles chosen by Jesus needed an occasional adjustment. Peter had a problem with his impetuousness. Thomas needed an adjustment of that vertebra that pinched off so much of his faith that he became a doubter. Judas had trouble with his loyalty which caused him to malfunction as a betrayer. Jesus was called the great physician. He healed the people's blindness, cured their leprosy and took away their lameness, but he also straightened out their thinking and believing, and adjusted their functioning in those important areas of honesty, fairness and devotion. He gave the unprofitable servant a rather vigorous adjustment for his fear. He treated others for their sloth, their unbelief and their sin.

Our present-day medical knowledge makes us almost immune to physical diseases. But in the past we haven't always made the right adjustments in our behavior, our attitudes, our faith, our spirituality, and our rejection of evil. Our crime waves, our atheism, and our sins indicate that a lot of things are out of joint along our moral backbones. Just suppose that we go down our own religious spines and assign each one of our 24 spiritual vertebrae to promote some particular part of our conduct, such as our physical backbones promote the welfare of our bodily organs. We might make the first ten vertebrae responsible for developing the positive aspects of the Ten Commandments so that there would be no malfunction in these 10 very important areas. We might also designate a golden rule vertebra. We could put another vertebra in charge of promoting our faith, and make another responsible for integrating it with our works. We need two good strong vertebrae to give the two greatest commandments a proper place in our lives. We might put another in charge of always maintaining the right mental attitude. When we had each of the twenty-four properly assigned, charged, trained, and focused, then we could take a picture of them occasionally to make sure that they were all keeping in line and that none were saying, "I have no need of thee." We have too many spiritual cripples because of a lack of adjustments in crooked backbones and those necessary traits of godliness and righteousness are being pinched off. It is from our own bad adjustments to law that we develop the devastating crime waves, the ridiculous sickness of vandalism, and the damaging blight of atheism that is making us so miserable.

If we let these distortions go uncorrected for a long enough period our backbones may become so crooked that we may almost need a sledge hammer to get them back into line again. One of our most pitiful examples of maladjustment is seen in an unfortunate group of people sometimes described as beatniks and moral ne'er-do-wells. They form in groups of weird-looking, evil-smelling human beings with uncut hair, dirty bodies and unsightly dress. They have strange manners and exhibit unhealthy attitudes about life, success and God. Some call themselves "Hell's Angels," or "Do Nothings," or "Hippies." They wade around in the immorality of their love-ins and make excursions in the enchanted land of glue sniffing and drug addiction. They want happiness without earning it. And many people have been impressed that even to have crooked backbones might be preferable to having no backbones at all. What a great benefit would come into the world if we could get some real convictions about success, and then all make a more happy adjustment to cleanliness, morality, ambition, and faith.

We have many wonderful reasons to rejoice in our good fortune of having been formed in the image of God. Certainly we should cling to our inheritance, and constantly reaffirm it in our lives. The beast goes down on all fours and thus his vision is cast upon the ground. Snakes have the undesirable assignment to crawl around on their stomachs in the dust and dirt of the earth. The jellyfish can only shiver and shake as it conforms to the environment around it. But man was created upright in the image of his Maker that he might look up to God. And one of the greatest glories of man is his strong backbone and the magnificent brain which crowns its top and directs its affairs. It was a mentally unadjusted Richard Speck who had the slogan "Born to raise hell" tattooed on his left arm. Actually man was not born to raise hell; he was born to become like God, his Eternal Father.

And as we progress from the weakness of childishness to the strength of godliness, it requires some proper adjustments made on the higher levels of our lives. To get from failure to success requires adjustments. We must adjust to school, marriage, righteousness and perfection. If we are going to live in God's presence, some of us are going to need to adjust our faith, our attitudes and our activities from those of sinners, beatniks and ne'er-do-wells. To be well adjusted does not mean to be on a friendly basis with crime, booze, immorality, selfishness, and disbelief in God. Or how can we expect to qualify for the magnificent presence of God if we are adjusted to hate, atheism, Satan and indecency?

When someone is thinking of becoming a "crook," he might try to imagine what a picture of his moral backbone would look like on the lighted surface of God's examination screen. This might stimulate us to keep in mind the many ways in which some of these dislocations can occur. Many years ago a man came into possession of a tract of land that greatly increased in value. Apparently this good fortune had so whetted his appetite for wealth that it pinched off his integrity and severely damaged those nerves regulating his honor. In trying to be a sharp businessman he went back on his word whenever he thought that that would serve his own selfish purposes. Now because people won't trust him, he thinks they are persecuting him. This criticism has weighed so heavily upon him that in many ways he withdraws from people and lives a lonely, unhappy life. His wife has tried to help him but this only agitates him further. It is sometimes pretty difficult for one to see his own crooked backbone. We need some way to get a better picture of these infirmities that are so clearly revealed by the X-ray. Certainly we need someone to go up and down our spines occasionally with the right kind of pressures and straighten out our backbones so that we will not become too crooked. Of course, we should remember that it is pretty hard to get any satisfactory adjustment unless we ourselves are ready. And if we let our infirmities get too far along it may take some pretty hard punches to straighten us out.

In Shakespeare's *Julius Caesar*, Cassius says to Brutus, "Therefore good Brutus be prepared to hear, and since you cannot see yourself so well as by reflection, I your looking glass will be and will modestly discover to you qualities of yourself that you yourself know not of." (I-II) This looking glass function is the one that parents are supposed to perform for their children, and teachers for their students, and husbands and wives for each other. This is the job that employers are supposed to do for their employees, and friends for friends. However, each of us is primarily responsible for himself. And occasionally we need to compare ourselves with the divine gospel program, which has been established to help bring about our own perfection. What a great goal it is to become straight and clean and solid, and then to take the necessary adjustments to see that we don't get too far out of line! Jesus even made the narrow way that leads to eternal life straight. God also said, "I will make darkness light and crooked things straight." (Isa. 42:16) That is a great idea for us to follow.

We might well be proud of our physical backbones when the doctor gets all of the kinks and crooks out of it. And we hope that with a few of the right kinds of spiritual and moral adjustments we will also be able to stand straight and have perfect spiritual functioning when the time comes to enter the presence of God.

The American Image

SOMETIMES PEOPLE ARE criticized for thinking or speaking too favorably about themselves. This also frequently applies to groups, races and nations. Occasionally people are so proud of their ancestors that they may annoy others by an over-recital of family virtues. When Americans travel abroad, and sometimes even when we remain at home, we often offend others by being too lavish with certain kinds of praise involving ourselves and our country. Everyone recognizes that America and Americans have a great many things to be humble about. Our crimes, delinquencies, political blunders and sins are such as should give us genuine concern. However, with all of the things pulling us down we also have many things that should be lifting us up.

It would be very harmful if either our national or our individual image were unduly damaged by the downgrading effect of envy or some other unreal fault attributed to us by others or by ourselves. When anyone, including ourselves, cripples our own point of view unnecessarily, or turns our virtues into ashes, we may be making a more serious error than in being overly conscious of them. We are aware that the most widespread disease in the world is an inferiority complex. There are many overly conscientious individuals who have lost confidence in themselves because some real or imagined weakness has been allowed to prey upon their minds. There are some Americans who have all of the American advantages, but their love of country has been poisoned by the scoffs and sneers of a reverse and false propaganda. Sometimes our own doubts and fears can be magnified until they destroy our patriotism, our national loyalty, and even our love of God. Communists would like nothing better than to have us believe that in their activities in abolishing the church, fighting against God, dealing in blood baths, slavery, and every kind of deception, their country is behaving more properly than is ours. And sometimes those who fail to adequately express their gratitude for their blessings run a serious risk of losing their benefits as well as the ability to produce them. The scriptures say that we should love God with all of our hearts, might, mind and strength, and for similar reasons a genuine love of country will also strengthen and ennoble us as individuals. When we exert an earnest desire to make our country better it will automatically improve our own lives. When people fail in their religious devotions, family loyalty, or in their national patriotism, their individual lives will also show a decline.

In his *Lay of the Last Minstrel*, the immortal bard, Sir Walter Scott, sang:

> Breathes there a man with a soul so dead,
> Who never to himself hath said,
> This is my own, my native land!
> Whose heart hath ne'er within him burned,
> As home his footsteps he has turned
> From wandering on a foreign strand?
> If such there breathe, go, mark him well,
> For him no minstrel raptures swell!
> High though his titles, proud his name,
> Boundless his wealth, as wish can claim,
> Despite those titles, power and pelf,
> The wretch, concentered all in self,
> Living shall forfeit fair renown
> And, doubly dying, shall go down
> To the vile dust from whence he sprung,
> Unwept, unhonored and unsung.

There are a great many advantages in possessing the right amount of love of country, and in honoring the special obligations that always go with it. There is great significance in our national Pledge of Allegiance in which we covenant "One nation under God, with liberty and justice for all." It must be evident to all thinking people that America is not an ordinary nation. In the Constitutional Convention wise old Benjamin Franklin accounted for much of our national success when, in addressing the President, he said, "I have lived a long time, sir, and the longer I live the more convincing proofs I see that God ruleth in the affairs of men."

He also quoted another great truth in which he said, "If a sparrow cannot fall to the ground without his notice, certainly a great nation cannot rise without his aid." And we should know that the uniqueness of America did not come about by chance.

To begin with there is no question but that the United States is the world's chief sponsor of freedom and Christianity and human dignity. And we may be sure that these virtues and an assignment to go with them came from God. The world's second most powerful nation is Russia; it bears a different kind of fruit and identifies a different kind of nation. The Russians are trying to destroy religion and banish God. Their rule is one of force and intimidation. The dictators who rule the people, seize their power from each other, and practice slavery, deceit and trickery on others wherever they can. America was settled by old-world refugees, who came here seeking an asylum from tyranny. They wanted a place where they could worship God according to the dictates of their own conscience.

And in all of our long history we have had no Stalins or Hitlers or Napoleons. No one tries to liquidate those who disagree with them, or use gas ovens, blood purges, or secret police as national instruments of their own selfishness. One of our greatest blessings is our God-given government. This is best described as a government *of* the people, *by* the people, and *for* the people. An American election develops a great emotional strain in centers of power, and yet we do not expect that even *one* life will be lost, or even *one* person's property will be destroyed. No politician in this country ever thinks of taking over the government by the kind of force or intrigue that is common in so many other places.

After a United States election is over, the half of the people who lose forget their grievances and support the half who win. Someone has referred to this regular transfer of power merely as the "changing of the guard." And along the way there are no rebellions, no uprisings, no efforts to forcibly unseat those in power, and no attempt to impose the will of any individual or group upon the people. We have none of the difficulties and blood-spilling in removing an unwanted leader from office that is common in many nations. This wonderful stability in American government has gone along unchanged since our nation was founded nearly two centuries ago, and we hope that we will not have any serious problems in this connection in the foreseeable future.

There is also a different attitude in America about ruling or conquering other peoples. After World War II the German nation was divided. Since that time East Germany has been ruled by the Russians who have drained off German resources and man-power to help support themselves, whereas America has poured millions of dollars into Western Germany to help it become one of the world's most prosperous nations. It is probable that one of the best things that ever happened to Japan was to be con-quered by the United States. For instead of further enslaving her the United States has materially assisted the Japanese to make their nation strong enough to compete with us in world trade. This is not the usual relationship that so often exists between the victor and the vanquished. There is also a different attitude in America about the sacredness of human life. Mr. Mao is reported to have said that he would welcome an atomic war, for even if it killed many millions of the people that are living in his overcrowded country there would still be plenty left.

The United States has the highest educational standards ever known in the world. America is the world's center of inven-tion, manufacturing, and scientific progress. America is the birth-place of the radio, the automobile, the airplane and the electric light. One of the greatest wonders of our world is modern Ameri-can business. Some business procedures and manufacturing tech-niques that are commonplace to us are unheard of in some other places. We also spend more money in helping to feed, clothe, train, and assist other people economically than all of the other nations combined.

There is a different attitude here about religion and funda-mental human righteousness. This situation has more than ordin-ary significance and gives strength to the faith of the founding fathers that this nation was established under divine guidance as the citadel of freedom and the stronghold of righteousness. Our American motto says, "In God We Trust." What an inspiring philosophy!

It is interesting to know that America had a great history before Columbus rediscovered it. A great civilization flourished here for some two thousand years with divine prophets equaling those who lived upon the eastern continent. These people left a volume of pre-Columbus American scripture called the Book of Mormon which, with the Bible, is binding upon everyone as the word of the Lord. This is the stick of Joseph, referred to by the prophet Ezekiel in the 37th Chapter of his book. The Lord said to Ezekiel, "Son of man, take thee one stick (book) and write upon it for Judah, and for the children of Israel his companions, (the Bible) and take another stick (book) and write upon it for Joseph, the stick of Ephraim, and for all the house of Israel his companions (the Book of Mormon), and join them one to another into one stick (book) and they shall become one in thine hand." And *both* the Bible and the Book of Mormon tell of the great role that America is yet to play in bringing about God's purposes in the earth.

Two thousand five hundred years ago when Daniel foretold the latter-day knowledge-explosion his vision was centered in America. God said to him, "shut up the words and seal up the book even to the time of the end; many shall run to and fro and knowledge shall be increased." (Dan. 12:4) When Daniel saw the stone cut out of the mountain without hands that should roll forth until it filled the whole earth, he was seeing the progress being made by the gospel after its restoration in latter-day America. (Dan. 2:34)

Daniel also saw the earthly thrones being thrown down and the "ancient of days" sitting to judge his posterity. The ancient of days is Adam, the earth's oldest man, and the assemblage that Daniel saw was taking place in Adam's own land, America. When John the Revelator said, "And I saw another angel fly in the midst of heaven, having the everlasting gospel to preach unto them that dwell on the earth, and to every nation, and kindred, and tongue and people," he was seeing the time when the angel Moroni, a resurrected prophet of ancient America, should play his part in the restoration of the gospel of Christ in America. And when John the Revelator saw the New Jerusalem coming down from God out of heaven, he was describing one of the latter day glories of America. (Rev. 21:2)

In their visions of the last days Isaiah and some other eastern prophets almost lived in *our* day in America. But a great deal of information also comes from the prophets of ancient America themselves. Mormon, one of the greatest of pre-Columbus American prophets, had an intimate knowledge of us and our civilization as the successors of his own people who were to be destroyed. In one of his important writings he said, "I speak unto you as if ye were present, for behold Jesus Christ hath shown you unto me and I know your doings." (Mormon 8:35) We need to get more of the divine into the real American image.

When one walks across the deserts of Arabia, or climbs the slopes of Mount Sinai, the consciousness that he is in the land of Moses gives an uplift to his spirit. Or when one makes his way from Nazareth up to the Holy City of Jerusalem, he is raised above the squalor of his present-day environment by remembering that he is traversing the land of Jesus. And what a thrilling thought that the dark curtain hiding America's past has now been lifted to let us know that America is a land favored above all other lands. It is the land where the Garden of Eden was located. It is a land that has been loved of God and many great American prophets. It is the place where Jesus himself came to organize his Church after his resurrection, and this visit is the source from which the ancient Americans obtained their knowledge of Christianity which has long troubled Christian scholars. America is also the place where so many wonderful things will happen at the second coming of Christ and during his millennial reign upon the earth. This is also the place where we have been granted that inestimable privilege of spending that important period of our own mortality.

We frequently sing "God Bless America" and we pray that God will guide the President of the United States in directing the affairs of this great nation. But God has given us the ability to answer many of our own prayers in carrying out the American assignment of keeping freedom and righteousness alive in the world. God offered to spare Sodom if fifty righteous people could be found therein. But we need some two hundred million righteous people to satisfy God's purposes in America. May God help us to be great Americans in the most exalted meaning of that term, for then our Creator will again be able to look out upon our land and call it "very good."

Bunker Bean

IN 1912, HARRY LEON WILSON wrote a novel of some 300 pages entitled *Bunker Bean*. It is an intriguing story about a man who was tricked into believing in himself.

Most people suffer throughout life from too mean an estimate of their own abilities. Consequently they spend their strength on small tasks and never put their real powers fairly to trial.

The experience of Bunker Bean makes the potential power of believing more clearly visible. There is a part of our literature that comes under the heading of "useful fiction." Throughout all history the myth, the fable, the allegory, the novel have been used with great effectiveness to teach principles. A remarkable thing about a parable is that it does not need to be true as an actual occurrence. It is of far greater importance that the truths it teaches and the principles it illustrates are true and clearly recognized. In the parables of the Bible many of life's vital experiences are captured and their messages made timeless with a universal application.

Bunker Bean's parents died when he was but a child, and he was left alone in the world. He "roamed the earth in rags and lived timidly through its terrors." Because he was inferior many of his friends made fun of him. And his mind was full of fears. He was afraid of policemen; he was afraid to ride in the elevator, as each time the elevator seemed to fall he suffered the sensations of dying. He was afraid of the future, afraid of situations, afraid of things, afraid of life — even afraid of himself.

Then one day a false spiritualistic medium moved into the cheap boarding-house where Bunker Bean lived. This man had a book on reincarnation, and he persuaded young Bunker Bean to believe that as we cast off our worn-out shoes and replace them with new, so we cast off our worn-out bodies and reclothe our spirits by this process of reincarnation.

Bunker Bean believed wholeheartedly in the teaching of his new-found friend. He was convinced that the friend possessed some extraordinary powers given to him from another world.

This man persuaded Bunker Bean that in return for his savings and a part of his wages over a long period, he could tell him about his (Bunker Bean's) previous incarnations.

After a considerable delay and seemingly with great effort on the part of the medium, Bunker Bean was surprised and delighted to learn that he, the weak, timid Bunker Bean, had once been the great Napoleon Bonaparte, the master of the world. It was quite a shock to learn that once people had been afraid of *him*. When he had been Napoleon the world had trembled before him. Then policemen had been to him as insects.

This he could not understand, and so he inquired of his friend why it was that Napoleon had been so courageous and Bunker Bean so timid. The medium explained that life went in vast karmic cycles. Napoleon had lived on the upper half of the cycle when the qualities of courage, initiative and power had been in the ascendancy. But Bunker Bean lived in the lower part of the cycle that was characterized by timidity, fear and weakness. Therefore Bunker Bean possessed the exact opposites of the great Napoleonic courage and self-confidence.

But there was some wonderful news awaiting Bunker Bean. He was told by his friend that the lower part of the cycle was just now being completed and he was re-entering that period in which he had lived so famously as Napoleon the Great. He was assured that it would not be many days before he himself would know this truth. He would soon feel a strange life stirring within him, for he was even now well on the way to becoming his own inspired, courageous, determined self again — strong, self-reliant, fearless and successful.

Even the *thought* of who he really was made Bunker Bean expand his chest. He straightened his shoulders and studied himself in the glass. Now that he thought about it, there was a certain majesty in his look. The thought of who he was and of his former accomplishments made him vibrate with a strange, fresh power never known before. He went to the library, where he secured and enthusiastically read every book about Napoleon, his former self. He devoured every idea and absorbed the ambition of the mighty Bonaparte, for he, Bunker Bean, was now determined to prepare himself to give full play to those great qualities which were beginning to reappear in his life. At all costs he must learn immediately the secrets that had previously brought him such overwhelming success.

He collected pictures of Napoleon and hung them around his little attic room where he could feast his mind upon them. He imitated the speech, thoughts and acts of his former self. He *was* about the same height as Napoleon, and he now remembered for the first time that he did possess some of those qualities of character that had distinguished the great general.

When he meditated and concentrated long enough he could almost remember Marengo. In those days he had been the one who had been in command, and now when he was tempted to be afraid he thought, "What would Napoleon have done?" And he knew that Napoleon would have been contemptuous of the groundless fears which had so terrorized the early life of Bunker Bean.

One of the historians had said that Napoleon had "won his battles in his tent." That was good enough for Bunker Bean. He would also plan and organize and think the problem out before it came to trial, just as Napoleon had done. Like Napoleon he would see to it that nothing was left to chance. Napoleon had permitted no exceptions to success. Bunker Bean had a colored picture of Napoleon sitting on his great white horse on an eminence overlooking a crucial battle which he was directing with masterly waves of his sabre. Bunker Bean thrilled at the thought that this same great power still lay hidden within his own breast, just waiting for expression.

This mental stimulation proved a powerful tonic for the ailing ego of Bunker Bean. He sat up all night to read the book entitled *The Hundred Days*, which described Napoleon's battles. True, it told of defeat, but also of how gloriously his former self had taken it; of his escape from Elba, his return to France, the march on Paris, conquering by the sheer magnetism of his personality wherever he passed. Bunker Bean's spirit bounded as he read of the frightened exit of the enemy of Napoleon, that puny usurper who went down in defeat before the mere rumor of Napoleon's approach. Then he had been magnificent. He had been willing to stake everything on his own judgment and skill. But finally there had come Waterloo and deathless ignominy. He heard again the choked sobs of "the old guard" as they bade their emperor farewell. He felt the despairing clasp of their hands as those strong bonds were finally severed that had held them together these many years.

Alone in his little room high above the glaring street lights, the timid boy read *The Hundred Days* and thrilled to a fancied memory of them. Now his breathing was stronger, his blood ran faster in his veins as it went to nourish a body that contained the essential portion of the great Bonaparte. Napoleon's contemporaries had called him an upstart, but the historians had said that upstarts were men who believed in themselves. And Bunker Bean now believed with all his heart. As he read about himself, he forgot his mean surroundings and the timidities of spirit that had brought him thus far through life almost with the feelings of a fugitive.

Napoleon had exhibited his greatest powers as he led men to conquest. Inasmuch as there were now no wars to be fought, Bunker Bean must find some other outlet for his extraordinary abilities. He had been employed in a minor position in a business undertaking. It seemed to him that this was the greatest field of adventure in which to employ his peculiar genius. Bunker Bean knew that what he had once accomplished on the field of battle he would now repeat in the field of commerce. He began to think about making money. He knew nothing about the specific processes involved, but he felt sure that if he followed the principles that had been so productive in the past, he could not fail in the future.

The historians had said that Napoleon "had known human nature like a book." Therefore, he resolved to study human nature. The historian had said that "with Napoleon, to think was to act," also that Napoleon was "merciless in driving himself." Therefore Bunker Bean would do again all of these things which had prevously laid the world at his feet.

He had been working for small pay, but as he began to think about and develop these Napoleonic qualities of initiative and courage, amazing things began to happen. He was soon a different person. And other people began to notice the changes that were taking place in him. As a consequence, he was given more important work assignments, his pay was increased, and he began to advance with great rapidity up the positive incline of his success cycle. Now he knew that his friend had told him the truth.

Then he was struck by another thought. He knew that for a short period of 52 years, he had been Napoleon. But certainly he should have some information about himself over a longer period.

Who was he before he had been Napoleon? With these questions he again confronted his friend, and now that prosperity and money were coming his way, he could pay the medium well for whatever additional information could be obtained.

And he was not disappointed, because after the money had been paid, he learned to his further astonishment and delight that before he had been Napoleon he had been the greatest of the Egyptian Pharoahs. He had had a long and wonderful reign and had died at the age of 82 years. His death was deeply mourned by all of his people. He, Rameses, had been a ruler of great strength and character. He had been stern at times, but always just. His remains received the burial customary in those times, and his body was even now interred in the royal sepulchre, covered by the sands of the centuries.

As the Pharaoh, he had been tall and handsome. He was so impressed with the account of the magnificence of the physical bearing of the Pharaoh that he immediately employed the best tailor and had his clothing cut in such a way as to give him the appearance of perfect physical development. The effect produced so improved his form that he unconsciously strove to develop the appearance that the garment gave him. He expanded his chest, drew in his waist and stood erect. "In beggar's rags most men are beggars; in kingly robes all men can be kings." And he must achieve that kingly behavior that is said to distinguish royalty.

He had been thrilled by his deliberate acts of courage because they stiffened his spine. Now he would add to them royalty and grace and mental power. He understood that such a marked advance in his spirit could not all be made in a day. Such progress could only come after long dwelling in thought and practice upon the qualities that were responsible for his splendid past. He was a king and he must do what kings did. Kings were rich; therefore he would be rich. No sooner would his kingship be proclaimed than money would be in his hands. Money would come to him now as it had previously come to him on the banks of the Nile centuries before. He did not question how or when — he only knew that it would come.

No longer would he play the coward before trivial adversaries. He would direct large affairs; he would think big and he would live big. Never again would he be afraid of death, or life, or policemen, or the mockery of his fellows. Under this mental discipline his spirit grew tall and its fiber toughened. He knew that he was a king and others could not help knowing it also.

He sometimes thought about his present employer, and it occurred to him that had his employer lived with him back in Egypt he would probably have been a royal steward, a keeper of the royal granaries perhaps, or a dependable accountant. But he never could have risen very high because his "lameness of manner was an incurable defect of the soul." He pitied his employer for his weakness. Though his employer was successful and well-to-do, Bunker Bean was in a different class. He was a king. But money and power came not only to kings, but to the kingly. Bunker Bean had been born to riches; he had been born a king, and would also do the things that characterized greatness.

Strength seemed to flow into him from his mental image of the strong, calm demeanor of the Pharaoh. When reliving his previous experiences he could believe no weakness of himself. He had once ruled a mighty people in Egypt. But also centuries later he had been Napoleon and had made Europe tremble under the tread of his victorious armies. He had made some mistakes in those earlier appearances. These he would not make again. Bunker Bean believed himself to be both a wise king and a courageous soldier. He thought courage at night and he awoke in the morning with a giant's strength. His thoughts were like a great inpouring of phosphorus into his personality. This gave him an iron will.

Then one day Bunker Bean made a tragic discovery. The medium was a fake. None of these important things that he had believed were true. He had been cheated for the sake of his money. Then he realized that he was not a king, that he was only weak, timid Bunker Bean, mean and insignificant. What a tremendous let-down! What an occasion for dejection and discouragement!

But in the years that Bunker Bean had believed himself a king, he had formed the habits that go with success, and habits are not easily broken. It was now natural for him to do the things that great men did.

And then Bunker Bean made another great discovery, and this time he was not deceived. He learned that great spiritual philosophy that, "As a man thinketh in his heart, so is he." And so it had been.

When he had believed himself to be a king, he had been a king. When he had believed himself weak, he had been weak.

Had he not discovered the deception and gone on believing in himself, all would have been as before. Then he learned this great truth, that "believing is all that matters."

A new, molten, luminous, inspiring truth now ran through the mind of Bunker Bean. During these years no one had known that he had believed himself to be Rameses and Napoleon except himself and his former friend. But Bunker Bean had become wealthy while he had lived this myth of imagining himself to be great. He had gained wealth, power and prestige by believing in himself. Rameses and Napoleon had been only a crude bit of scaffolding on which he had climbed to success.

But the confidence that he had developed in himself could now endure without the help of the scaffolding. He would still think big and live big and be big. In spite of the discovery, his faith would still continue. The Corsican's magnetism would still prevail, and he, Bunker Bean, the lowly, would still have the power to magnetize, to thrill, to lead, and to accomplish. He would still remember that money, power, success and leadership came not only to kings, but to the kingly. The world would always be at his feet "if he could only believe."

Later he visited the tomb of Napoleon to pay his tribute to the man who never lost faith in himself. Even in those last sad days on the prison rock of his lonely island, his spirit had remained unbroken. How greatly Bunker Bean had profited from that courage and faith. He had developed a certain grim sureness of himself which would survive.

Emotion surged into the eyes of Bunker Bean, threatening to overwhelm him as he contemplated these great truths that "every man is born a king." "Every man is born to riches." "To believe is all that matters."

LOOKING UPWARD

I raised my eyes to yonder heights
And longed for lifting wings
To bear me to their sunlit crests
As on my spirit sings.

And though my feet must keep the path
That winds along the valley's floor,
Yet after every upward glance
I'm stronger than before.

—Nautilus

Caesar's Ransom

T HERE IS AN OLD legend to the effect that during the early conquests of Julius Caesar he was once captured and held for ransom by a group of barbarians. During his forty-day confinement he won their. admiration by his coolness, friendliness and wit. However, when he learned that they had set his ransom at $55,000 he laughed at them because they didn't understand the value of their prisoner. Caesar suggested that they raise their sights, and the ransom figure was reset at $550,000. He also laughingly promised to crucify each of them as soon as the ransom was paid. This promise he faithfully carried out immediately after his release.

But even $550,000 is a small amount to pay for a Caesar. He put together the greatest empire ever known in the world. He developed Rome's military power, improved her government, upgraded her education, and filled her coffers with wealth.

It is interesting to note, however, that these barbarians are not the only ones who have been bad judges of human values. Joseph was sold into Egypt for 20 pieces of silver, which was the equivalent of eleven American dollars. Then Joseph built granaries and stored up enough corn in the years of plenty to avert the long hard famine that followed. And thus for eleven dollars two nations were saved from starvation.

But Judas Iscariot probably made the most fantastic miscalculation in human values when he sold Jesus to his enemies for 30 pieces of silver. Jesus became the Savior of the world and the Redeemer of men. In the Council of Heaven the Lord had spoken of all of the people who would live on the earth and had said, "I will ransom them from the power of the grave." His was the only life with sufficient value behind it to redeem us all from death.

Caesar's ransom was very important to the Romans. But this practice of paying ransoms is still big business. Not long ago some evil people kidnapped little Bobby Greenlease of Kansas City, Missouri. The next day the kidnappers wrote his parents a letter and said, "We will let you have him back for $600,000.00." The money was furnished and I am sure that if they could, they would have been willing to pay 600 million or 600 billion to get their son back. But Jesus placed the value of human life far beyond any of these. He compared the worth of one human soul to the wealth of the entire world, which would be many hundreds of trillions of dollars, and the price he paid should help us to appreciate that his atonement and our ransom is the most important event that has ever taken place upon this earth, and we should be prepared to make the most of it.

The fall of man made us all subject to eternal death and only by shedding the blood of the Son of God could we be redeemed. Therefore, in appreciation and gratitude, we join with Charles H. Gabriel in singing his hymn of worship saying:

I stand all amazed at the love Jesus offers me,
Confused at the grace that so fully he proffers me,
I tremble to know that for me he was crucified,
That for me a sinner he suffered, he bled and died.

Oh it is wonderful that he should care for me
Enough to die for me,
Oh it is wonderful, wonderful to me.

I marvel that he would descend from his throne divine
To rescue a soul so rebellious and proud as mine.
That he should extend his great love unto such as I
Sufficient to own, to redeem and to justify.

I think of his hands pierced and bleeding to pay the debt,
Such mercy, such love and devotion can I forget?
No, no, I will praise and adore at the mercy seat
Until at the glorified throne I kneel at his feet.

Oh it is wonderful, that he should care for me
Enough to die for me.
Oh it is wonderful, wonderful to me.

But one of the most wonderful things about our ultimate eternal success is that we ourselves may have a part in bringing it about. The Savior did that which we could not do for ourselves when he broke the bonds of death. And "as in Adam all die, even so in Christ, shall all be made alive." But this is not all there is to salvation and the degree of our eternal exaltation depends upon our own obedience to God's laws. As the Lord has said, "For

behold, my blood shall not cleanse them if they hear me not."
(D&C 29:17)

Our responsibility is indicated in a great revelation which
says, "For behold, I, God, have suffered these things for all, that
they might not suffer if they would repent; But if they would
not repent they must suffer even as I; Which suffering caused
myself, even God, the greatest of all, to tremble because of pain,
and to bleed at every pore, and to suffer both body and spirit
— and would that I might not drink the bitter cup, and shrink —"
(D&C 19:16-18)

This word *ransom* has several interesting meanings. The
dictionary says that to ransom is to redeem. It may be the act
of releasing a captive by the payment of a consideration. Usually
when we owe someone a great debt, they are given a mortgage
on our securities. And before we can get back a clear title to our
property, we must pay those amounts that are outstanding against
it. We also redeem our lives in about the same way.

The first mortgage is held by our Creator. Paul says, "Ye
are not your own, ye are bought with a price." Under the
arrangement made in the council of heaven, if we are obedient
to God's laws this mortgage will be paid by the atonement of
the great Redeemer. But for various reasons most of us pile
up other liens against our lives which must also be paid. When
one commits a crime against the state and doesn't want to be
confined in jail he is sometimes given the privilege of ransoming
himself by paying an equivalent fine in cash. But in one way
or another every law carries a penalty for its violation. If we
violate the laws of health, a fine is imposed. There are also millions of people who are in bondage to alcohol, and in order to be
redeemed each must pay the ransom demanded. It may be
exacted in effort, suffering, expense, repentance, or all of these
combined.

A group of the ancients had an interesting way of punishing
crime. If one became a murderer his punishment was to be
chained to the corpse of his victim, so that there was no way
he could possibly disentangle himself from the result of his evil
deed. Wherever he went for evermore he must drag the dead
body of his victim with him. If later he should decide to kill
again, another corpse would be added to his oppressive burden.

Such a punishment seems severe, and yet life has a program
of retribution that is closely akin to it. Everyone is always

chained to his sin. When one violates the law of temperance a ruinous driving thirst attaches itself to push him further and further down the road to despair. The sentence of one who tells lies is that he eventually becomes a liar. If one neglects the laws of learning, a sentence is imposed that he is forever chained to his ignorance. And who can imagine a more dreadful bondage than to be compelled to drag his foul load of sin with him until the payment is made. The Apostle Paul probably had this ancient custom in mind when he cried out, "O wretched man that I am! who shall deliver me from the body of this death?" (Rom. 7:24) And we might echo, Who indeed?

One of our most serious problems is, How are we going to be redeemed from the dreadful bondage of such things as atheism, immorality, dishonesty, and disobedience to God? The price of redemption from any sin is always terribly high. Think of the great fortunes that have been lost and the sufferings that have been endured while dragging around the oppressive burdens of alcohol, dishonesty and drug addiction. The Romans thought that it was worth $550,000 to redeem Caesar, but how much is it worth to us to be ransomed from our ignorance and freed from our sloth and pardoned from our guilt? It has been said that the best way to break a bad habit is to drop it. But how can one drop nicotine or indifference or sin, after they have their chains tightly wrapped around him? Any wealthy man would pay a very large sum to be excused from suffering out a 20-year jail sentence under the miserable conditions always existing in any penitentiary. But how much more would it be worth to be bailed out of an eternal sentence in Hell. To be ransomed from Hell is not only to be relieved of the suffering but also to be freed from the depressing company of a miserable group of sinners.

If we actually spent a few months in Hell getting a taste of its torments and suffering the misery of an enforced association with evil, then the thought of being ransomed, redeemed and sanctified, with all of our debts paid and our suffering ended, might have a much greater appeal than at present. If it was worth $550,000 for Caesar to get away from the pirates and live those extra few years in Rome, what would it be worth to us if we could fully enjoy the comfort, peace of mind, beauty, and happiness of our heavenly home forever. We usually appreciate a thing more when we know its value, and surely our own ransom is something that we should not only understand but start working at to bring it about. Those who get the full benefit of the great atonement made by Christ will not only have their souls redeemed, but they will be sanctified and glorified as well.

We ought to get clearly in mind some tangible thoughts about how much our own soul is actually worth. The soul is described in the scriptures as the spirit and the body when they become inseparably connected. The body is the lesser part of this combination, but even it has tremendous value. Satan and his followers were forever denied the privilege of having bodies as a part of the punishment for their antemortal rebellion against right. Yet every spirit child of God hungers for a body. We remember the evil spirits who appeared to Jesus in his day, who preferred the bodies of swine to not having any bodies at all. What is even worse, Satan and his followers can never hope for any redemption. We would not like to lose a leg or an eye or a brain on this earth, yet certainly it would be far more terrible to lose them hereafter.

John D. Rockefeller, the world's first billionaire, had a bad stomach. He once offered his chauffeur half of his wealth to trade stomachs with him. A prominent British neurophysicist recently said that you could not construct an electronic computer for three billion dollars comparable to the human brain.

A utility linesman once paralyzed his left side by coming in contact with a live wire. In the lawsuit that followed he was asked to smile before the jury, and because he could only smile on one side of his face, the jury awarded him $100,000 in damages. If half a smile is worth a hundred thousand dollars what would a whole smile be worth? But if we are not redeemed what will there be to smile about? Suppose then that we get a total for ourselves by adding up our half-billion dollar stomach, our three billion dollar brain, our two hundred thousand dollar smile, and then add in an appropriate amount for a couple of billion dollar eyes, two willing hands, a miraculous voice, and the godly power of the human will. How much would this body, formed in God's image, be worth if we didn't have one? To this sub-total we might credit a few hundred billions for an immortal spirit and have it inseparably joined together with the body, that we might have eternal joy.

But then just suppose that this marvelous creation formed in God's image is in hock to sin, mortgaged to the hilt for an amount that we are completely unable to pay. Then suppose that someone should tell us about this magnificent atonement made by the Son of God, and that the price had been paid so that our lives could be ransomed, redeemed, glorified, celestialized, and eternalized, and in every way fully qualified to live forever with God in eternal glory. Who can even comprehend the value of the peace, happiness and joy of this situation? Then suppose that we ask ourselves what we would be willing to do in order to bring it all about. One of the great facts of life is that we may have every blessing that we are willing to live for. It is a pretty good guess that even now Satan is laughing at us because we don't know our own value as the children and heirs of the eternal God. Some of us are still going blindly on our disobedient way, putting one mortgage on top of another until we are so deep in bondage and so unable to repent that his blood will not cleanse us and even the fires of hell may not be able to burn out the dross. Caesar crucified *his* captives, but Satan has a far worse fate in store for *his*. And all of those who remain forever unredeemed will fall into his hands. It is an interesting fact that we don't need to wait until eternity to get started on this most important project of redemption. We are presently operating under a kind of lend-lease arrangement, and only after this life has been finished will we be turned over to ourselves and "have eternal glory added upon our heads forever and ever." But in the meantime we can redeem ourselves from ignorance through study. We can redeem ourselves from sloth through self-motivation; we can redeem ourselves from sin by repentance and self-mastery, and the great Redeemer will pay the ransom for our souls if we are obedient to him. And may God help us so to do.

Discrimination

THERE IS A LEGEND that has come down to us from the ancient Chinese, saying that if you were visiting in one of their homes and you expressed admiration or love for some particular article that they possessed, you may find that they would wrap it up and send it to you as a present. This custom may seem a little bit unusual to us, and yet life has a procedure that is exactly like it, as life has decreed that whatever you love hard enough and long enough you make it your own, and then life wraps it up and sends it to you free of charge. That is, if you love honesty, you get honesty. If you admire industry, you get industry. If you develop a love of beauty and success in your heart, that is exactly what you get in your life. It is one of our most important opportunities, that anyone can go into the great department store of life and pick out as many good things as he wants, and then by exercising his love and appreciation he may make them his own. This is an ability that makes the golden touch of king Midas pale into insignificance. However, because this great gift has no discrimination, it also has a negative aspect, and it takes no responsibility either for the lack of judgment in the one doing the selecting, or for the quality of those things that we may fall in love with.

That is, if we love immorality, drunkenness, irreverence and hate, life also wraps them up in packages and sends them to us with its compliments. Therefore, to give this gift its greatest value, the receiver himself must accept the responsibility for developing his own good taste and supporting it by an effective ability to discriminate. However, it frequently becomes a little bit difficult to properly direct the forming of these attachments. We live in a world where good and evil, success and failure, truth and error are often mixed up together. Sometimes in loving some good thing we may be developing an appetite for the evil that is associated with it.

Shakespeare's comedy *A Midsummer-Night's Dream*, has to do with some fairies living and frolicking in the woods. There was one mischievous sprite named Puck who found a magic flower. When the juice of this flower was dropped onto the eyelids of a sleeper, it would make him fall violently in love with the first creature that his eyes rested upon after awakening. This little character went around through the woods putting these magic drops onto the eyelids of those whom he found resting or asleep. When they awoke some of them found themselves involved in the most ridiculous emotional mix-ups. Then Puck watched gleefully as pairs of formerly ardent lovers were broken up by strange new attachments. Beautiful ladies made violent love to some absurd creature, and even the most devoted prospective mates did not always see each other first upon awakening.

But that is about the same trick that life frequently plays on some of us. And no matter how ridiculous the things are that we fall in love with, life puts title to them in our name and sends them to us as our own. Puck could remove the spell from those whom he had enchanted by treating their eyes with the juice of another flower. But this is something that those who have fallen in love with alcohol, idleness and dope, for example, are not always able to do.

The reason for the perfect life of Jesus was that he always fell in love with the right things. He had the finest sense of values and was always able to effectively discriminate between right and wrong. It is interesting that much of his teaching was upon this subject of discrimination. God hates evil and loves good, and Jesus was always pointing out the differences between failure and success. He discussed the problems involved in separating the sheep from the goats, and the wheat from the tares. One of the most important events that will take place at his second coming will be the destruction of the wicked and the rewarding of the righteous. This involves discrimination in what will happen at the great and final judgment. The occasion when every man must be rewarded according to his works will also require that the sheep must be clearly distinguished from the goats.

One of the helpful teaching instruments used by Jesus was the parable. The easiest way to learn discrimination is by comparison or contrast. We can see dark things best when they are exhibited on a light background. The best way to be impressed with how crooked a stick is, is to lay a straight one down beside it. And we can more easily understand the defects of an old worn-out automobile by driving one that is brand new. We are also able to better understand good traits in human character and personality by comparing them with the bad. In getting people to understand the greatest religious truths, Jesus frequently used non-religious terms because they were more clearly understood. He illustrated great spiritual values by telling the stories of the good Samaritan, the prodigal son, and the unprofitable servant.

In one of his best known parables, Jesus tells of a certain farmer planting his crop by the primitive methods used in ancient times. As some of the seeds fell in areas where the soil had inadequate depth, they died for lack of nourishment. Some fell in stony places where they didn't have a chance to grow, and consequently were eaten up by the birds. Some seeds fell among the thorns and thistles and were choked to death by those plants that made up their evil environment. But some of the seeds fell in good soil where they produced an abundant crop and repaid the original investment many times over. But even among the healthy growing plants, the farmer still had a problem of making decisions, for an enemy came by night and sowed tares among the wheat. This seriously complicated the situation as the roots of the tares were soon intertwined with the roots of the wheat, and the farmer could not pull out the weeds without disrupting the grain. Yet the tares took a lot of strength out of the soil that was intended for the wheat. However, the farmer decided to let the weeds and the wheat grow together until the time of the harvest. Then the tares were sorted out, tied in bundles and burned, and the wheat was threshed and the grain was put in the bin.

I thought about this parable the other day as I was shown a great modern wheat farm. The plowing was done by giant machines pulling many plows. Other machines prepared the seed bed and kept the land free of weeds. Then great drills planted the seed wheat deep enough that the sun could not wither the sprouting plants and the seeds were also put beyond the reach of the birds. The rocks had all been removed and no thorns or thistles were permitted to jeopardize the growth of the wheat. An abundance of fertilizer not only assured a big crop but also enriched the grains with the right kind of vitamins. I thought of the many changes that had taken place since that time when our forefathers plowed their ground with a wooden stick and struggled against the rocks and the weeds with their bare hands in order to reap a meager harvest of food. But the thing that impressed me most was the differences in the harvesting process. Instead of using a sickle to cut a handful of grain at a time, this farmer had a giant combine harvester that cut a twenty-foot swath across the field while moving as fast as a man could walk. Each hour hundreds of bushels of golden grain were cut and threshed and made ready for the granary. This one farmer could probably produce as much grain in a year as ten thousand of his ancient ancestors. I was also very interested in how this giant machine solved its sorting problems. The harvester has a built-in ability to pick out the golden kernels and yet eliminate all of the straw and chaff. If by mischance some tares were found growing in the field, the harvester made short work of them by blowing them out with the other waste. I was impressed that this separating operation being carried on so expertly by this harvester is also about *our* most important problem in life. Dividing the good from the bad is necessary because we cannot afford to gather in all experience indiscriminately.

When it was first discovered that strychnine would kill, it became forever unnecessary for any individual to have any more personal experiences in that field. Nor is it any longer required that anyone must sit on a red hot stove to discover that it is unpleasant. Our civilization itself is being wasted by the tares because we have failed to separate the good from the bad in our environment. As a consequence many people on judgment day may find themselves tied up in the bundles that will be prepared for the fire.

Thirty-four hundred years ago, God came down upon the top of Mount Sinai and, to the accompaniment of lightnings and thunders, gave us a talk on discrimination. In ten great commandments he told us about a lot of things that we just must not do. We must not permit that juice of evil on our eyelids that keeps us falling in love with false gods, false religion, immorality, profanity, covetousness, Sabbath day violations, dishonesty, unfairness, and atheism. If we put as much righteousness on our eyelids as we do eye shadow, eye liner, eyebrow pencil, and mascara, we may be able to more effectively fall in love with the great virtues of industry, fairness, honesty, courage, temperance, reverence, and obedience to God. With a little more faith and singleness of purpose on our eyelids then God would probably wrap up some of his greatest gifts and send them to us with the titles registered in heaven in our names.

But in every department of life, the sheep and the goats, the good and the bad must be separated, and in all of our activities we are continually asked to perform some kind of a combine harvester function. For example, so many of our failures and successes come from reading, and sometimes without effective discrimination we load up our lives with the crime and sin contained in our newspapers or the immorality and pornography of the movies and magazines, rather than getting the good that may also be found in these places. As the world has read about the so-called "new morality," the alcoholism, the nicotine addiction and the atheist views of the so-called intellectual free thinkers, it has brought on some of the crime waves and psychiatric problems that are now being registered in our names.

A fine young salesman recently showed me a lewd picture with an appropriate sales slogan beneath it. He thought it might be a pretty good way to get more prospect attention. Yet to build this kind of a spirit around even the best salesman will always kill far more sales than it will ever make, and in addition it will also tend to destroy the salesman. In a good salesman, as in a good automobile, it is the *clean* engine that produces the power. Some salesmen tell questionable stories because they are sure to bring a laugh from certain people. But all of the time a by-product of carbon and gum is accumulating in his cylinders. And as a result of his loose discrimination he will always find a lot of tares in his granary with the wheat. There are many things that come within our experience every day that ought to be blown out with the chaff. When we set our life's machinery to retain even the best of the tares we are headed for trouble.

In this connection, I have been very interested in the discrimination in a reading operation carried on by a friend of mine. This is necessary as all of the things even in the best books are neither good nor important. In my friend's intellectual harvesting operation he always reads with a pencil in hand, as reading is like even the most valuable wheat plant which is made up of roots, stems and leaves, as well as kernels. And even Shakespeare wrote some things that have in them very little mental nutrition. Yet Shakespeare was one of the greatest writers who ever lived. He looked with keen insight into human lives, and effectively recorded many of the good and many of the bad things that he found there. Therefore a wise reader, like a good combine harvester, goes through each volume eliminating the harmful and unimportant, but at the same time marking into his own notebook a kind of concentrate of good from which all of the chaff and straw has been eliminated. Only those things are retained that are thought to be of great value to him personally. Then he goes over these ideas again and again after they have been put in the granary. Many of them are memorized and placed in active service in his own mind and personality.

This process might also be compared to a mining operation — because no ore comes pure, it is run through the smelter and under intense heat the dross and the valuable metals are separated. Because of this separation the one in charge of smelting gold ore ends up with nothing but pure gold. Then this becomes a part of his own financial resources and begins working for him.

Even the most effective separation process has no value if no use is made of the gold afterwards, and some people do this smelting without any profit to themselves as the gold never finds its way into the treasury. There would be no point in having a combine harvester if the wheat and chaff were separated but left unused on the ground. A grain truck and a granary are necessary parts of every profitable threshing operation, and a good idea bank should be a fundamental possession of everyone who would be wealthy in ideas, ideals, and ambitions.

Our lives themselves are the soil in which this most valuable of all crops is grown. We need the best possible equipment to keep out the tares. We need some good fertilizing to enrich our grain with vitamins, and then we are in business on a profitable basis.

The Doll Library

IN A RECENT number of the *Readers' Digest*, Robert O'Brien tells of a unique international doll library established by Samuel Pryor in Greenwich, Connecticut. Then in trying to answer the question, why a doll library, Mr. Pryor says that "every doll is like a book and has a story to tell." He says, "You can look at a doll and read history in the way it is dressed." He points out, "that dolls tell volumes about a country's culture, customs, religion, and family life. A doll is a kind of miniature representative of mankind. And a doll library may be a kind of small scale library of people."

It is a significant fact that most things are not important only for themselves alone; frequently they are even more important for what they stand for, or make us think about or motivate us to accomplish. Our world is full of symbols and emblems and insignias that represent things more important than themselves. We treasure the pictures of people, because of who and what they make us think about. Occasionally we dress ourselves up in the costumes of the pilgrims and the pioneers. As we represent them physically, we can more easily re-think their thoughts and re-enact their lives. The primary importance of books is to remind us of something else, and this is also the purpose of these miniature representations of human beings that we refer to as dolls. As children we live largely in a world where dolls, toy soldiers, and other symbols are substituted for the real thing. But even in later life we put on a uniform, or we put a ring on the finger, or a flag in the sky, or a light in the window to remind us of something. We enrich our lives by means of our representations. At Christmas and Thanksgiving time we decorate our home with certain symbols that produce the particular spirit that we desire to possess us for that period. After we remove the symbols, that particular spirit largely disappears also.

Through the door of this Doll Library one enters a timeless enchanted world of people, represented by dolls of various sizes and ages from every country under the sun. June Anderson

Douglass serves as the Curator of the Doll Library and from the description cards she reads many interesting histories. These dolls were loved by young and old alike. Caressing human hands once petted them, dressed them, brushed their hair, rocked them to sleep, and generally reacted to them. And now they seem to fill this enormous room with longing. "Hold us," they seem to say. "Only as you touch us and love us can you bring us back to life again."

High on the east balcony, where the dolls out of America's historic past are grouped, there are two dozen tiny figures with a strange tale to tell. They are made of gleaming white china, their dark hair is parted in the middle and their arms are outstretched in rigid appeal. These are "frozen Charlottes," named for the heroine of a ballad composed in the 1830's by a Vermont folk singer. One sub-zero New Year's Eve fair Charlotte, and young Charlie her sweetheart, set out in an open sleigh for a holiday ball. Rather than cover her beautiful gown, Charlotte spurned the proffered blanket and froze to death as a result. The children who lived a hundred years ago pampered these little china dolls, trying to make up to frozen Charlotte for the sad thing that had happened to her in the ballad.

As in real life each of these dolls have been the center of many important life plays. The children who owned them and loved them also grew by their association. They assumed in their childhood the imagined virtues of maturity as they cared for and loved these children of their hearts.

So often our dolls and other playthings bring about the fundamental development of our lives. The lovely personality of a beautiful doll stimulates the imagination of the child mother and she thereby generates a greater love in her own heart. The boy who associates with manly toy soldiers is incited by them to play the part of a patriot, hero, and statesman. And he will become a different kind of man than the boy who plays at being a bank robber or a desperado.

It was pointed out in this article that the hobby of collecting dolls is growing rapidly among all kinds of people of all ages including men, women, and children. And as each centers his mind upon an ideal represented by this little image, each comes to love the ideals and ambitions pictured in his miniature associates. As he reacts to them he builds the roadway on which

his future success will travel. Some dolls have performed a divine
mission by molding the future of their principals who loved them.
And each doll is particularly fitted by its personality to fill a
certain kind of need.

One day in 1953, 300 dolls that had been willed to him by
a friend arrived at Mr. Pryor's door. He said, "Suddenly here
were all of these wonderful little people looking to me for a
home. Among them were Spanish dancers, Japanese wisteria
maidens, rugged Chinese coolies, Turkish band players, Peruvian
Indians, and bejeweled Russian princesses." Mr. Pryor took
them all in and made them welcome.

In their strangely timeless world, like the principals they
represent, dolls have widely different missions to perform. Some
are entertainers; some are puppets and marionettes. There are
French mechanical dolls from the time of Napoleon III. Turn
the brass key and a petite French miss flutters her eyelids as
her bosom rises and falls. Her fingers strum a little lyre as a
hidden music box supplies a tune. Again like their principals,
some dolls are deeply rooted in religious ceremonies. There are
brightly painted and befeathered Hopikachinas, carved of cotton-
wood to represent gods of the sun, of rainbows, of west winds, of
life-giving rains. There is a Madonna of the Bullfighters twelve
inches tall. Hundreds of years ago, matadors prayed to her for
safety in the bullring. Now she looks out over the enormous room
from her place on the mantel, serene and regal — worlds away
from the bullring chapel, and the deaths that took place in those
long-ago afternoons.

The Egyptian carved cedar ushabti is the Library's oldest
and perhaps rarest doll. It is about nine inches tall and carved in
the shape of an Egyptian mummy with wide eyes painted on the
face giving the little figure an aura of silence and mystery. This
particular doll was buried nearly 3100 years ago in an Egyptian
tomb. Like all ushabti dolls, its function was to accompany the
deceased to the next world, to perform whatever manual labor
might be required.

In the collection are many portrait dolls, miniatures, and
caricatures of noted personages. Here we meet in a bizarre con-
frontation with Sigmund Freud, Shirley Temple, Franklin D.
Roosevelt, Henry the VIII, Harriet Beecher Stowe, Topsy, and
General Charles DeGaulle. A doll named Fanny sits in a wing

chair wearing a merry look and a garland of ivy in her hair; a note tucked in her satin brocade dress, says that the captain of a Yankee trading schooner brought her home to his wife from a foreign land. Generations of the captain's descendants had loved and cared for Fanny, and then a few years ago she became a part of the Library. Now she sits by the fireplace as if hearing beloved voices, and she may even be remembering those days of old.

In his imagination Sam Pryor likes to think that his dolls can remember. He feels that in some poignant way, when the Library's doors are locked for the night and the enchanted museum is quiet, the dolls then somehow stir to life and remember the voices that they once heard, and feel again the arms that once held them in tender embrace.

In recent years this idea of portrait dolls has been expanded in a little different direction. All over the country some interesting wax museums have recently come into existence. Life-size wax figures have been made of many of the famous people of history, depicting the important events in which they had a part. They seem so lifelike and real that we tend to more fully re-feel their emotions and relive their experience. Like the members of the Doll Library these wax creations are also timeless. Sometimes through them in a more real way than in a book we may see and associate with Christopher Columbus, George Washington, Abraham Lincoln, Colin Kelly and Douglas MacArthur. Each is a stand-in and is playing the role of his chief for our benefit. Each is made to look so real that we sometimes get a strange feeling that we are actually associating with the principal. Then we more effectively relive their experiences. With Napoleon, we may wait out those last sad lonely hours of life on the isle of St. Helena where, with one hand crossed behind him, he gazes out across the sad and solemn sea toward the land of his former glory and triumph. Napoleon often expressed the hope that when he was dead his spirit would be able to talk things over with such idols as Alexander, Hannibal, Caesar, and Frederick the Great. It was also one of the wishes expressed by Tennyson's Ulysses that he might touch the happy isles and see the great Achilles whom he knew.

But probably without always realizing it, each of us gathers together some kind of a library or museum of his own. There we gather around us the things that represent our own most important ideas and the people that we love the most. As we get older we become a little more prone to indulge this temptation of going back into the past. For example, I have a drawing that was made of my daughter when she was five years old by a sidewalk artist in Arizona. To me this has become something of a priceless treasure. I also have a plaything that my son loved when he was just a little boy. I helped him to obtain it on a very pleasant occasion many years ago while the family was on a trip together. Somehow this plaything represents the particular happiness and family solidarity that characterized that outstanding occasion. Among all of our happy memories there are some that we are more than ordinarily anxious to preserve, and we can best hang onto them through some kind of visual representation. I have a treasured keepsake that my mother loved. A colored picture taken when she was only eighteen years old contains this treasure which now belongs to me. Because my mother loved it then, I love it now. It is sacred to me because her hands touched it, and her heart placed its value upon it. I like to think of my mother at other periods of her life when I knew her personally. But somehow I am particularly attached to this period when she was a young girl, and I would not like to lose this connecting link in my association with her before I was born.

We also have other ways to represent great ideas and feelings to ourselves. Sometime ago the *Readers' Digest* published a book called *Great Lives, Great Deeds.* This book is a kind of word museum containing written portraits of 80 of the greatest people who ever lived. It is a kind of doll library or wax museum of great lives where we can not only get acquainted with, but also come to love, those wonderful souls who have so greatly enriched our world generally as well as us personally.

I have always been something of a hero-worshipper and I am sustained and built up by going in friendly association from one of these great lives to another. Every one of them has some personal contribution to make to us. In a very personal way we may have the music of Beethoven, Bach, and Mozart, the philosophy of Socrates, the drama of Shakespeare and the religion of Jesus. We go through the scriptures and each of its great characters takes his own place in the library of our hearts: we receive the radiations from their devotion and faith. We actually derive health from Louis Pasteur, we get honor from Abraham Lincoln, light from Edison, and good humor from Will Rogers.

Sometime ago while receiving the benefit of a radium treatment, I thought of Marie Sklodowska Curie with a kind of personal love and appreciation. I could see her with numb fingers and empty stomach as she worked tirelessly in an old leaky shed year after year without equipment or funds in order to isolate radium for my benefit. After the experiments had met with success, inquiries about the use of radium came from many lands, and the Curies must now decide whether they would give away their new life-giving product without reserve to benefit everyone, or whether they would patent the process for their own good. But this was not a serious problem for the Curies. Their work had always been done for others, not themselves, and besides, as Marie pointed out, to patent this great discovery would be contrary to the scientific spirit. For 35 years Mme. Curie had been handling radium, and breathing in the powerful substances which it radiated. As a consequence she had received many painful burns and finally a deterioration began in her own blood. She paid little attention to the fever which began to bother her. But in May 1934 she went to bed, never to arise from it. Her great heart ceased to beat and she had given her life for our benefit.

May we be worthy of association with those eternal spirits who are our best friends and greatest benefactors, who make up the libraries of our lives.

The Dropout

T HE RESULTS OF a statewide survey were recently published having to do with the large number of young people who discontinue their schooling before the end of the twelfth grade. The purpose of the study was to determine, if possible, the cause and cure of this serious human problem.

Surprisingly enough it was found that most of the dropouts were not bothered by either physical or mental handicaps. Many had rated above average in their intelligence examinations, although a large number had habitually made low grades.

The dropouts themselves gave different reasons for failing to finish their education. Some said they had quit school in order to earn more money, some wanted to get married, some planned to go into military service. Many didn't like either the school or its teachers. Some felt that they had not been treated very well by their fellow students. All wanted to bring about a more pleasant, *present* situation for themselves.

It is very likely that if this survey could follow these dropouts through life, it would reveal an unpleasant trail of disappointment and heartbreak. Certainly a very large percentage of the marriages of these teenagers will go on the rocks. The premature job holders may not like their employers any better than they did their teachers. Most of those who quit school to make more money will be disappointed. The traits that prompted them to quit school as teenagers may also prompt them to quit many other things as adults before the end of their lives. These dropout decisions are almost always based on a false premise. Those who want to make more money should stay in school and better their preparation. The time spent by a woodcutter in sharpening his ax is usually his most profitable investment. And the student who feels deficient should not drop out of school, but should go to school that much longer.

The most wide-spread disease in the world is the inferiority complex. This is a condition that should be corrected, not run away from. Feelings of inferiority and failure are life's signals warning us to redouble our efforts, not to drop our preparation. Whether we are young or old our biggest problem is our reluctance to pay the price demanded by success. The easiest thing in the world to do is to quit, and when one has the attitude and aptitude of a quitter he is always headed for disappointment.

The financial losses alone incurred by dropouts amount to a staggering sum. But there are also some mental, social, spiritual and personality losses. These cannot be measured in money. The self-discipline that one receives from the struggle itself has a substantial cash value. The refining influences derived from the association with other students and teachers can also be most valuable. But whatever the lifetime reward may be of a good day spent in school, it is certainly one of the most worthwhile ways to invest these preparatory years of our lives.

The most important part of this problem is that the dropout drops the wrong things. Before one becomes a dropout from school it is probable that he has already become a dropout from church, and a dropout from responsibility. It is a little bit ironic that while one is dropping his education, his ambitions and his faith, he is usually hanging on for dear life to his inferiority, his discouragements, his laziness and his ignorance. What a pity that it is so easy to quit the school, the church and one's high ideals, and yet so difficult to quit smoking, wrong thinking, immorality and general delinquency! There are very few people who ever quit life's good things because they are incapable of doing the work involved. The reverse is usually true, that they can't do the work involved because they are quitters. And yet quitting only aggravates their problems. A confirmed dropout jumps from one job to another, from one divorce to another, and from one location to another, and usually he doesn't learn very much that is good from these unfavorable experiences. The third wife usually doesn't suit him any better than the first or the second wife.

On December 10th, 1963, the UPI News Service carried a story about the bankruptcy proceedings of a certain Hollywood actor. This 41-year-old screen star had a very large income almost from the time he was born, and yet he couldn't pay his bills. However, his manager proudly told the court that he had never shirked his responsibility to support the children of his present wife, or the children of any of his four previous wives.

Dropout tendencies not only increase our personal problems but they make our national record a disgrace. Our marital problem is not just one of finding the right person, it is also one of being the right person. That is also our biggest occupational problem and our biggest problem in life generally.

Sometime ago a prominent magazine made a survey of the older occupational dropouts. It said that 75 per cent of all workers hate their jobs. That would not be so alarming if they just hated one job, because they could quickly get a job that they liked and the problem would be solved. But we usually hate the tenth job as much as the ninth, and the twentieth as much as the nineteenth. It isn't that a dropout just hates his present job, he frequently hates all jobs. One reason is that we never really like a thing until we learn to do it well. But among dropouts we have so many starters and so few finishers.

Some years ago it was announced that an occupational school would be conducted among the members of a certain industry. This contemplated a training that filled a long-recognized need. Excellent teachers were provided. Great interest was shown immediately in the program. The classes were arranged so that they would not interfere with regular employment. But even before the classes started the dropouts began to appear. A large group of those who claimed to be interested never got involved enough to register. Some were not quite ready, others were too busy, still others didn't have the tuition.

However, the classes began with 164 students. Then as assignments required that lessons must be prepared, the real dropout rush began. Some got behind in their home work. Others were assailed by doubts as to whether or not this study was really worthwhile. Distractions made attendance irregular for others. Some didn't like the teachers, and some had already changed their employment. These dropout influences cut down the class membership until only seven remained to take the two parts of the final examination; of these, two members passed both tests, two failed both tests, and three failed one and passed one. Of one kind or another almost everyone had become a dropout. They were dropouts from study, dropouts from purpose, dropouts from ambition, dropouts from attitude and dropouts from industry.

Recently I saw some moving pictures of an automobile endurance race. Immediately after the starting gun the casualties began to show up. One racer blew out a tire, one couldn't quite negotiate the curve, there were a couple of collisions and some had engine trouble. When the race was over there was one winner, a few others had run a good race, but most of the participants were strewn along the track as casualties.

This is about what happens in the race of life. Everyone wants to be successful and happy. But some never get sufficiently involved with life, and some don't care enough to pay the price. Others become victims of indecision and inertia. Some never really get their tuition paid to life, and others just do the wrong things along the way. We look at the greener grass on the other side of the fence. We are assailed by doubts and fears. Unforeseen problems that we can't handle are sure to arise. So we drop our resolutions and our righteousness and get a listing among life's casualties.

Isn't it strange that with so many wonderful ideas and ambitions, we allow ourselves to be victimized by this terrible weakness that makes us quitters. What a thrilling ability to be able to stick to our guns and our wives and our faith and ideals and our jobs! It has been said that "genius is only the power to make continuous effort." It's the follow-through that makes men and women great. We *can learn* to love our wives, our faith and the work that life has given us to do. The prophet Mahomet is supposed to have said, "If the mountain won't come to me then I will go to the mountain." If we can't get a dinner to suit our taste then we should get a taste to suit our dinner.

I would like to share with you some inspirational lines by Douglas Mallock, called "Bill Brown."

> Bill Brown made a million, — Bill Brown, think of that!
> A boy, you remember, as poor as a rat,
> He hoed for the neighbors, did jobs by the day;
> But Bill made a million, or near it, they say.
> You can't understand it? Well, neither could I,
> And then I remembered, and now I know why:
> The bell might be ringin', the dinner horn blow.
> But Bill always hoed to the end of the row.
>
> Bill worked for my father, you maybe recall;
> He wasn't a wonder, not that, not that at all;
> He couldn't out-hoe me, or cover more ground,
> Or hoe any cleaner, or beat me around;
> In fact I was better in one way that I know,
> One toot from the kitchen and home I would go;
> But Bill always hoed to the end of the row.

We used to get hungry out there in the corn.
When you talk about music, what equals a horn,
A horn yellin' dinner, tomatoes and beans,
And pork and potatoes and gravy and greens?
I ain't blamin' no one for quittin' on time;
To stop with the whistle, that ain't any crime,
But as for the million — well, this much I know:
That Bill always hoed to the end of the row.

There may be better success formulas than this ability to finish the job, but I don't know just what they are. Any man shows a great character strength when he keeps on in a good cause, in spite of distractions, difficulties or unpleasantness. In fact, most real success is actually built upon failure.

Thomas A. Edison failed 5,000 times in his attempt to invent an electric light, but he learned a little bit from each failure until finally there was nothing left but success. Abraham Lincoln was defeated for almost every office but he kept on trying until he became President of the United States. It has been said that in her wars, England usually loses all of the battles except the last one, but the last battle is the important one.

Mohandas K. Gandhi also had a habit of winning the last battle. He had so many problems to overcome that he finally called himself a self-remade man. But everyone should be a self-remade man, with a constant remodeling job always going on. And an important part of his construction should include this ability to stick to the job. It requires neither brains, character nor industry to quit, and this is a temptation that confronts everyone.

During the bitter days of the Revolutionary War, George Washington wrote to a kinsman and said, "Such is my situation that if I were to wish the bitterest curse on an enemy this side of the grave I would put him in my place. I see the impossibility of doing any essential service to the cause by continuing in command, and yet I am told that if I quit the command inevitable ruin will follow from the distractions that will ensue." He said, "In confidence I tell you that I never was in such a divided, unhappy state since I was born." But it was only because Washington didn't quit that he became the father of his country.

Many years ago on one of the islands in the St. Lawrence, a multi-millionaire began building a replica of a famous ancient castle. He employed the best architects. He went around the world looking for materials. But early in the building, construction was allowed to stop. Today the partially completed castle still stands on the island as a mecca for curious tourists who go there to see the remains of this unfinished dream. But unfinished dreams are all about us. It may be the foundation of a home that was never built. It may be a discontinued program for character development. It may be the plans for a godly life that was abandoned in the face of some distraction. We are all capable of great dreams but the test comes in getting them finished.

Jesus was speaking of the most worthwhile of our unfinished castles when he talked about our mansions in Heaven. And again and again he repeated the formula saying, "He that endureth to the end shall be saved." With our eternal salvation, as with everything else, it is the follow-through that is most important. It has been said that the fifth principle of the gospel is endurance. Faith, repentance, baptism and the gift of the Holy Ghost are all wonderful, but even they lose much of their value if we lack the ability to stay on the job. We need more of this ability to overcome difficulty, this ability to remain faithful and keep believing, this ability to keep building the castle of our eternal lives! I close with the words of the old hymn which says:

> Things may not look well,
> But then you never can tell,
> So carry on, old man, carry on.
> Be proud of your mission;
> Greet life with a cheer.
> Give it all that you've got,
> That's why you are here.
>
> Fight the good fight,
> And be true to the end;
> And at last when you die,
> Let this be your cry —
> Carry on, my soul, carry on.

El Dorado

THERE IS AN INTERESTING story told about the early Spanish explorers who came to the Western Continent in search of gold. They had heard stories of a legendary treasure-city called El Dorado. They believed that this golden city was located somewhere in the northern part of South America. It was supposed to be inhabited by a tribe of enormously wealthy Indians. On every hand these sixteenth century Spaniards heard exciting tales about this fabulous wealthy city of gold. It was even said that at their yearly festival these wealthy El Dorado Indians covered their entire bodies with gold. However, search as they would, the Spaniards were unable to locate this golden city of their dreams.

In addition to being an interesting story, this account involves an important trait of human nature. Men have always had a ravenous hunger for gold. Jason went in search of the Golden Fleece. We have legends of the golden apples of Hesperides, and the fable about the goose that laid the golden eggs. We are still a little envious of the golden touch of King Midas, and the underground store house filled with gold that was possessed by Ali Baba and his forty thieves. We even have our own buried city of gold at Fort Knox, Kentucky.

The ancient kings used to reward their heroes by putting chains of gold around their necks, and rings of gold upon their fingers. For a hundred years prior to January 31, 1934, the monetary system of the world was based on the gold standard. We have conducted some gold rushes to California, the Yukon, and the New York stock exchange. Since gold was discovered on the west coast in 1848 we have referred to California as the El Dorado state. Some of these excitements still smolder under the surface of our lives. In our imagination we still cling to the hope of finding some golden city.

But this interesting word El Dorado has also been used to describe some other kinds of riches. Each year the golden state of California takes many times more wealth out of her soils than ever came out of her gold mines. Yet the greatest values are not in the ground at all, but in the people who live upon it. The wealth that came out of the mind of Thomas A. Edison has surpassed the value of all of the earth's gold put together. And either Henry Ford or John D. Rockefeller could make Ali Baba, Jason and the Spaniards altogether look like paupers. But it has been said that the most severe poverty as well as the greatest riches are largely of the spirit.

Every human being has buried within himself a natural vein of greatness. And, in addition, he may become rich in material things, rich in wisdom, rich in the spirit, rich in personality traits and rich in the possibilities of eternal life. In each case he needs only to learn how to command the shaft in order to draw out the gold. God has placed inside of every human being the very things that he seeks. If we seek for great faith we have in our own hearts the seeds of faith, waiting only for us to make them grow. If we need courage we have only to develop that which we already have. Talents can produce wealth but wealth cannot produce talents. Therefore, talents are greater than wealth. And the greatest of all talents are the religious talents.

No one can find success and happiness by merely going to Paris or London, or New York, or California. For if one doesn't find peace, success and wealth within himself, he will never find them any place. Man himself is the most miraculous of all treasure houses. And everyone is sitting on his own acre of diamonds. Each of us has a bonanza under his own feet. Everyone's lucky days are already at hand. In his own hands each holds the keys to the front door of a gold mine and each owns a power plant with its powers still unutilized. And everything is within — nothing is without.

Jesus said, "The Kingdom of God is *within* you." A note in the King James version says that he meant the Kingdom of God is *among* you. And that may be what he did mean. But the phrase "Kingdom of God" has at least three meanings — one is a place, one is an organization and one is a condition. So far as the condition is concerned the Kingdom of God is within you. Peter said that faith is more precious than gold and so is righteousness, devotion, truth and godliness. These are all in people. Jesus taught us to pray, "Thy kingdom come. Thy will be done on earth, as it is in heaven." This prayer will be fulfilled when the condition and the organization bring about and become part

of the place. In his great vision of the future, John the Revelator
saw the time when our earth would be sanctified, immortalized
and celestialized to become the eternal dwelling place of those
who had earned the right to live here. Then our El Dorado will
be an actual fact. There is a thrilling description of this future
dwelling place in the book of Revelations. John said, "And I saw
a new heaven and a new earth: for the first heaven and the
first earth were passed away; and there was no more sea. And
I, John, saw the Holy City, New Jerusalem, coming down from
God out of heaven, prepared as a bride adorned for her husband.
And I heard a great voice out of heaven saying, Behold, the
tabernacle of God is with men, and he will dwell with them, and
they shall be his people, and God himself shall be with them,
and be their God. And God shall wipe away all tears from their
eyes; and there shall be no more death, neither sorrow, nor cry-
ing, neither shall there be any more pain: for the former things
are passed away. And he that sat upon the throne said, Behold,
I make all things new. And he said unto me, it is done. I am
Alpha and Omega, the beginning and the end. I will give unto
him that is athirst of the fountain of the water of life freely.
He that overcometh shall inherit all things; and I will be his
God, and he shall be my son." (Rev. 21:1-7)

John saw twenty-four elders seated around the throne
clothed in white raiment having crowns of gold on their heads.
"And before the throne there was a sea of glass like unto crystal."
(Rev. 4) John also describes our glorified earth as a sea of glass
mingled with fire. (Rev. 15:2) He mentions that it will be lighted
by the glory of God. He says that the light was like unto a stone
most precious even like a jasper stone, clear as crystal. He said,
"And the building of the wall of it was of jasper: and the city
was pure gold, like unto clear glass. And the foundations of the
wall of the city were garnished with all manner of precious stones.
The first foundation was jasper; the second, saphhire; the third,
a chalcedony; the fourth, an emerald; the fifth, sardonyx; the
sixth, sardius; the seventh, chrysolite; the eighth, beryl; the ninth,
a topaz; the tenth, a chrysoprasus, the eleventh, a jacinth; the
twelfth, an amethyst. And the twelve gates were twelve pearls;
every several gate was of one pearl: and the street of the city
was pure gold, as it were transparent glass. . . . And the city had
no need of the sun, neither of the moon, to shine in it: for the
glory of God did lighten it, and the Lamb is the light thereof.

And the nations of them which are saved shall walk in the light of it: and the kings of the earth do bring glory and honor into it.

". . . there shall be no night there. And there shall in no wise enter into it anything that defileth, neither whatsoever worketh abomination, or maketh a lie; but they which are written in the Lamb's book of life." (Rev. 21:18-27)

John says, "And he shewed me a pure river of water of life, clear as crystal, proceeding out of the throne of God and of the Lamb. In the midst of the street of it, and on either side of the river, was there the tree of life, which bare twelve manner of fruits, and yielded her fruit every month: and the leaves of the tree were for the healing of the nations. And there shall be no more curse: but the throne of God and of the Lamb shall be in it; and his servants shall serve him: And they shall see his face; and his name shall be in their foreheads." (Rev. 22:1-4)

Since the fall of Adam, our earth has existed in its fallen or telestial state with a curse upon it. But at the glorious second coming of Christ the earth will be cleansed. The curse will be removed and the earth will be restored to the paradisaical state such as it was before the fall. During the Millennium Christ will reign personally upon this earth which will then be terrestrial. The final change in the earth will be brought about at the end of the one thousand years when the earth will be celestialized and become the permanent abode of those of earth's inhabitants who qualify for celestial glory. As you read the description of the future glory of this earth try to imagine something that compares with it. The early Spanish adventurers left their homes to die in the wilderness of South America seeking an imaginary golden city that did not exist. But God is offering us the most wonderful golden city in which we may live for eternity. We must make ourselves into celestial people, otherwise we will not be eligible to live on a celestial earth. One of our biggest problems is not only that we half-believe that "God is dead," but most people don't even think of eternal beings as real people or of eternal locations as real places. God is a real person. Our glorified earth will be a real place as solid and as material as is our present telestial earth. And blessed will we be if we have earned the right to dwell upon it. But even above the glory of the earth will be the glory of the people who dwell there. The great being who gave John this revelation also gave a revelation of himself.

John said that he was in the spirit on the Lord's day when he heard a great voice behind him as of a trumpet saying, "I am Alpha and Omega, the first and the last: and, What thou seest, write in a book." John turned to see who had spoken to him and he said that he saw . . . "one like unto the Son of man, clothed with a garment down to the foot, and girt about the paps with a golden girdle. His head and his hairs were white like wool, as white as the snow; and his eyes were as a flame of fire; And his feet like unto fine brass, as if they burned in a furnace; and his voice as the sound of many waters. . . . And his countenance was as the sun shining in his strength." (Rev. 1:13-16) That is a challenging picture of a glorified being.

Someone has said that an inspired book needs an inspired reader, and a glorified earth must have glorified people to live upon it. By our faith and devotion we must get a little more of this glory into *us* before we can get into *it*. And why not! God is giving us herewith our greatest opportunity. Our resources are inexhaustible, our potential power is overwhelming, and our blessings will always follow the use of our talents. We need only to develop the faith and the will to achieve

Everyone has sometime said to himself, "If only I could change my circumstances," or "If only I could do better with my 'things'." Recently a 64-year-old man said, "I wish I could live my life over again." Millions of people merely sigh over the years that are never used. And many of us will present before the judgment bar of God a life that has only been partially lived. God wants us all to be wealthy. In the greatest sermon ever preached Jesus talked about laying up for ourselves treasures in heaven. But most of us put off getting started.

I recently heard a man accused of being unfriendly. More than anything else in the world this man wants to be friendly, but he just doesn't know how. So far as I know everyone wants to be successful and happy. We all want to be faithful, deserving and live in God's golden city, but mostly we just don't know how. One man wants to be financially successful by sharp practices, another tries to get his satisfactions from being immoral. We all want to change our circumstances, but few are willing to change themselves. Frequently those who fail don't even know the reason for their problem. We look for our El Dorado in the wrong places. Happiness is never found in wickedness, nor is rest found in idleness, nor is there peace in selfishness, nor is there glory found in disbelief. All of these talents must first be developed in our own lives. Jesus said he that loseth his life shall find it. We get happiness by making others happy. We get love by giving it away. We know the way to the liquor store, but we lose our way to the church. We want to succeed but we are usually so vague and indefinite in our faith. We need to be more familiar with the word of the Lord and know where we are going. Benjamin Disraeli once said that genius is the power to visualize the objective.

The legendary city of gold was never discovered by the Spaniards, and the real one may be missed by us unless we discover and use these God-given talents that he has planted in us for this purpose. Each year the moving picture industry is sending out hundreds of talent scouts trying to discover someone on whom they can lavish $2,000 per week for talents which the person himself may not have been aware of. But all of us also need a discoverer. Like the unprofitable servant mentioned in the parable we mostly just hide our talents in the ground and forget about them. Or we put our lights under a bushel so that no one can find them. Jesus was a discoverer. He found some unlearned men who were fishermen, tax collectors, etc., and made their lives rich by changing them into saints and apostles. He enlarged their faith, aroused their courage and stirred up their testimony and ambition, and he will help us to discover ourselves if we dig down into the darkened areas of our lives and utilize those golden talents that he has hidden there. Our power of believing can help us qualify for God's golden city, and may he also help us to discover ourselves in it.

Examination Day

ONE OF THE MOST important experiences in life comes under the heading of education. It might be said that all of life is education and all of education is preparation. We prepare for school, we prepare for marriage, we prepare for our life's work, we prepare for death. In our antemortal existence we prepared for this life. In this life we prepare for the next life. From the beginning of life to its end it is as though we are passing through one long progressive schoolroom.

One of the most productive aids to our education is the device known as the examination. In fact the examination or check-up is one of the most important parts of any worthwhile accomplishment. The dictionary says that an examination is a search, or an investigation. It is a process of scrutinizing that has been designed to determine how successful we are being in our quest for truth. The examination is also designed to test the qualifications and objectives of the learner. One's personal success is his most important possession, and the examination is probably the best way we have of proving ourselves to ourselves and to others. It is also the best way of checking up on our actual performance. By the examination we are able to establish a basis for an accurate evaluation to supply us with the information on which the most expert future planning can be based. The examination may also help to provide the motivation for reaching our success. The check-up takes advantage of our inborn desire to do well. That is, there is a powerful motivation in being on or ahead of schedule. Those engaged in both public and self-education might well be judged by how effective they are as examiners. There are many kinds of examination, some are oral, some are written, and some are based on an actual accomplishment. There are term examinations, monthly examinations, weekly examinations and daily examinations. Some are given by a teacher, some are given by an employer, some are given by ourselves and some are given by God. Every day we are being checked upon by our critics, our enemies, our friends, our families, and life itself. The primary purpose of the examination is to see to it that each day's assignments are fulfilled and converted that day into accomplishments. The examination is successful when the words "mission accomplished" can be written at the end of each success period. Most students, employees and citizens are strong enough to carry the burdens imposed by success for one day. However, when we let our loads accumulate they can soon become unbearable. To begin to fall behind is at best temporary failure. And a good set of preliminary examinations gets us ready and keeps us on schedule for the finals. The term "final examination" has a feeling and a sound of great consequences, but probably no more than it deserves. "Final" means about what its name implies. The finals are final! They may determine forever whether or not we have made the grade.

The examination for the semester of the term may not be quite as challenging, for we usually have another chance. But their frequence and regularity are intended to protect us against our natural weakness of procrastination. Most people have a tendency to postpone the consideration of things to a date when they will have more time. And it is a part of our human nature that when we put off the check-up for any considerable period we discover that we have lost ground. There is a serious defect in our perspective that makes everything in the future seem easy. It is so natural to feel that somehow we will be less rushed in the future and our lessons will be easier later on. Then we will have more money to solve our financial problems and more ability to relieve our personal needs. But usually when we arrive at the place where we expected to find our Utopia, we may discover ourselves buried under an impossible mountain of accumulated problems. Then we are aware that we should have kept a tighter rein on ourselves with some kind of an effective "pay as you go" schedule. A good salesman needs to make a daily work audit in order to know where he is slipping and how far he may be behind schedule. By a conscientious use of the daily examination one can usually keep the day open until we are able to hang out a finish sign.

An old Chinese proverb says, "The superior man uses the night in which to prepare for the day." And the work of the day should be finished before we let it go. To have a daily program of measuring each day's accomplishment against that day's plans is also a good way to increase our sense of urgency. At best, life is very short. And the hazard of failure is increased by this deception in our perspective. If we are to achieve in full measure we must be in more of a hurry than we ourselves may feel is necessary.

We will only have enough time to complete our lives if we finish each day as we come to it. To let our work accumulate, and hope that by some cramming process we will be able to solve the problems of many days in one day, is a poor substitute for a daily program of steady accomplishment. If we could only develop the attitude for each week throughout the year that most students have during the week of the finals, then our success would rest on the most solid foundation. When the finals are on then everyone is on the job. We are in a better position to understand the need of the "checkup". During the week of the final examination it is easy to form the resolution that in the future each day's work should be finished that day. Then our better attitude is more likely to prompt us to turn on enough extra pressure to keep our lives on schedule.

Things seem to have a clearer meaning and a greater value on examination day. When our efforts are tied closer to our accomplishments by a regular schedule it tends to magnify our interest. With no time for procrastination or meandering we tend to keep our objectives in better focus and more accurately in our sights. The week of the finals is also the one period when we tend strictly to business. Then day-dreaming and mind-wandering are out of the question. Certainly this idea of a regular examination is a very profitable one, and its applications reach into many departments. In court the witnesses are examined before they are qualified to testify. Prospective customers like to make an examination of the products they purchase. We are well advised when we make check-ups on our health with regular physical examinations. The Boy Scout program recommends that all scouts do a good turn *every* day. But as great as this program is, it would lose most of its value without a daily checkup. A Boy Scout who gets six months behind on his good turns will be in serious trouble with his program. He will not *only* have lost the spirit, but he will also have lost the good turn *habit*, and the size of the pile of his overdue good turns will discourage his effort and kill any hope of accomplishment. On the other hand the greatest motivation always comes out of performance. Nothing succeeds like success. We never quit while we are ahead. No one ever gets tired while he's winning. But there are even greater reasons why we need a regular check-up on our *religious* progress. The religious examination is more important because greater consequences depend on the results. Everything, including the welfare of our souls, depends upon how we come out in our religious finals. Failure in religion is so much easier than other failure, inasmuch as religious objectives are usually a little further down the road, and in the deception of distance they look smaller and less important. There is also less pressure and a smaller amount of urgency than attends such needs as those of meeting our financial obligations or of getting an occupational increase. Some of the most powerful ordinary pressures usually do not attend the meeting of a religious obligation. This is especially true because more than in other things we are required to check up on ourselves. The lack of urgency and the deferred nature of the reward makes religion one of the easiest things for most of us to postpone for later consideration.

A Sunday School teacher once asked her students how many of them wanted to go to heaven. All raised their hand except one boy. The teacher said, "Bill, wouldn't you like to go to heaven someday?" And he said, "Oh sure, someday, but I thought you were getting up a group to go tonight." Everyone wants to do great things and be a fine person someday, but we don't always have a lot of pressure urging us to do it now. In fact someone has said that "Hell is just truth seen too late." It is the function of the check-up to help us to do the important things *now*.

A professor at a great American university was recently interviewed by some newspaper men who wanted to know about his faith. He told them he didn't have any faith. They reminded him that when he had come to the university five years previously he had been known as a man of faith. He explained to them that when he had come to the university he had been impressed with the great amount of educational work that he would have to do and that he wouldn't have time for religion. He decided that the best thing to do would be to temporarily put his faith in cold storage. He said it was as though he had opened a drawer and put his faith in it, and then closed the drawer. He had expected to come back five years later and reopen the drawer and reinvest himself in his faith, much as he would redress himself in his last summer's suit. But five years later when he opened the drawer the faith was gone. There *is* no such thing as *preserved* faith.

Faith can't live in isolation. When you take away the works — the faith always dies.

Sometime ago a Dr. Betts talked to a group of young people about their interest in their church. Many of them replied that the activities of the church were something that could be attended to later on in life, and they felt that there was no need to devote themselves to it in their youth when there were so many other interesting things to do. But when one becomes a dropout from religious activity he soon becomes a dropout from religion itself. It is interesting that to commit such sins of omission as ignorance, indecision and indifference you don't need to do one single thing wrong, you just don't do anything at all. Many people actually apostatize from the Church by doing nothing. They merely let their interest die a natural death by getting too far behind schedule. Some people are ten years and some are fifty years behind in their religious lives. If anyone ever got that far behind in his finances or his medical school studies there wouldn't be very much left. This is also true of religion.

To prevent this from happening the Apostle Paul made an interesting suggestion about the check-up to the members of the Church at Corinth. He said, "Examine yourselves to see whether or not you are still in the faith." That is one of the greatest ideas. Before anyone can be accepted into the Church he is required to pass some entrance examination in faith, repentance, and baptism. Then he is given the gift of the Holy Ghost.

Each week we have a program for re-examining our goals and recommitting ourselves to our objectives by partaking of the sacrament of the Lord's supper. Each time our temple recommend is renewed we pass a new examination in our faith. And each day we should prove our good turn by our works. We should give ourselves a frequent critical self-examination, rather than waiting for some serious crisis to force us to check up upon ourselves. If we haven't examined ourselves for ten years we may find that we quit going to church 9½ years ago, and became a part tithe payer eight years ago, and started drinking six years ago, and stopped believing in God five years ago, and now we may find that we are so far away from the straight and narrow way that we have lost interest in getting back. So frequently we are like the sheep in the parable that just nibbled its way into getting lost. The sheep went too far without a check-up.

Thomas Carlyle once said that "A man's religion is the most important thing about him." That is what he believes in and thinks about and lives by and fights for. That is the thing on which everything else depends. And we need to examine ourselves frequently to make sure that we are still in the faith, and that we are somewhere near the middle of the straight and narrow way. We should have in mind now that someday there is going to be a great judgment day; that will be a day when everyone will be examined to see whether or not he is still in the faith. Then everyone will be judged according to his works. We can be absolutely sure that it will be a sorry day for us if we get a low score in life's finals.

John the Revelator frightens us just a little bit as he describes this interesting final examination day. He said, "And I saw the dead, small and great, stand before God; and the books were opened: and another book was opened which is the book of life: and the dead were judged out of those things that were written in the books, according to their works." (Rev. 20:12) "And whosoever was not found written in the book of life was cast into the lake of fire." (Rev. 20:15) That will be a day to remember, and if our names are not going to be found written in the book of life we ought to know it as soon as possible so that we can do something about it. For above everything else we will want to pass our entrance examinations for the celestial kingdom.

Failure

FOR AS LONG AS anyone can remember we have been telling ourselves the world's great success stories. We have memorized stimulating success poems, meditated over inspiring scriptures, absorbed helpful philosophies, and stamped and painted the pictures of success into our minds. As someone has excelled in some good thing, we have held up his example to motivate our own accomplishment.

A hundred years ago, Horatio Alger wrote some 235 books of the "rags to riches" kind of success stories. These have increased the success quotient of thousands of lives. Unfortunately, however, all of our vicarious experience does not carry the success image. Life itself is made up of opposites. We see white objects most clearly on a dark background. The Lord himself has pointed out that if we did not know the bitter, we could not understand the sweet.

Whether the villain performs in the theater or on the stage of life itself, he often serves our best interests quite as well as does the hero. The hero shows us which road to travel, while the villain points out the quicksands to be avoided. Jesus talked of hell about as much as he did of Heaven, and we must learn to deal effectively with both the good and the bad.

One of the great books of the world is Dante's *Divine Comedy*. In those days a comedy was not something that was funny. It was something with a happy ending. A more understandable title for our day would have been the *Divine Experience*. Based on the scripture, and stimulated by his imagination, Dante took his readers on a trip through the lower regions, with a happy ending in Heaven. But Dante believed that it was his mission in life to show men hell, that they might be better informed about the misery caused by those things that should be avoided. Because it shows us failure at its worst, Thomas Carlyle said that in his opinion *The Divine Comedy* was the most remarkable of all books. Certainly the one business of life is to succeed. We were not placed here to waste our lives in failure. But because no one can afford a personal experience in either hell or failure, we should learn as much success as possible by studying its opposites as they appear in the lives of the great failures.

The Bible itself would not be complete without the experiences of Cain, Lucifer, Nebuchadnezzar, Jezebel, and Judas Iscariot. For us to effectively feel the pain of those who have made their own lives miserable may be like developing an antitoxin to prevent that particular evil from forming in our own lives.

Most of life's tragedies develop around this short two-syllable harmless-appearing little word called failure. Primarily we are frightened only by those ugly giant sins. However no one ever *starts out* to be a sinner, and no one ever *plans* to be a failure. We fail only because goals are not achieved, plans are not carried to completion, and righteous ambitions are neglected or allowed to go unfilled.

The dictionary says that "to fail" is "to waste away," "to decline," "to dwindle," "to miss the mark," or "to become insolvent." It is to be weighed in the balances and found wanting. Frequently we are found wanting in faith, or industry or righteousness. It is bad enough to fail in our health or in our occupation, but the greatest tragedy is to fail in our lives.

Very few people ever miss the success mark by chance or accident. We fail because we don't do the right things in the right way. No one is a failure merely because he falls down occasionally. There is an old proverb that says, "He who rises quickly and continues his journey is as though he had never fallen." The failures are those who surrender their courage and stop trying. Nations fail when they allow unrighteousness and decay to destroy their vitality and thwart the better impulses of their people. There is always a dark, dismal despair dogging the footsteps of nations or individuals who lose their ideals or distort their sense of right.

A breakdown in character is usually followed by a breakdown in occupation, public confidence, family solidarity and self-respect. A survey recently conducted at Stanford University showed that among those who were fired from their jobs, over 94% were fired for some reason not even remotely connected with job competence. They lost their employment because they had allowed idleness, sloth, dishonesty, immorality, and bad attitudes to infiltrate their lives.

But like most things failure can be prevented if precautions are taken against it in advance. Someone once said that he wished he knew where he was going to die, for then he would never go around the place. If we fully understood failure as it manifests itself in others, a personal indulgence for us would then be unnecessary. Because failure is unpleasant, we sometimes try to avoid thinking about it by hiding our heads in the sand. But failure doesn't cease to exist merely because it is ignored. Like other diseases, the more the problem is neglected the more vigorously the trouble grows.

Aristotle once said that we never really know a thing until we know it by its causes. Every success has a cause, and every failure has a cause. Indigestion has a cause, toothache has a cause, overweight has a cause, unhappiness has a cause, a poor marital relationship has a cause. If we can discover what causes success, we can reproduce it. If we can find out what causes failure, we can eliminate it.

Not only do people become alcoholics and other varieties of failure without meaning to do so, but they usually insist that they have no problem — until their wills have been taken captive, and they have gone beyond the point of no return. It is interesting to remember that the mysterious hand that wrote about Belshazzar's failure in the plaster of the palace wall is still in business. Belshazzar was the head of the greatest government of that day and he drank his wine from golden goblets, yet he was found wanting in God's balances.

Of course, there are no cases of either *total* success or *total* failure. Failure is like physical disability which the government counts as a percentage. One man may be 10% disabled, another 20%, and another 90%, and whether we are thinking either of this life or of the next, rewards and punishments are handed out according to our fraction of success. We might try to understand what the Psalmist had in mind when he spoke of the lowest hell, or what Paul was thinking when he mentioned the third heaven. Paul elaborated on his idea by saying, "There is one glory of the sun, and another glory of the moon, and another glory of the stars: for as one star differeth from another star in glory, so also is the resurrection of the dead." What a tragedy it would be to receive only a fraction of our possible blessings, when God places before us the possibility of "a fullness of the glory of God."

It has been said, "He is idle who might be better employed" and everyone fails to the extent that he misses his maximum success possibility. When anyone allows himself to become frustrated, discouraged, or unrighteous, this lessening process immediately begins to take place. Then something goes out of him, so that his morale begins losing altitude.

General MacArthur once said that "old generals never die, they just fade away." But an ambition and a zest for living can also fade away.

A few years ago a drought in a certain area caused a heavy crop failure. The people concerned had spent an entire year at hard labor. They needed a good crop, but conditions outside themselves made that impossible. As a result considerable misery and unhappiness was caused. But the most severe misery and the worst unhappiness is caused when the failure is in us.

During the war the government spent large sums of money training fighter pilots. Whenever a crackup occurred, the government lost a large investment in the aircraft and in the pilot. A survey indicated that 6% of the losses were caused by mechanical failure, and 94% by man failure. Worry, liquor, or trouble at home, caused more crackups than all of the mechanical defects combined. In government, in business or in life itself most of our problems come from "man failure." When we fail to differentiate between good and bad, we have about the same problems as a mixed-up aviator flying in a storm with an erratic compass. A failure in righteousness, or a conscience failure, or a failure in reason can easily cause a crackup. Lawbreakers, alcoholics, sex deviates or those with insufficient concern for the word of the Lord can quickly destroy their own success. Usually failure has little to do with one's intelligence quotient. Success is more a matter of "I believe" and "I will" than of I.Q. For example, Satan was one of the most brilliant among all of the hosts of heaven, but he rebelled against God and became a colossal failure. He not only failed for himself, but he also led one-third of all of the hosts of heaven to their downfall.

Suppose that we make a list of some of the great failures and see if we can determine what caused their trouble. These failures will be found among the rich and the poor, the ignorant and the educated, the wise and the foolish. Through the scriptures we might try to understand how the guilt of the publicans and sinners differed from that of the chief priests and Pharisees. Or we might examine those in the very highest strata. The first king of the United Nation of ancient Israel was Saul. He was selected by God himself, and yet he didn't work out very well as king. He first began failing in his obedience to God, then his courage began to fail. Failure has a way of feeding upon itself, and soon Saul became depressed and melancholy. Then the scripture says that an evil spirit came upon him. His decline continued until he finally committed suicide by falling on his own sword.

Next upon the throne was King David, who was called a man after God's own heart. Yet in spite of his great qualities he committed two of the most serious sins. Solomon was the third and last king of the United Nation of Israel. He was blessed with greater wisdom than any man who had ever lived, and yet in spite of his advantage he died an idolator very much out of favor with God. God had said to Solomon's father David, "If thy children take heed to their way, to walk before me in truth with all their heart and with all their soul, there shall not fail thee (said he) a man on the throne of Israel." (I Kings 2:4) But because Solomon made such serious mistakes, the kingdom was divided and his people became the slaves of foreign powers. But more or less we all become slaves when we insist on doing the things that bring slavery about.

We have an interesting manner of speaking where we add the important stipulation "without fail." The Lord has also attached some "without fail" signs to his commandments. Through Ezra he said, "Take heed that ye fail not." (Ezra 4:22) What a great idea it would be to add a "without fail" to our diligence, our righteousness, and our obedience to God. To the exact extent to which we violate the laws of God we become failures.

In doing their part of the work of the world, medical men are trying to wipe out disease, government leaders are trying to wipe out poverty. Our greatest opportunity should be to wipe out sin and failure from our own lives. In an interesting prayer quoted by President Franklin D. Roosevelt an early Chinese addressed the Creator by saying, "Reform the world and begin with me." Each one of us has the power to reform himself by conforming his own life to divine standards, and only as we succeed in this can we stop this tremendous useless human waste and prevent ourselves from flinging back into the face of the Creator a life that has been only half used. With devotion to God and a strong will we may live a "good life, without fail."

Night swoops on me with blackest wings
    But I'll succeed.
I see the stars that darkness brings
    And I'll succeed.

No force on earth can make me cower
Because each moment and each hour
I still affirm with strength and power
    I shall succeed.

Fathers and Sons

ONE OF THE MOST important parts of our lives is our human relationships. Man is a highly gregarious being. He is at his best when he is living and working effectively with others of his kind. God's statement that it is not good for man to be alone could have several significant meanings. When people try to live as hermits, their faculties and senses always deteriorate. But the more pleasant and constructive any human relationship is, the better it is for everyone. The present world hate existing between nations and individuals has caused an increase in all kinds of financial, mental and emotional problems. On the other hand, great benefits accrue when people get along well together. Honest friendships bring a substantial return in success and happiness. Where there is real confidence and trust between individuals or groups, everyone becomes more prosperous materially and spiritually.

Of course the primary and most important human associations usually develop within the family unit. Some of the most worthwhile relationships exist between the parents and their children. We have instituted some Mothers' days and some Fathers' days to promote these tremendous associations. The father is the head of the house and as such he has several significant responsibilities to all the rest of the family members. He is their provider, protector, educator, companion, friend, and example. Our literature has some inspiring stories that stimulate good relationships between fathers and sons.

In 1853 Matthew Arnold wrote a great Father and Son poem entitled Sohrab and Rustum. Rustum, a powerful young Persian War Lord, had met and married the daughter of the King of the Koords. Before their son, Sohrab, was born, Rustum was called to a faraway field of battle, and because his wife feared that he might seek out their son to train for war, she sent him word that the child which had been born to them had been a sickly girl. But Sohrab's warrior inheritance and the stories of his father's heroism led him to adopt the profession and develop the abilities of his famous father. And Sohrab was called into the military service of the Tartars among whom he lived, although they were the enemies of Persia.

However, above everything else Sohrab longed to know his hero father. In all of his travels he was possessed by only one thought and that was to find Rustum. One day the Tartars met the Persians by the River Oxus. With his general's consent, Sohrab challenged the Persians to match him in single combat with their greatest champion. Because of Sohrab's fame he hoped that the Persians would not dare to send anyone against him but the mighty Rustum himself. This proved to be the case, and not knowing that young Sohrab was his son, Rustum was persuaded to take up the challenge, although he insisted on fighting unknown. As the two met, Sohrab had a faint hope that the great warrior figure planted before him upon the sand was his father, and he ran forward and embraced his knees and clasped his hand and said, "Art thou not Rustum?"

Rustum thought that Sohrab falsely claimed to be his son, and while he had earnestly longed for such a son as Sohrab, yet he feared what the motive of this young man might be. He felt that it may be that the mighty Rustum (who had never faltered on any field of blood) was being tricked into compromising the challenge, so that his fellow Persian lords might be shamed through him. Rustum was the mightiest leader of them all, and the stern old warrior felt that he must insist that the young challenger either make good his vaunt or yield.

Never had Rustum lost a single fight, and never had a single antagonist ever been saved. But Sohrab had seen battles too, and had waded foremost in their bloody waves. Kindling under Rustum's taunts, he decided to fight it out. As this battle of giants proceded it seemed that even the very elements themselves took part in that unnatural conflict. Sohrab would have won; but as hope still filled his soul he let his chance for victory pass, and as he heard the great name of his father shouted in his battle cry, he instinctively lowered his shield — and was transfixed by Rustum's sword. As he lay dying he showed his erstwhile unbelieving father the sign of Rustum's shield, that as a baby his mother had tattooed upon his arm. Rustum knew this was a proof that could not lie. Then, with a great cry of recognition and pain, Rustum said, "O Boy, thy father!" In his terrible grief he half consciously drew his sword as if to slay himself. But Sohrab saw his thought and crawled to where he lay, and put his arms around his father's neck and kissed his lips and said, "Come sit beside me on the sand before I die, and take my head betwixt thy hands, and kiss my cheeks, and wash them in thy tears and say "My son," and let me feel that I have found my father."

Matthew Arnold thrills us with the tremendous feeling of love, hero-worship and confidence that can dwell in the heart of a son for his father. However, there is an equally powerful counterpart for this emotion that a father can feel for a wonderful son. Fighting was the business of this particular father and son. They were both trained to love courage, skill and the ability to make war successfully. All people feel pride in their soldier heroes, and in Sohrab's heart this feeling of devotion, pride and love for his soldier father had almost grown to the proportions of worship. He knew that his father Rustum was the best there was in his field. Very frequently the pride of some young boy may impel him to say of *his* father, "My dad can lick anybody." Life actually magnifies sons and fathers in each other's eyes and therefore enlarges this feeling of love and confidence. For his entire life Sohrab had lived by contemplating these great manly warrior traits as they lived in his father. They were the qualities that had made his father loved, honored, followed and successful wherever he went. Even the quality of worship could hardly have produced a greater adoration in Sohrab's heart. But Rustum was also heart-hungry for a son, one who was capable of fighting by his side, being his confidant, and sharing his fame as a companion in arms. What an exciting thrill it would have been for Rustum to have been engaged in some great cause, with his magnificent son fighting by his side capable of carrying as great a load as his father. Even as he thought about Sohrab after his death, it must have been a source of great pride and joy to him to know that his son was even a better man than his father. It is doubtful if a stronger emotion will ever be discovered than for a successful, devoted father to feel that a righteous son excels him in accomplishment.

When I was a high school freshman, I had an almost unlimited confidence in the ability of a football player who held down the quarterback position. I felt that if it were humanly possible to move that ball across the goal line, he could do it. In war, or in football, or in life, winning is often of overwhelming importance. And what a tremendous power can be built up in children's hearts when they have such confidence in the purpose, righteousness, responsibility and faith of their father.

The story is told of a young father who had been killed in the war. His two little daughters used to comfort themselves with the idea that they would not have been left hungry and poorly clothed if their father had lived. Many lives are broken because children do not have confidence in their parents. This lack of faith can give children nervous disease, mental illnesses and cause serious psychological problems. But what strength comes to children who have faithful, devoted parents, whose ability and purpose can be thoroughly depended upon!

This mutual trust is illustrated by two brothers who fought in World War I. They loved each other — they had gone to school together, they had grown up together, they had joined the army together and they had gone "over the top" many times together. One morning after an excursion out into no-man's land, one of the brothers did not return. Jim immediately went to the officer in charge and said, "Sir, I would like permission to go out into no-man's land to find my brother." The officer said, "Permission is denied — your brother is probably dead and it would be a useless waste." A few hours later Jim returned to the officer and said, "Sir, I would like to go out into no-man's land and find my brother." Again the request was refused. Then just as it was getting dark, Jim again returned to the officer and said, "Sir, I would like to go out into no-man's land and find my brother." Impatient and irritated, the officer said, "All right, it's your own life. If you want to throw it away, go ahead."

So Jim climbed out of the trench, and on his hands and face crawled under the barbed wire and disappeared into the darkness of no-man's land. Hours passed and he didn't return. Midnight came and went with no sign of Jim. Then just before daylight the sentry noticed something moving out in the darkness of no-man's land; and after Jim had satisfied the challenge he was helped down into the trench. As he approached the officer to report his return, the officer said, "Well I hope you're satisfied. He's dead isn't he?" Jim said, "Yes, he's dead, but he wasn't dead when I found him!" Then he told how he had retraced their course of the night before, and all night long he had searched among the dead of yesterday's battle. And finally in a shell hole he had found his unconscious brother. He washed the dirt from his face with the water from his canteen. Then, as he cooled his

parched lips and give him a drink, his brother opened his eyes.
He regained consciousness before he died just long enough to
say five words. As he looked up into his brother's face he said,
"Jim, I knew you'd come." Then Jim said to the officer, "Sir,
I would rather have died a thousand times than to have had my
brother die in disappointment while out there in no-man's land
expecting me."

Among the most thrilling incidents that I know of in the
holy scriptures are those describing the relationship between God
the Eternal Father and his Son Jesus Christ. The first begotten
and most worthy son of God in the spirit was known as Jehovah,
who had ruled with God in the presidency of heaven. Sometimes
a father who loves a particular work has the thrill of having his
son come into his business with him. God is a creator. And about
his Son, Jehovah, Elohim said, "Worlds without number have
I created — and by the Son I created them, which is mine only
begotten." (Moses 1:33) What Jesus referred to as "My Father's
business" is that most important enterprise of bringing about the
eternal salvation of God's children. And here also battles have
had to be fought and won. And Elohim also had a soldier son.
Before the Son of God was the Prince of Peace, he was Jehovah
the Warrior, and led the hosts of heaven against the rebellion
of Lucifer. The brilliant Son of the Morning rebelled against God
and sought to institute force as the governing principle among
God's children. The forces of Jehovah won the battle. Then with
a kind of leave of absence from the ruling council of heaven,
he volunteered to come to earth to give his life to redeem his
Father's other children from death on condition of their repentance. How pleased God must have been with his wonderful Son!
All of God's children did not turn out well. Many of them caused
God serious heartache. Cain became a murderer; Judas a betrayer; and others have been weak, sinful, cowardly and disloyal.
But how different was Jehovah! He could be trusted. He was
always righteous. He came to the earth to do the most important
job involved in the eternal salvation of God's spirit children. He
did his job without error, and he himself lived without sin. On
four known occasions — including his baptism and his transfigura-
tion — what joy must have been in God's soul when he was
heard from heaven saying, "This is my beloved Son in whom I am
well pleased." (Matt. 3:17)

God has planted this same joy instinct in every human heart, and the best way to have joy is to be righteous, and feel confidence and love for others. The prophet said, "Man is that he might have joy." God has provided that every time that we do a good thing we feel pleasure. We enjoy getting good marks in school; we like to win football games; we are pleased to receive well-earned praise and acclaim. This ability to have joy in success and righteousness is most highly developed in God himself. The scripture says that there is great joy in heaven when even the most humble sinner repents. Then try to imagine the intensity of God's love and joy in having a perfect Son. A Son in whom he had extreme pleasure and great pride. Or what ambition in us could be greater than to make it possible for God to get joy from also saying about us, "This is my beloved son, in whom I am well pleased." And what a great joy it may be for us if, like Sohrab, we can really find our eternal Heavenly Father before we die! To this end we need to appropriately commemorate each year our Heavenly Father's fifty-two days.

Fear God

THERE ARE MANY seeming contradictions in our world of opposites that sometimes tend to get us confused. Even the meanings in the dictionary and the Bible are not always clear. In the dictionary we sometimes find as many as forty different definitions for the same word; and some 250 different Christian denominations each claim to get their conflicting religious doctrines from the same Bible. There is an interesting phrase repeated in several forms in the scriptures indicating that we should "fear God." But the Bible also uses other phrases such as "fear not," "be not afraid," "why are ye troubled?" or "why do thoughts arise in your hearts?"

One of the most severe censures ever given by Jesus involved the unprofitable servant who confessed his sin by saying, "I was afraid and hid my talent in the ground." The Master said to him, "Thou wicked and slothful servant." Then he said to his associates, "Take the talent from him and give it unto him which hath ten talents . . . and cast ye the unprofitable servant into outer darkness: there shall be weeping and gnashing of teeth." The unprofitable servant had become the victim of a useless fear that had paralyzed his effort and destroyed what otherwise might have been a substantial accomplishment. Jesus also vigorously condemned those kinds of fear that produce sloth, indifference, lethargy, and tend to lessen good. One of our chief problems comes in our failure to discriminate. Sometimes we cultivate the wrong kind of fear, or we fear the wrong things. The great Psalmist had this discrimination in mind when he said, "Whom then shall I fear — and of whom shall I be afraid?" (Psa. 27:1) When we can properly answer that question, we can solve most of our other problems.

Fear is like "love" or "money" or "industry": it is good or bad depending on how we use it. We should try to overcome those fears that do us harm, and be appropriately afraid when that is in our best interests.

The Apostle Paul speaks of a "godly fear." (Heb. 12:28) This is a fear that serves the best purposes of all concerned.

In Melville's great whaling story *Moby Dick*, the captain in charge of the boat sent out to harpoon whales said to his crew, "I will have no man in my boat who is not afraid of a whale." He knew everyone would be in trouble if his crew had too much of the spirit of careless bravado. The captain wanted men who understood danger, and knew how to make the most effective preparation against it.

Someone recently reported a group of teenagers who played a game of outdaring each other. In driving their cars, and in some immoral situations, their praise went to the one who would take the greatest risks and do the things that others were afraid to do. This kind of courage does not make one a very good prospect for a life insurance policy, nor does it readily promote his own character development. Alexander Pope described such a person when he said, "Fools rush in where angels fear to tread." President James A. Garfield was showing a much more praiseworthy emotion when he said, "I am afraid to do any evil thing." Shakespeare describes this godly fear as "the fear that reason leads." Every virtue must have some fear to give it strength. And the most worthwhile of all fear, is the fear of the Lord. The Psalmist said that "the fear of the Lord is the beginning of wisdom." And developing this fear can be as highly profitable for us personally as developing any other great virtue.

One of the greatest of scriptural passages was written on this subject by the wise man Solomon. In summing up his important Book of Ecclesiastes, he said, "Let us hear the conclusion of the whole matter: Fear God, and keep his commandments: for this is the whole duty of man." This is a rather all-inclusive statement and has considerable importance, coming as it does from one reputed to have had such great wisdom. Solomon didn't put any qualifications or limitations in this scripture. He didn't merely say that it was *important* to fear God and keep his commandments, or even that this was the *most* important thing to do. He said that to fear God and keep his commandments was man's *whole* duty. However, this kind of fear is the constructive kind. It is not the crippling variety that many of us are bothered by. The Bible commentary describes this kind of fear as a combination of love, awe and reverence leading to obedience. We know that God is very wise: he makes his laws only in our interest and we should be very afraid to go against his judgment. He is also a gracious Father and if we loved him we would certainly be afraid to let him down. Taylor said, "Fear is the mother of foresight, implanted in us to guard us from evil." We are also stronger when we are afraid. Fear produces a greater amount of adrenalin in the blood, making it possible for us to run faster, fight harder, think quicker and be more capable.

The ancient Romans had such a feeling on this subject that they built a shrine called "The Temple of Fear." That might suggest a pretty good idea for us to give some attention to. We benefit greatly from our temples of learning and our temples of faith. What would be wrong with a temple of fear dedicated to the philosophy of Solomon, that the whole duty of man comes in fearing God and keeping his commandments? It would naturally follow that we should learn the thing of which we should be afraid and how much we should be afraid. Angelo Patri, a noted American educator, once described the best education as being afraid at the right time. The right time to be afraid is not after we have been destroyed by the whale. And we should not just be a little afraid of a whale. Ignorance gives a baby great courage in the presence of a rattlesnake. Enough ignorance can also give us great courage in the presence of sin. Yet we would not rate one's intelligence very high who carried rattlesnakes around with him to prove his courage. And a very little sin can cause us more suffering than all of the rattlesnakes in the world put together. A sin that we are not at all afraid of may readily consign our souls to hell.

In older generations ministers of the gospel used to talk a great deal about hell and eternal torment. However, we have become so courageous and unbelieving that we are not now particularly concerned over such things. However, without the opiate of ignorance no one could possibly be unafraid of the terrors of hell. Jesus himself talked as much of hell as he did about heaven. One is as much a part of Christan doctrine as the other. And probably the thing that we need more than about anything else, is to be able to feel enough hell each week to give us a substantial scare of evil.

However, hell has never been a very popular subject for discussion among sinners. If we think about it at all, we usually bolster up our complacency with enough ignorance, disbelief and indifference to kill any possible fear. However, like death, or taxes, or the penitentiary, hell does not cease to exist merely because it is ignored. If a little fear is a good thing to help us prevent cancer or murder, or the devastation of a killer whale, it might also help us to limit ourselves in disregarding the great laws of God. We might increase our safety factors by imagining what it would be like to bear the torment of some excruciating physical pain. Or what would it be like to bear the tortures of humiliating shame, or eternal death, or the regret of some wasted opportunity, or the mental oppression caused by a divided unhappy family? Suppose that this pain lasted for eternity, or even for a hundred years. No one has ever yet discovered the extreme limits of mental suffering. We do know that it can be intense enough to derange our minds or actually kill our bodies.

An ancient American prophet, speaking about certain sins, said, "Therefore, if that man repenteth not, and remaineth and dieth an enemy to God, the demands of divine justice do awaken his immortal soul to a lively sense of his own guilt, which doth cause him to shrink from the presence of the Lord, and doth fill his breast with guilt, and pain, and anguish, which is like an unquenchable fire, whose flame ascendeth up forever and ever. And now I say unto you, that mercy hath no claim on that man; therefore his final doom is to endure a never-ending torment." All of our reason tells us that we should be seriously scared by this possibility. The prophet continues by saying, "O, all ye old men, and also ye young men, and you little children who can understand my words . . . I pray that ye should awaken to a remembrance of the awful situation of those that have fallen into transgression." (Mos. 2:38-40) If we develop a proper understanding we can get the most constructive good from those scriptures outlining the disadvantages of suffering in hell. If we were wise enough to get a godly fear into our hearts, it could prevent the worst misfortunes. Someone has said, "Oh, my brethren, it makes my blood run cold to think that some of you may be excluded from those glorious mansions of love."

In the early 1930's with the financial depression at its worst, President Franklin D. Roosevelt said, "The only thing we have to fear is fear itself." Of course, he was thinking of those paralyzing devastating forms of fear where we throw up our hands and stop trying. I would like to paraphrase the president and suggest that about the only thing that we have to fear is our own reckless lack of fear under many conditions. Courage is wonderful but it is not enough and by itself it sometimes has many disadvantages. In the first place we usually do not understand what it is. Courage is not merely the absence of fear. Actually courage can only be developed in the presence of fear. Someone has said that the only one who doesn't know fear is an idiot. We must know fear in order to develop courage. If we knew no fear there would be no motivation to develop our other virtues. We practice health principles when we are afraid of disease. We get an education because we are afraid of ignorance. We work because we are afraid of poverty. We don't rob banks because we are afraid of the penitentiary.

The scriptures say that we should all work out our salvation "in fear and trembling before God." (Phil. 2:12) The reckless fearlessness of one who dares to scoff at righteousness, jeer at punishment and jeopardize the welfare of his own soul may expect to have some serious problems. How unfortunate are those who are brave enough to drink and swear and disbelieve in God! Certainly one has a destructive kind of courage who dares to say that how we conduct our lives doesn't matter. Fear is an instrument of caution and our greatest producer of happiness and we need to work regularly on developing it properly.

Burt says, "An early and provident fear is the mother of safety," and "good men have the fewest fears." Witherspoon says, "It is only the fear of God that can deliver us from the fear of men." And just as we can build up the kind of appetites and loves that can make us great, so we can build up enough fears to overcome our ignorance, lethargy and indifference to righteousness. Certainly fear was put into the human personality to be one of the most important parts of our success. As physical fear rings a bell in our minds to warn us of the approach of danger, so a godly fear stirring in our souls is the signal to rally our defences.

In capitalizing on the Psalmist's question "of whom shall I be afraid?" we might make a list of the things that should incite fear in us. We should be afraid of evil and even the smallest temptations. No negative or foreign matter should ever be allowed in the mind, as it is the mind that makes the body sick. Rags, tatters, and dirt always exist in the mind before they appear on the body. Doctors have prevented many diseases by an early injection of an anti-toxin into the blood. And we might use the thoughts of pain and mental torture as anti-toxins to prevent some more awful pain that may follow if our evil is not corrected. Recently I heard a man say that he had been in hell for two months. Because of problems that had arisen he had felt an awful torment and suffering which in his mind was comparable to the pains of hell. Dante believed that if everyone went through hell in his imagination it might help to keep him out of hell actually. Just as everyone who doesn't want to die from a dread disease should be inoculated, so everyone who doesn't want to go to hell should cultivate some of the right kinds of fear.

Listen to some of the Bible's arguments about the importance of fear. It says, "The fear of the Lord is clean, enduring forever." (Ps. 19:9) "The fear of the Lord is to hate evil, pride, arrogance and every evil way." (Ps. 8:13) "The fear of the Lord prolongeth thy days; but the years of the wicked shall be shortened." (Pro. 14:27)

In the days of Moses the Lord said, "O that there were such an heart in them, that they would fear me, and keep all my commandments always, that it might be well with them, and with their children forever." (Deut. 5:29) If this process of godly fear is properly used we can make ourselves stronger than anything that can happen to us.

One man said, "I am afraid of what I may do in the future." Actually his fear is not great enough. He is still uncertain about his course. This man is still carrying his rattlesnakes around with him. He is still in danger because his fear of evil is only about equal to his desire to sin.

In an ancient covenant God said, "I will put fear in their hearts that they shall not depart from me." "A new heart also will I give unto you, and a new spirit will I put within you." If we repent in the right spirit then according to this ancient covenant God will put enough of his fear into our hearts to prevent any repetition. Here is one of our wonder of wonders in action.

God has promised that our past evils will be forgiven, and our righteous futures will be guaranteed by that wondrous miracle of godly fear which will make us new creatures with new hearts that are strong enough to withstand any future evil. Certainly we should get the words of Solomon in our hearts, and say with our lives, "Let us then hear the conclusion of the whole matter — fear God and keep his commandments, for this is the whole duty of man."

A Felony

AMONG THE MOST distinguishing characteristics of our day are our crime waves, and our increases in delinquency.

The Bible says that sin is the transgression of law, and the dictionary says that a transgression of the law is "some forbidden act or omission that is punishable by death, imprisonment, fine or removal from office." The three subheadings of crime include treason, misdemeanors and felonies. Treason is usually considered the most serious, and the dictionary gives the example of Benedict Arnold bargaining to sell West Point to the British during the Revolutionary War. But in many ways there are people who are still selling out our national interests to our enemies. The most serious limitations placed upon our abilities to fight our foreign foes are because the enemy within our own borders so greatly reduces our strength. Probably no one believes that any foreign foe could ever militarily defeat the United States. But many of our enemies are actually expecting an American overthrow by the weaknesses and divisions caused by the traitors existing within our own borders. In a most real sense the agitators and the marchers and the banner wavers, as well as every murderer and every trouble maker and every liar and every alcoholic and every idler, is committing treason against his country by cutting down its strength and destroying it character and morale.

However, another serious category of our crime comes under the heading of felony. Felonies include such crimes as embezzlement, extortion, forgery, fraud, grand theft, rape, abortion, assault, arson, bigamy, burglary, prostitution, pandering, receiving stolen property, riot and robbery. Giving a check without sufficient funds is a felony, punishable by imprisonment for a period up to five years.

But the punishment for any felony is, of course, terribly severe. One man spent a total of over 20 years in Ohio State penitentiary for theft, who never got more than $63.20 at any one time. But in addition to the imprisonment, think of the waste of his life's reputation and happiness that is also involved. What a severe fine is imposed by the idleness, the heartbreak of family and friends, and the losses to unsupported children. There are also a great many expenses involved in the detection, trial and support—as well as the bad example—of the felon. Crime is such a perfectly stupid way to try to make a living. It does not pay in a material way, but it is also very hard on the nervous system and the life expectancy. It is sometimes pointed out that criminals are not always caught. But whether one is caught in the first, second or third offense, or even if the criminal is never caught by the police, yet *all* criminals are *always* punished. There is a basic law in the universe that says that sooner or later all wrong must be paid for. And no one can do an evil deed without paying for it, any more than he can do a good deed without receiving a reward. There is an invisible avenger that constantly stands guard in the world to see to it that no sin goes unpunished. But wrong is punished in so many ways. We are punished *for* our sins and *by* our sins. We are punished in body, in mind and in spirit. We are punished financially and socially, and we are punished here and hereafter. And the most fortunate criminal is the one who gets caught in the first offense. Even if one commits a wrong that is not on the statute books, yet a punishment still takes place. It may not be against the law to get drunk, and yet no alcoholic ever goes unpunished.

However, the most severe punishment for evil is not what we have to pay *for* it, but what we become *because* of it. There are millions of people who tell lies who may never be placed under arrest. But think of the friends they disappoint, the self-respect they lose and the ill will that they bring upon themselves. But the most terrible punishment for one who tells lies is that he becomes a liar. As one becomes an alcoholic a ruinous driving thirst attaches itself to push him further and further down the road to despair. Every alcoholic becomes a slave and a hundred other unpleasant things that he doesn't want to be. What comfort can it ever give us to think of filling our great beautiful world with drunkards, vandals, criminals and sinners? What pride can we take in being dishonest, immoral, unfair and burdened down with a guilty conscience?

Recently, in Grinnell, Iowa, a district court judge sentenced two juveniles on charges of car theft. In the process of pronouncing sentence, the judge indicated the tragedy that can sometimes

lie hidden behind some thoughtless deed. He said "Both of you
young men come from good homes. George, I've known your
father for many years, and I have as much respect for him as for
any man I know. . . . Since your arrest he has gone about his
work with more sorrow in his heart than if there had been a death
in the family.

"He still loves you, but you will never again have his full
respect and confidence. There will never be a time when you
are away from home that he will not have a feeling of fear and
wonder about what you are doing.

"John, I am told that your family is equally as good as
George's. And the things that I say apply equally to both of you.

"Both of you have been convicted of a felony. A felony is a
crime for which you might be sent to the penitentiary. In this
case I do not have to send you to the penitentiary. . . . I am
permitted to give you a parole.

"But even if you never see the inside of any penitentiary, you
cannot escape from the penalties of your crime.

"The record of your conviction will be here as long as the
courthouse stands. No amount of good conduct in the future can
ever erase it. Next year, or ten years from now, or even when you
are old men, if you are ever called to be witnesses in any court of
law, some lawyer will point his finger at you and ask this question: 'Have you ever been convicted of a felony?' And you will
hang your head and admit that you have, because if you deny it,
the record of these proceedings will be brought up and read to the
jury, and doubt will be cast on all of your testimony, as convicted
felons are not very readily believed.

"It may be that some day some great opportunity will be
available to you in one of the expanding countries outside of the
United States. Then it will be necessary for you to apply for a
passport. But no passport will be granted. Because of this record,
no country will allow you to become one of its residents.

"This felony has already made your world much smaller than
it was before, and some future mistake could further shrink its
size until its dimension would be the size of a single cell in solitary
confinement. Some day you may seek a position in the civil
service of your state or of the nation, but on the application blank
you will find this question: 'Have you ever been convicted of a
felony?'

"In two years you will be 21 years of age and your friends will have the right to vote, but you will not. Even if your own father is a candidate for office, you will not be allowed to vote for him. You will be of no value to your political party and will have no voice in the management of your country's affairs.

"Your country may be calling men to the colors. It needs strong men to defend liberty and justice and right. But neither the Army nor the Navy nor the Air Force will ever accept you. Military men are proud to wear the uniform of their country. They are proud to serve this great land that they love. But your country will not permit its flag nor any of the services to be debased by having a convicted felon in its ranks.

"I am going to grant both of you a parole. But a parole is in no sense a pardon. You will report to your parole officer as often as he may require. Your own convenience will not be a matter of any considerable importance.

"You will also be required to obey your parents. If your parents desire to send you to bed at 9 o'clock you must go without complaint. Your parole is a fragile thing and you must perform such tasks as will be assigned to you.

"Should the slightest complaint of your conduct reach this court your parole will be immediately revoked, and you will begin serving your sentence. You will not be brought back here for questioning or explanations. You will be picked up and taken to prison without notice to you and without delay."

Naturally we feel very sorry for anyone who would be so unwise as to spoil his opportunities without hope of any compensating profit. By this process of committing some crime a person can wreck his prestige, ruin his hope and destroy his greatest opportunities to do good in just a few minutes. The guilty one will forever be kept aware of the fact that he is a felon, and that whoever he meets and wherever he goes his unpleasant record will be in the minds of people. But a stigma always attaches itself to wrong doers, whether they are branded by the court or not.

I know of a woman who ran over and killed a little four-year-old girl. Of course, the parents were heartbroken. Officers of the law charged the woman with reckless driving, but because nothing could be done to bring back the life that had been taken, the parents did not bring charges against the driver. These two families live less than a mile apart and frequently see each other.

They never speak of their tragedy, but they are constantly being reminded of it. How many hours this woman has spent in regretting her recklessness! Because of her, this little girl will forever be deprived of the privilege of having a family, of feeling love, of knowing success, and of doing any of the things that she was born to do. There is another woman whose loose moral standards have influenced several younger people to leave the path of virtue. As a direct result of her bad example, one of these has illegitimately brought a child into the world. Through the recklessness of one woman a life was cut off from its blessings; and through the recklessness of another, a life was brought into being under very severe handicaps. In both cases a chain of offenses have been set in motion that can never be stopped, and someone has become a felon before God. Jesus said, "He who offends one of these little ones . . . it were better for him that a millstone were hanged around his neck, and that he were drowned in the depth of the sea." Everyone must be responsible for his own sins, and also for his unrighteous influence. If two boys steal an automobile, the idea and leadership may belong to one and then he involves the other. Many felons would not be felons without the evil influence of a companion. No one learns to drink or smoke or be profane or be immoral by himself. Someone provided the leadership and the example. No one ever smoked until Columbus found some half-savage American Indians going around with rolls of tobacco leaves burning in their mouths. But think of the lung cancer, the heart disease and the wasted resources that have resulted from the bad example of a group of ignorant, near-naked Indians.

The power of example is indicated by a recent newspaper headline which said, "A Fad of No Socks Sweeps U.S." The article said, "The pictures of Brigitte Bardot marrying German playboy Gunther Sacks is presently haunting American sock manufacturers. Mr. Sacks spells his name S-A-C-K-S and pronounces it SOCKS. When he led Miss Bardot to the altar in Las Vegas last summer, he treated witnesses and the world to a glimpse of his bronzed bare ankles." According to the *Wall Street Journal*, the result has been the elimination of socks from the everyday garb of many university men across the country. The newspaper says that to many thousands of students, going without socks is now the cool, hippy and sexy thing to do. The fad is raging from New York to Texas. The Gunther Sacks example apparently accelerated a trend toward the bare look which last year cut sales of socks by more than one million four hundred thousand pairs. Even without meaning to do so Gunther Sacks got people to go without socks, and without meaning to do so some uncivilized American Indians started a cigarette craze that causes millions of deaths and untold misery. One boy makes an automobile thief out of his friend, and brands him as a felon. Then by our bad example we induce others to be delinquents before God. Gunther Sacks discarded his socks and millions followed him. Someone else discards his ideals with the same effect.

So frequently someone speaks of the "new morality," and is actually leading others into immorality or causing them to have no morality at all. We sometimes say that each individual is a part of his environment and is not responsible for what he does. Thus we cheat our own souls and make ourselves and our friends felons before God. But that is not all, we still have this basic fundamental law which says that we must balance up our lives and pay for all of our wrong deeds and evil influences. We sometimes say that what we do is our own personal affair, but life is not that simple.

What will our settling-up day be like if it is reported that some of God's felons received their inspiration from us? It is a much better idea to live our lives as citizens of God's kingdom and not as felons before him.

The Fifth Gospel

ONE OF THE MOST valuable possessions of our world is the four gospels. These are four inspired New Testament histories telling of the life and teachings of Jesus of Nazareth. The English word *gospel* comes from an Anglo-Saxon word meaning "the good-tidings" or "the God-story." Later, this word was specifically applied to these four books which were written for the purpose of spreading this important "Christ Message." The first three gospels are called the synoptic gospels. They give a synopsis or make a general presentation. These three gospels have a common point of view, with many agreements in subject, order and language. They were written some 30 years after the resurrection. Each of the gospel authors had a different purpose for writing. Matthew wrote his account for the benefit of his Jewish countrymen. Mark wrote the second gospel primarily for the Romans. Luke was in Greece when he wrote the third gospel for the benefit of the Greeks. Then many years later John wrote the fourth gospel to help the Christians and provide some training in the faith for those who had entered into the the new kingdom of Christ.

However, all four gospels together fall far short of exhausting the possible gospel subject matter. If all of the words spoken by Jesus as recorded in the four gospels were put together into one account they could be read in about thirty minutes. Whereas in concluding his book John says, "And there are many other things which Jesus did, the which, if they should be written every one, I suppose that even the world itself could not contain the books that should be written." (John 21:25)

What a wonderful help it might be if we had some of this additional material! There is nothing that has ever happened on our earth that is one thousandth part as important to us as the life and ministry of the Savior of our world. Certainly it is more important than the Cuban invasion, or the Israeli war, or some of the other things that get so much of our attention. The coming of the Son of God to the earth was looked forward to by the prophets for four thousand years, and they have discussed every part of its importance in advance. And we have been looking back upon it for nearly two thousand more years. However, we now have some new light on the life of Christ in the interesting book of Third Nephi, which someone has called the Fifth Gospel. This is a magnificent account of the visit of the resurrected Jesus upon the Western continent. It was written in ancient America for Americans by an American prophet named Nephi.

Some 600 years B.C. a group of Israelites were led away from Jerusalem under the leadership of a prophet by the name of Lehi, to re-people the western continent. They brought with them many Old Testament scriptures and other sacred writings. And, like all believers in Old Testament prophecies, they looked forward to the coming of the Messiah who would redeem all men from death on condition of their repentance. During his ministry in Palestine, Jesus made reference to these people when he said, "Other sheep I have, which are not of this fold: them also I must bring, and they shall hear my voice; and there shall be one fold, and one shepherd." (John 10:16) And while he was not understood by those to whom he spoke, yet when he arrived here he said to them, "Ye are they of whom I said: Other sheep I have which are not of this fold." (III Nephi 15:21)

In the year 5 B.C. a Lamanite prophet promised the people in ancient America that in five years the Lord would give them a sign of the birth of the Redeemer in Bethlehem. He said, "For behold, there shall be great lights in heaven, insomuch that in the night before he cometh there shall be no darkness. . . ." As the end of the five years approached, wicked people were persecuting those who believed in the promised sign. It was claimed by them that the date given for the sign had passed, and preparations were being made to execute the believers. In desperation the Prophet Nephi cried mightily unto God to spare their lives. Then the voice of the Lord came unto him saying, "Lift up your head and be of good cheer; for behold, the time is at hand, and on this night shall the sign be given, and on the morrow come I into the world." (III Nephi 1:13) Then as the sun went down that night there was no darkness and throughout the entire night it was as light as at midday. (III Nephi 1:15)

We know that on the eastern continent some unusual events marked both the Savior's birth and crucifixion. As he hung on the cross there was a strange darkness that covered the land. (Matt. 27:45) The record says that from the sixth to the ninth hour the earth did quake and the rocks were rent and the "veil of the temple was rent in twain from the top to the bottom." It also says, "And the graves were opened; and many bodies of the saints which slept arose, and come out of the graves after his resurrection, and went into the holy city, and appeared unto many." (Matt. 27:51-53) But this ancient American gospel tells us that for the three hours that Jesus was on the cross there were severe storms accompanied by violent upheavals of nature which shook the western continent so that the whole face of the land was changed, and the more wicked part of the people were destroyed. (III Nephi 8:5-19; 10:12) Then a voice came from heaven announcing the damage, and reminding the people that it was their own wickedness and disobedience that had brought this punishment upon them. It seems too bad that the information given about the ministry of Jesus is so brief. Only Matthew mentions the opening of the graves and he uses only 33 words in telling us about it. And yet these resurrected people appeared to many others in the Holy City. And how interesting it would be if we had some of their testimonies! None of the four gospels mentions what Jesus was doing while his body lay in the tomb. However, this information is briefly supplied by Peter, who says that while his body lay in the tomb, his spirit went and preached unto those spirits in prison who had been disobedient in the days of Noah. (Peter 3:18-20, 4:6) And this very interesting and important American gospel gives us a thrilling additional and independent witness of the divinity of Jesus Christ, and it tells us many other things that we would not have known otherwise.

Soon after Jesus had ascended into heaven from the Mount of Olives he appeared in ancient America in fulfillment of the promise already referred to. He came to a group of people who were gathered around their temple in a place called Bountiful. They were surveying the damage and talking about the terrible destruction which had so recently taken place. While they were conversing, they heard a voice as if it came out of heaven. They cast their eyes round about, for they understood not what the voice said. It was not a loud voice, neither was it a harsh voice, but notwithstanding it was a still small voice, it seemed to pierce them to the center and cause them to quake. The voice came a second time, and again they heard the voice, but again they understood it not. But the third time the voice came they did open their ears, and their eyes were toward the sound thereof;

and as they looked steadfastly towards heaven they heard the voice say unto them, "Behold my Beloved Son, in whom I am well pleased, in whom I have glorified my name — hear ye him." Then they saw a man clothed in a white robe coming down out of heaven, and he descended until he stood in their midst. The resurrected Jesus introduced himself. He invited them to inspect the nail prints in his hands, and the sword wound in his side. Then he taught these people, who were also members of the House of Israel, the principles of the gospel as he had done to the Jews in and around Jerusalem. As he taught them he gave them specific instructions to write the things which he had said, and thus in point of time the "Fifth Gospel" was actually the first one written, and it was also directly and specifically authorized by the Lord himself. (III Nephi 16:4)

In the days that he ministered among them he called twelve special disciples, (III Nephi 12:1-3, 6, 27, 24, 25) and organized his Church, just as he had done in Jerusalem. He gave them authority to baptize, and carry on all of the work of the Church. (III Nephi 11:22) He gave them an interesting direction as to what the name of the Church should be. The record says, "And they said unto him, Lord, we will that thou wouldst tell us the name whereby we shall call this church; for there are disputations among the people concerning this matter. And the Lord said unto them: Verily, verily, I say unto you, why is it that the people should murmur and dispute because of this thing? Have they not read the scriptures, which say ye must take upon you the name of Christ, which is my name? For by this name shall ye be called at the last day; And whoso taketh upon him my name, and endureth to the end, the same shall be saved at the last day. Therefore, whatsoever ye shall do, ye shall do it in my name; therefore ye shall call the church in my name; and ye shall call upon the Father in my name that he will bless the church for my sake. And how can it be my church save it be called in my name? For if a church be called in Moses' name then it be Moses' church; or if it be called in the name of a man then it be the church of a man; but if it be called in my name, then it is my church, if it so be that they are built upon my gospel.' " (III Nephi 27:3-8)

In addition to teaching them the gospel and organizing his Church, he blessed their children and healed their sick. (III Nephi 17:7) He told them some things about modern America, and that the new Jerusalem should be built here in the latter days. (III Nephi 21:23)

What a thrilling new witness for the divinity of the life of Christ, and what a great deal that life means to us! This Fifth Gospel testifies that Jesus did not go out of business when he finished his work in Jerusalem. He ascended into heaven from the Mount of Olives, but he descended again to minister to his people in America. This Gospel makes clear that Jesus was not just a great teacher, but in very deed the literal Son of God. And that his interest was not confined to those few people who lived in Palestine in his own day. God is the God of the whole earth, and all of the earth's inhabitants are the children of God. In a day when people are saying that God is dead, it is very thought-provoking to have this testimony that Jesus can descend to the earth as well as ascend into heaven, and it teaches us to look ahead to the time when he will come again in power and great glory. When Jesus left these ancient Americans he told them that he was going to visit the lost ten tribes. He said, "And verily, verily, I say unto you that I have other sheep which are not of this land, neither of the land of Jerusalem, neither in any parts of that land about whither I have been to minister. . . . but I have received a commandment of the Father that I shall go unto them, and they shall hear my voice, and shall be numbered among my sheep. . . ." (III Nephi 16:1-3) He said, "But now I go . . . to show myself unto the lost tribes of Israel, for they are not lost unto the Father, for he knoweth whither he hath taken them." (III Nephi 17:4) And as he was about to leave them he said, "And now I go unto the Father." (III Nephi 27:28)

But before he ascended, he asked his newly appointed disciples what they desired of him after he had gone to the Father, and nine of the twelve said, "We desire that after we have lived unto the age of man, that our ministry, wherein thou hast called us, may have an end, that we may speedily come unto thee in thy kingdom. And he said unto them: Blessed are ye because ye desired this thing of me; therefore, after that ye are seventy and two years old, ye shall come unto me in my kingdom; and with me ye shall find rest." When he had thus spoken he turned himself unto the three and said unto them: "What will ye that I should do unto you, when I am gone unto the Father? And they sorrowed in their hearts, for they durst not speak unto him the thing which they desired. And he said unto them: Behold, I know your thoughts, and ye have desired the thing which John, my beloved, who was with me in my ministry, before that I was lifted up by the Jews, desired of me. Therefore, more blessed are ye, for ye shall never taste of death; but ye shall live to behold all the doings of the Father unto the children of men, even until all things shall be fulfilled according to the will of the Father, when I shall come in my glory with the powers of heaven. And ye shall never endure the pains of death; but when I shall come in my glory ye shall be changed in the twinkling of an eye from mortality to immortality. . . .

"And again, ye shall not have pain while ye shall dwell in the flesh, neither sorrow save it be for the sins of the world; and all this will I do because of the thing which ye have desired of me, for ye have desired that ye might bring the souls of men unto me, while the world shall stand. And for this cause ye shall have a fullness of joy; and ye shall sit down in the kingdom of my Father; yea, your joy shall be full, even as the Father hath given me fullness of joy; and ye shall be even as I am, and I am even as the Father." This teaching answers one of the Master's greatest questions when he said to these ancient Americans, "What manner of men ought ye to be?" And then he gave a thrilling answer to his own question when he said, "Verily I say unto you, even as I am." (III Nephi 27:27) We are invited to have a part in that work in which God himself spends his entire time, and it is one of the most important parts of the "God-message" that if we are faithful, the offspring of God may eventually become like their eternal parents. May each of us also effectively answer this all-important prayer in his own behalf.

The Glory of Christmas

E ACH YEAR AS we commemorate Christmas we are conscious of a spirit that distinguishes this season from all others. This difference might best be described as "The Glory of Christmas." We catch something of this spirit when we read those seven scriptural verses written by Luke in which the birth of Christ is announced to the world. Luke says, "And there were in the same country shepherds abiding in the field, keeping watch over their flock by night. And, lo, the angel of the Lord came upon them, and the glory of the Lord shone round about them: and they were sore afraid. And the angel said unto them, Fear not: for, behold, I bring you good tidings of great joy, which shall be to all people. For unto you is born this day in the city of David a Saviour, which is Christ the Lord. And this shall be a sign unto you; Ye shall find the babe wrapped in swaddling clothes lying in a manger. And suddenly there was with the angel a multitude of the heavenly host praising God, and saying, Glory to God in the highest, and on earth peace, good will toward men." (Luke 2:8-14)

What a great experience it must have been in that long ago Christmas night for these shepherds to see and hear an angel from the presence of God! We are not told who the angel was. It may have been the same who had previously announced the coming of John the Baptist, and informed Mary of her mission. To Zacharias the angel introduced himself by saying, "I am Gabriel, that stand in the presence of God; and am sent to speak unto thee, and to shew thee these glad tidings." (Luke 1:19) The messenger came in great glory, authority and power to deliver his message. But God's glory also enveloped the shepherds who received the message.

Some form of this term "glory" appears in the scriptures over 400 times. It is used to describe that quality of radiance and magnificence in the personality of God, as well as to picture God's dwelling place. But glory is one of the qualities distinguishing the entire idea of Christmas, and when we get it into our hearts it lifts us above the ordinary events of the rest of the year.

The dictionary says that glory is a resplendent beauty, or magnificence. It is a state of splendor, or absolute happiness. Glory also means exalted praise, honor or distinction. It is something that makes a person illustrious. The scripture speaks of some people being "glorified." This is an act or process of exaltation. God is the most exalted of all beings, and therefore the most glorious. God is such a glorious personage that no one can endure his presence unless quickened by his spirit.

We remember that after Moses had visited with God upon Mount Sinai, that the glory of God rested upon Moses with such intensity that the children of Israel could not endure his presence, and therefore a covering had to be placed over his face to make it possible for them to communicate with him. In the Garden of Gethsemane on the last Thursday of his life, Jesus said to his Father, "I have glorified thee upon the earth, I have finished the work which thou gavest me to do and now, oh, Father, glorify thou me with thine own self, with the glory that I had with thee before the world was."

On the following Sunday morning as he came forth in the resurrection, a part of this prayer had already been answered, and in his *immortal* presence the soldiers whom Pilate had placed on guard to maintain the security of the tomb became as dead men. These were not timid, easily frightened men; these were hard, bold, courageous, seasoned soldiers of Rome, who had learned to stand in the presence of death without a quiver of emotion. But now that they stood in the presence of a resurrected glorified life they became as dead men.

But the purpose of Christ's mission to the earth was to redeem and glorify all of us. If we live as we should it is reasonable to expect that the offspring of God might eventually hope to become like the eternal parent, and we need to get started on this important process as soon as possible. In speaking about this to the Thessalonians the Apostle Paul says, "We are bound to give thanks always to God for you, brethren, beloved of the Lord, because God hath from the beginning chosen you to salvation through sanctification of the Spirit and belief of the truth: Whereunto he called you by our gospel to the obtaining of the glory of our Lord Jesus Christ." (II Thes. 2:13-14) We need not wait until eternity begins to start acquiring this quality. Christmas is to help us to get some of this glory into our lives now.

When I was in my earliest school years, a part of the first day after the Christmas holidays was used in having each student stand up and tell the other members of the class what he had received for Christmas. For the children from well-to-do homes this seemed a pleasant experience, but the members of poorer families were sometimes a little embarrassed because they didn't always have as much to talk about. Sometimes when a large family lives under difficult financial conditions there aren't always enough presents to go around.

But even as adults we still have the same question asked and answered many times at Christmas. Someone is sure to ask "What did you get for Christmas," and we may still feel a little bit bad if we don't have an acceptable answer at least to ourselves. Everyone enjoys getting nice presents, and of course Christmas means so many different things to so many different people, and actually there are many kinds of Christmases. There is the child's Christmas — its symbol is the toy, and its chief characteristic is excitement. Then there is the world's Christmas. Its symbol is the Christmas tree, and its chief characteristic is festivity. There is the drunkard's Christmas — its symbol is the bottle, and its chief characteristic is sin. Then there is the Christian's Christmas. Its symbol is the star, and its chief characteristic is the kind of righteousness that leads to the glory of God.

While God's glory surrounded the shepherds, the angels sang their Christmas anthems saying, "Glory to God in the highest and on earth peace, good will to men." When this glory is lacking in the world, then to that extent unrighteousness and unhappiness prevail. Christmas can be and sometimes is a very lonely time, for some people under some circumstances. Some people might answer this question of "what did you get for Christmas?" by listing a sour stomach, a drunken headache, a mental depression, and the consciousness of a few extra steps taken along that broad road that leads to death. Those who celebrate Christmas the wrong way might feel a little bit embarrassed if they were asked to stand up and report before the class. And while we generally think of Christmas as a happy time, yet it is not always so: It can be a very serious tragedy when no one remembers us with a Christmas present, or a letter of love, or an expression of good will. It can also be tragic to have a memory of a Christmas without any glory in it.

We try to get glory into our lives at Christmas time by lighting up our cities, our homes and our Christmas trees. This might in some way represent the glory that lighted up the Judean hills and the manger in Bethlehem on that long ago Christmas night. But there are other Christmas lights that shine out through people's faces, or well up out of their hearts. It would be difficult to think of God, or Gabriel, or others from God's presence without their glory, but *we* are God's children and we have been so created that glory may also be made to shine in us.

Archibald Rutledge once wrote a delightful little book entitled *My Colonel and His Lady*. In his book he tells of an interesting experience which he had as a lad on the Santee River in Central South Carolina. This particular occasion has to do with an old Negro riverboat captain who piloted the ferry boat *Foam*. The boat was dirty, odorous and badly kept. But one day when Dr. Rutledge went down to the river he found the *Foam* completely transformed. It was clean from stem to stern. It fairly glistened and gleamed in the sunlight. The boat's brass had been polished until it shone like so many mirrors. The bilge water had disappeared from behind the seats, and the deck had been scoured to the raw wood. No less miraculous was the transformation in the Negro captain himself. He was shining and immaculate. His face beamed, his eyes sparkled, as he sat behind the *Foam's* wheel with an open Bible on his lap.

When Dr. Rutledge asked him the reason for this wonderful transformation, he said, "I got a glory." That is, some great ideas had gotten into the Captain's thinking and some great aspirations had gotten into his blood stream. These had made him a different man. He now had the glory of a lighted mind, and the glory of a quickened personality. He also had the glory of a righteous ambition. Religion had touched him effectively in exactly the right places. But the transformation that was so apparent in the river boat, was only a manifestation of a more important transformation in the Captain. The nature of his work itself had not changed, he was still a riverboat captain. But he was now the best riverboat captain on the Santee. Henceforth whatever he did would indicate his own change of life, and his life's work would indicate his life's glory.

But the story of the Negro riverboat captain is the story of everyone who gets a glory into his life. And what a great Christmas this would be if we all cleaned up our riverboats and got the glory of Christmas into our hearts. Like so many other things a glory comes because of what we do. If one isn't glorious in what he does, then he isn't glorious. We can't get a glory in our hearts while the bilge water is still under our seats and in our attitudes. We can't have a glory and a chronic case of unrighteousness at the same time.

We have several descriptions of the physical glory of immortal beings. John gives us one in his Book of Revelation. While on the Isle of Patmos some 60 years after the Savior's crucifixion on Calvary, John says that he was in the spirit on the Lord's day when he heard a great voice behind him as of the voice of a trumpet saying, "I am Alpha and Omega, the first and the last." John turned to see who had spoken to him and he said he saw "one like unto the Son of man, clothed with a garment down to the foot, and girt about with a golden girdle." He said "his head and his hairs were white like wool, as white as snow; and his eyes were as a flame of fire; and his feet like unto fine brass, as if they were burned in a furnace; and his voice as the sound of many waters. . . . and his countenance was as the sun shineth in his strength." (Rev. 1:11-16)

We often describe a quality in people by saying they have a light in their eyes or their faces beam or their countenances glow. But here these qualities might be magnified a few million times where John could say, "His eyes were as a flame of fire." But the visits of heavenly messengers are not limited to Bethlehem and Patmos.

In the early spring of 1820 in upper New York State, the Father and the Son appeared to the Prophet Joseph Smith, who describes the experience as follows: He said: "I saw a pillar of light exactly over my head, above the brightness of the sun, which descended gradually until it fell upon me. . . . When the light rested upon me I saw two Personages, whose brightness and glory defy all description, standing above me in the air. One of them spake unto me, calling me by name and said, pointing to the other, 'This is my beloved Son. Hear Him.' " (Jos. Smith 2:16-17) Other heavenly messengers have also appeared upon the earth in our day. Joseph Smith describes a visit that he had with the Angel Moroni on September 21, 1823 as follows: "While I was thus in the act of calling upon God, I discovered a light appearing in my room, which continued to increase until the room was lighter than at noonday, when immediately a personage appeared at my bedside, standing in the air, for his feet did not touch the floor. He had on a loose robe of most exquisite whiteness. It was a whiteness beyond anything earthly I had ever seen: nor do I believe that any earthly thing could be made to appear so exceedingly white and brilliant. His hands were naked, and his arms also, a little above the wrist; so, also, were his feet naked, as were his legs, a little above the ankles. His head and neck were also bare. I could discover that he had no other clothing on but this robe, as it was open, so that I could see into his bosom. Not only was his robe exceedingly white, but his whole person was glorious beyond description, and his countenance truly like lightning.

"The room was exceedingly light, but not so very bright as immediately around his person. When I first looked upon him, I was afraid; but the fear soon left me. He called me by name, and said unto me that he was a messenger sent from the presence of God to me, and his name was Moroni." (Jos. Smith 2:30-33)

If God and angels had only been seen once, that would be proof that they still exist. One of the greatest glories of Christmas is the knowledge that God lives, and that Jesus Christ is the Son of God who came to earth to help us get his glory into our lives. Our greatest Christmas ambition should be that we might be successful in making our own lives glorious.

The Golden Rule

ONE OF THE THINGS that our success needs more than about anything else is to spend more time on an intimate basis with some good ideas. We have a helpful literature available that in some ways resembles a vast supermarket of thought. In it can be found all of the foods and vitamins necessary for our health, strength and growth, and yet most of these helpful materials remain unused by us. The difference between success and failure, happiness and misery, good and bad, largely comes as a result of the kind of thoughts, attitudes and ambitions that find their way into our minds. Of course, the greatest of the great ideas are found in the Holy Scriptures. The scriptures are God's ideas about the things that will make us successful, happy and righteous. But as in other fields, our problems with the scriptures are that most of us do not have a close enough association with them. There is some tendency in our modern times to regard the scriptures as old fashioned, and not worth our time. Religion itself has been so seriously downgraded in some quarters that we almost completely miss its benefits. However, there is another point of view that we may adopt.

Of course, it is one's religion that largely determines what he will become. If anyone fully accepts the philosophy advocated by the scriptures, his life can be greatly improved in every way. For example, there is one great scriptural line that by itself will add a great deal of wealth, happiness, success and righteousness to any life that spends adequate time effectively practicing it. Someone has called this idea "The Golden Rule." And while everyone is familiar with the title, there is a much smaller number of people who are familiar with the way of life that it represents. This Golden Rule idea might involve either a negative or a positive action, and the title may not be very descriptive of the idea itself. Several attempts have been made to express the opposite of this philosophy to fit the spirit of our times. With its negative aspect in mind someone has given us the descriptive title of "The Law of the Boomerang," and someone else has called it "the Law of Retaliation."

A little while ago the Chinese burned down the British Embassy building in Peking in retaliation for some real or imagined offense previously committed by the British. One reason that our bombs are getting bigger and more destructive is that each nation wants to be able to repay with compound interest whatever damage may be attempted against it. Of course, when we fight wars, or impose sanctions, or carry out threats, we always attract a greater damage in retaliation. Many people dig a pit for someone else, and end up by falling into it themselves. Our evil chickens always come home to roost, and we are usually hit with our own boomerang.

It is very seldom that anyone ever really hurts us except ourselves, and if we all tried to carry out the ancient law of "an eye for an eye" we would eventually end up by making everybody blind. The fact that the evil that we initiate usually recoils upon our own heads is the opposite aspect of the great idea contained in the Golden Rule. The positive application was given voice by Jesus in his Sermon on the Mount. However, the Golden Rule idea has been in existence since very early times. It has been an important part of almost every great philosophy, and was known and talked of by many great people for centuries before the days of Jesus. What we think of as the positive version of this rule says, "as ye would that men should do unto you, do ye even so unto them." These are probably the most powerful 15 words in any language, and can be the most constructive or destructive influence in our lives, depending upon how we use them. But the application that we make of this rule is frequently negative. People are always unfriendly to us when we are unfriendly to them. When we go around with chips on our shoulders, someone will always be found who is willing to knock them off.

If an individual or a nation desires to provoke a fight, the easiest way to do it is through this law of retaliation. Under normal circumstances every nation and every individual wants peace. Everyone knows that no one ever wins in a war. And very few people are willing to fight unless provoked by some aggression or threat from the other side. If you offered a nation money to get itself involved in any kind of a war, it would probably refuse, and it would be pretty difficult to recruit individuals to fight in an army of hirelings. But if one nation or one individual should attack another, then immediately a war is on.

If you asked someone to punch you on the nose he would think of it as silly, unchristian, and serving no useful purpose. If you offered to pay him to punch you on the nose it would seem just as ridiculous. But if you punch him on the nose first, his whole attitude changes. He then immediately forgets all of the disadvantages of fighting. His reluctance is forgotten, his most pressing duties are laid aside, his procrastination is overcome and his fear vanishes, while in retaliation he gives you a good hard punch on the nose. However, you may use this Golden Rule coin in your own interests by turning it over on its other side. If you want someone to invite you to his house to dinner, all you need to do is to invite him to your house to dinner. If you want him to send you a Christmas card, just put one in the mail to him on the 20th of December, and you will get one back on the 23rd.

These fifteen words will give anyone the greatest possible power who is willing to use them effectively. We can control people, we can get our own way, and we can reach about any objective by a practice of these fifteen simple words. If you want someone to like you, like them; if you want them to trust you, trust them. If you want the boss to raise your salary, do what you would want him to do for you if the circumstances were reversed. This gives one such great power that he may accomplish almost any goal. By using this rule, we can to a large extent even influence and determine the attitudes and actions of God himself concerning us. We know that God will be pleased if we live a righteous life. If we pay our tithing, he will prosper our efforts. If we keep the word of wisdom, he will bless our health. If we obey the Celestial law, we will be exalted in the Celestial Kingdom. In fact, the practice of this law is the secret of all marital, occupational, religious and personal success.

If a husband wants to get along well with his wife, the best way to do it is to practice these fifteen words. The best way to promote our selfish interests is by being unselfish. The best way to be loved is to love. When people forget the interests of others and always try to selfishly get their own way, they usually fail. However, if a man devotes himself effectively to making his wife or his employer or his associates happy, then the chances are overwhelming that he himself will be happy.

It seems a little bit peculiar that when such a powerful sure-fire tool is available to us, we use it so infrequently. Most individuals are still pretty well committed to the old idea of rewarding evil for evil, while relegating the Golden Rule to a minor role in their philosophy of life.

Sometime ago Dr. Max Rafferty, California Superintendent of Public Instruction, reported that in some areas of the United States 8-year-olds are being taught Karate. This is a Japanese word for "empty hand." It is a system for self-defense without carrying a weapon. One of the instructors justified giving this course by saying, "some of these kids live in bad neighborhoods where self-defense is a necessity. We teach them the basic techniques of blocking, punching, striking and kicking, and we show them just where to place their punches, strikes and kicks." He didn't seem to worry very much about the idea that the skills and the attitudes that went with these activities might lead to possible mayhem, or cause some tousle-headed youngster to liquidate another with a well-placed chop to the third cervical vertebra. This heavy handed instructor-expert emphasized to his students from the beginning class the lethal potentialities of Karate.

Instead of practicing the Golden Rule, so many of us are becoming experts in the art of chopping each other down. The riots throughout the country tell of too many young people with too much education in fighting the police, and in burning the property of others. By gang rule, or by organized vote, many people expect to take what they want regardless of the consequences. And this damaging state of mind is contagious. People all over the country are doing things that they have never done before. We have not advanced very far from the old days when people used to settle differences by fighting a duel. And while the principles involved are similar, the duel at least has in it some of the elements of honor and order. Of course, there is a place in our world for self-defense. But we may be going a little bit too far when children are expertly coached in how to rupture the carotid artery with the flat of one hand, while deftly breaking three ribs with the other.

But it may be even more serious when we teach the attitudes that are developing our riots, racial hate and irreverence for God. The Beatniks, the Nothings, the marchers, the burners and the Hells Angels, have carried us far beyond the place where our old-time sensibilities compelled us to stop. And what we are now in need of more than about anything else is to get out the scriptures and polish up that old-fashioned success instrument called the Golden Rule, and see if we can't get back into our blood stream some of the success devices associated with it.

A prominent sports writer recently wrote an article bringing out this need, when he told of the disregard for others that sportsmen frequently manifest as they hunt quail and other game on the private property of farmers and ranchers. These land owners are busy trying to make a living from their land, but along comes a group of irresponsible hunters who scatter herds, trample crops, and cause trouble generally in the name of recreation. Of course, it may still be true that 90% of the hunters would not think of disturbing sheep, tearing down fences, or peppering a building with buckshot. But this troublesome 10% sometimes seem as though they couldn't care less. In this they are selfish, short-sighted and in some cases downright stupid. And because they disregard the Golden Rule, they compel the thoughtful, considerate hunters, fishermen, campers and others who would like to enjoy the out-of-doors to suffer for their sins.

Jesus gave a far more important concept when he said that we should live by every word that proceeds from the mouth of God. He said, "love one another," "do good to them that hate you; and pray for them that despitefully use you and persecute you." What a great world we would have if we followed that direction!

Our world is already loaded down to the breaking point with troubles, and when anyone does any wrong thing he is just adding to the total. If the laws of the gospel of Christ were strictly followed by all of us, then this earth would be God's paradise and we would realize the condition for which the Master taught us to pray when he said, "Thy kingdom come, thy will be done on earth as it is in heaven." But when we quarrel, swear, smoke, get drunk, and indulge in hate and negative irrational thoughts, we cause problems not only for ourselves but for everyone else, including God. Our greed, immorality and idleness tend to make a hell upon this great earth that God has created for our pleasure and benefit. And yet, even though we are all aware of the unpleasant, unprofitable situation that we have placed ourselves in, our condition seems to be getting worse by the hour, and to plead for a return to religion sounds almost impossible in view of our perverseness.

However, if we desire, we have within our easy reach the ability to make ourselves successful and happy, by the practice of these fifteen little simple words. By living this one great principle that God has provided for our use, we can put ourselves back in favor with man and with God, and so we should frequently reenact the Golden Rule in which we get our lives themselves to say, "As ye would that men should do unto you, do ye even so unto them."

Hamlet

THE GREATEST treasures of our world are probably its literary treasures. Through our literature we accumulate and preserve for our use those great ideas and philosophies that motivate our lives for good. Our literature serves an especially important need in our day of culture and education. Culture gives us polish and pleasure, and all education is about ourselves. We study medicine to learn how to keep ourselves well physically. Psychology, psychiatry and the other studies of the mind, tell us how to keep ourselves well mentally. Sociology is how we live together agreeably. Law is how we keep our lives orderly. Business is how we deal profitably with each other. Then we have that great science of religion to teach us how to keep ourselves well spiritually. This is the branch of knowledge in which most of the real importance of our lives is centered. If we were to make a list of our greatest human concepts they would have to do with such subjects as:

The immortality of the human personality, and the eternal glory of the human soul.
Eternal Progression.
Fulfilment of our divine destiny as children of God.
The eternity of the family unit.
The free agency of man.
The concept of eternal happiness as life's chief object

The reason that the scriptures are so important is that they give the fullest and most authoritative treatment to these and other important subjects. And our great literature can be one of the finest aids to our total success.

A number of years ago an interesting literary survey was made by Daniel Starck. He interviewed 100 of the most competent literary judges in an attempt to identify the greatest books that had ever been written. Excluding the scriptures, the first ten books named in order of their popularity were:

1. Shakespeare's *Hamlet*, written in 1600 A.D.
2. *The Works of Aristotle*, written in 325 B.C.

3. Homer's *Iliad*, written in 800 B.C.
4. Darwin's *Origin of the Species*, written in 1859 A.D.
5. Dante's *Divine Comedy*, written in 1300 A.D.
6. Plato's *Republic*, written in 400 B.C.
7. Goethe's *Faust*, finished in 1808 A.D.
8. *The Writings of Confucius*, written in 480 B.C.
9. Milton's *Paradise Lost*, written in 1667 A.D.
10. Cervantes' *Don Quixote*, written in 1605 A.D.

Excluding those men who have spoken directly for God, most people usually think of Shakespeare as being the greatest writer who ever lived. Shakespeare looked with keen insight into human lives. He wrote 37 plays and staffed them with a thousand characters, each personifying some personality trait. He said his purpose was to hold the mirror up to life to show virtue her own image, and scorn her own likeness. In his plays we can see our own lives in miniature as we watch his players react upon each other. If *Hamlet* is the greatest of all Shakespeare's works, it may be helpful for us to think about the reasons why. The story of Hamlet is as follows:

Hamlet, the King of Denmark, was sleeping in his garden. His brother, Claudius, poured a quick-acting poison into his ear that went coursing through his blood, and caused his death. The report was given out that the king had been bitten by a serpent. In less than two months Claudius had married Hamlet's queen, ascended the throne, and taken over the rule of Denmark. Hamlet's son, Hamlet, was not a great admirer of his uncle, and he had a suspicion that something was wrong.

While the young prince was trying to find out what it was, the report came to him that the late King's ghost had been seen in the dead of night, stalking the gloomy battlements of the castle. In a terrifying encounter Hamlet learns from the specter that his father was murdered by his brother. The young prince is committed to revenge his father's death. The rest of the play has to do with him carrying out this oath, and in the process all of the principals in the play lost their lives.

In Shakespeare's day most plays were labeled as either comedies or tragedies. A comedy was not something that was funny. A comedy was something that had a happy ending. The fact that over one half of all Shakespeare's plays were tragedies may also indicate a ratio for human lives.

Shakespeare was a great author for many reasons. He understood human nature. He said, "Conceit in weakest bodies, strongest works." He knew how to appeal to human interest. Certainly he was not dull. He was great for the impetus he gave to self-improvement. He said, "Assume a virtue if you have it not." He dealt with these important subjects of life and death and success. He knew the place of good and evil in human lives. He was an architect of speech, and understood how to exalt and polish the most simple expression. He was an artist in making language beautiful and effective. Shakespeare was also a wise philosopher. He said:

> For to the noble mind rich gifts wax poor
> When givers prove unkind.

Again:

> Neither a borrower nor a lender be:
> For the loan oft loses both itself and friend,
> And borrowing dulls the edge of husbandry.

Again:

> This above all: to thine own self be true,
> And it must follow, as the night the day,
> Thou canst not then be false to any man.

Hamlet greatly loved his father. He said, "He was a man: take him for all in all I think I shall not look upon his like again." Again he said:

> What a piece of work is man! How noble in reason!
> How infinite in faculty! In form and moving how express
> And admirable! In action how like an angel! In apprehension
>   how like a God!

Shakespeare also made some great utterances that were centered in human weakness. And those human frailties in young Hamlet's weak-willed mother, helped to touch the young Prince with a case of melancholia where he contemplated suicide. He was restrained by fear of the penalty which God has attached to taking one's own life. In his dilemma of despondency he said,

> O, that this too, too solid flesh would melt,
> Thaw and resolve itself into a dew!

> Or that the Everlasting had not fix'd
> His canon 'gainst self-slaughter, oh God, God
> How weary, stale, flat and unprofitable
> Seem to me all the uses of this world!
> 'Tis like an unweeded garden
> That goes to seed; things rank and gross in nature
> Possess it merely.

Hamlet's doubt that life was worthwhile prompted the famous soliloquy in which he said:

> To be, or not to be: that is the question:
> Whether 'tis nobler in the mind to suffer
> The slings and arrows of outrageous fortune,
> Or to take arms against a sea of troubles,
> And by opposing end them? To die — to sleep —
> No more; and by a sleep to say we end
> The heart-ache and the thousand natural shocks
> That flesh is heir to, 'tis a consummation
> Devoutly to be wish'd. To die, to sleep;
> To sleep: perchance to dream: ay, there's the rub;
> For in that sleep of death what dreams may come
> When we have shuffled off this mortal coil,
> Must give us pause. There's the respect
> That makes calamity of so long life;
> For who would bear the whips and scorns of time,
> The oppressor's wrong, the proud man's contumely,
> The pangs of despised love, the law's delay,
> The insolence of office, and the spurns
> That patient merit of the unworthy takes,
> When he himself might his quietus make
> With a bare bodkin? Who would fardels bear,
> To grunt and sweat under a weary life,
> But that the dread of something after death,
> The undiscover'd country from whose bourn
> No traveller returns, puzzles the will,
> And makes us rather bear those ills we have
> Than fly to others that we know not of ?
> Thus conscience does make cowards of us all.

Hamlet had died in his sleep without any chance to repent. Therefore, according to a particular theology, his soul was sent to hell. In the midnight rendezvous with his son, the father touches our interest as he describes his situation. He said:

> Hamlet, I am thy father's spirit;
> Doom'd for a certain term to walk the night,

And for the day confin'd to fast in fires,
Till the foul crimes done in my days of nature
Are burnt and purged away. But that I am forbid
To tell the secrets of my prison-house,
I could a tale unfold whose lightest word
Would harrow up thy soul, freeze thy young blood,
Make thy two eyes, like stars, start from their spheres,
Thy knotted and combed locks to part,
And each particular hair to stand on end,
Like quills upon the fretful porpentine:
But this eternal blazon must not be
To ears of flesh and blood. . . .
. . . Now, Hamlet, hear:
'Tis given out that, sleeping in my orchard,
A serpent stung me;
But the serpent that did sting thy father's life
Now wears his crown.
O list, list, if thou didst ever
Thy dear father love,
Revenge his foul and most unnatural murder.

As the spirit scented the approach of morning air, and knew he must depart, he bade a quick farewell to his son by saying, "Hamlet, adieu, remember me."

Then under the stress of a most determined resolve the son replied,

"Remember thee?
Ay, thou poor ghost, while memory holds a seat
In this distracted globe. Remember thee?
Yea, from the table of my memory
I'll wipe away all trivial fond records,
All saws of books, all forms, all pressures past,
That youth and observation copied there;
And thy commandment all alone shall live
Within the book and volume of my brain,
Unmix'd with baser matter.

But first Hamlet decided to have more proof of his uncle's guilt. He reasoned that inasmuch as the devil had the power to assume a pleasing shape, the spirit he had seen may have been Satan trying to entice him to commit a murder in order to damn him. He said, "Yea, out of my weakness and my melancholy, Satan who is very potent with melancholy spirits, may be abusing me to damn me." A group of traveling players were then in the castle, and Hamlet arranged for them to enact a similar murder play before his uncle, while he watched his uncle's face for the telltale indication of his guilt. He said:

> I have heard
> That guilty creatures sitting at a play,
> Have, by the very cunning of the scene,
> Been struck so to the soul, that presently
> They have proclaim'd their malefactions;
> For murder, though it have no tongue, will speak
> With most miraculous organ. I'll have these players
> Play something like the murder of my father
> Before mine uncle, I'll observe his looks
> I'll tent him to the quick, if he but blench,
> I know my course.

He said, "The play's the thing, wherein I'll catch the conscience of the King." When the players reached the murder scene, the panic-stricken King arose from his seat, hastily broke up the performance, and left the room. Hamlet's chance soon came to kill his uncle when, unbeknown to Claudius, Hamlet entered his room. But he found Claudius on his knees praying aloud. Claudius prayed:

> O! my offense is rank, it smells to heaven;
> It hath the primal eldest curse upon it;
> A brother's murder! Pray can I not,
> Though inclination be as sharp as will:
> My stronger guilt defeats my strong intent; . . .
> What if this cursed hand
> Were thicker than itself with brother's blood,
> Is there not rain enough in the sweet heavens
> To wash it white as snow? . . .
> Then, I'll look up;
> My fault is past. But, O! what form of prayer
> Can serve my turn? 'Forgive me my foul murder'?
> That cannot be; since I am still possessed
> Of those effects for which I did the murder,
> My crown, mine own ambition and my queen.
> May one be pardoned and retain the offense?

Hamlet felt that if he killed Claudius while he was praying, the latter's soul would then be clean and would go to heaven, and his own revenge would be thwarted. He said:

> A villain kills my father; and for that,
> I, his sole son, do this same villain send
> To heaven.
> Why, this is hire and salary, not revenge.

Therefore he left the room to await a more appropriate time. However, the king himself was not satisfied that his prayer was of much help to him, as upon arising he said:

> My words fly up, my thoughts remain below:
> Words without thoughts never to heaven go.

Finally Hamlet killed the king with a poisoned sword point that the King had prepared for the Prince, and the tragedy of Hamlet came to an end. In pointing out a comparison, Shakespeare says, "All the world's a stage, and all the people in it merely players. Each in his time plays many parts." May each of us play his own part well, and may each of our lives have the most satisfactory happy ending.

He Is Not Here

OUR ETERNAL EXISTENCE has been divided into three important periods which someone has compared to a three act play. We had a long ante-mortal existence, which might be called the first act. This is followed by a short period of mortality, which is called the second act. Then we have an eternal, everlasting immortality which is the third act. Nothing is more clearly written in the scriptures than the fact that the life of Christ did not begin in Bethlehem, neither did it end on Calvary. Jesus said, "I came forth from the Father, and am come into the world. Again, I leave the world and go unto the Father." But it is just as certain that *our* lives did not begin when we were born, neither will they end when we die.

During our first estate we lived in heaven as the spirit offspring of God, and while we lacked mortal bodies yet then, as now, we were intelligent, personable men and women with abilities, ambitions, form and individual personalities. A spirit has a body as tangible as the one that we now know, but it is made of finer material and is not subject to some of the limitations that are presently imposed upon mortal bodies of flesh. However, God, angels, spirits and men are all of the same species in various stages of development and different degrees of righteousness. And about our progression during these three different periods of our lives God has said, "And they who keep their first estate shall be added upon, and they who keep not their first estate shall not have glory in the same kingdom with those who keep their first estate; and those who keep their second estate shall have glory added upon their heads forever and ever." Because we satisfactorily passed all of the requirements of our first estate, two-thirds of God's children were graduated into this life and were "added upon," with a body of flesh and bones. The other third were denied mortality because they followed Lucifer in his rebellion against God in the council of heaven. In our first estate we walked by sight. We all have seen God; he is our Father. We lived with him, but it was necessary for us to learn to walk a little way by faith, and we were born into this world of good and evil that we might learn to effectively distinguish between the two. It is helpful in this life if we know as much as possible about the purpose and accomplishments of our first act, as well as the possibilities of our second act and the eternal rewards of our third act.

Someone has said that if you went in the theatre after the first act had been finished and left before the third act began, you may not understand the play. The foundations of our lives were laid in the first act. In the second act we are not only "added upon" with a body, but we acquire the experience and obedience necessary to prepare us for the third act. God has given us a preview of our final estate in the holy scriptures. I have a relative who, when she reads a novel, always reads the last chapter first. She wants to know before she begins where she is going to be when she gets through. And that is a pretty good idea for life. But there is another part of our life's play that we should also understand, and that is a kind of intermission called death that takes place between the second and third acts. Sometimes in the theatre and in life we lose a great deal because we mistake the intermission for the end of the play.

Certainly one of the most important events of life is death. Death is not only the entrance to the third act, but also it is our only gateway to immortality and eternal life. The third act is where the happy endings are. That is where the rewards are handed out. We should understand that death is not a mistake, but because the spirit can best be given its final cleansing, education, and glorification while separated from the body, death can add some of the most important values to our eternal lives.

An ancient American prophet referred to this period of intermission by saying, "Now there must needs be a space betwixt the time of death and the time of the resurrection." It is significant that the time requirement is much greater for those who have lived unrighteously. In the case of Jesus, an interval of only three days elapsed between the time he laid his body down and the time that he took it up again. Immediately following his resurrection many others were resurrected.

The scriptures say, "And the graves were opened; and many bodies of the saints which slept arose, and came up out of their graves after his resurrection, and went into the holy city, and appeared unto many." We have evidence that many other worthy men and women have also been resurrected since that time. And yet some of the people who have been in their graves for a very long period will have to wait for resurrection until after the millennium. The scriptures tell us that the final part of the first resurrection will take place at the glorious second coming of Christ, when he comes to cleanse the earth of its sin in preparation for his millennial reign upon it. About this event Paul said to the Thessalonians, "For if we believe that Jesus died and rose again, even so them also which sleep in Jesus will God bring with him. For this we say unto you by the word of the Lord, that we which are alive and remain unto the coming of the Lord shall not prevent them which are asleep. For the Lord himself shall descend from heaven with a shout, with the voice of the arch-angel, and with the trump of God: and the dead in Christ shall rise first; then we which are alive and remain shall be caught up together with them in the clouds, to meet the Lord in the air: and so shall we ever be with the Lord." (I Thes. 4:14-17) But those who are less worthy will not be ready. A modern-day revelation says that when the Lord shall utter his voice out of heaven and the earth shall tremble, he shall say to the sleeping nations, "Ye saints arise and live; ye sinners stay and sleep until I shall call again." (D&C 43:18)

And John the Revelator says, "But the rest of the dead lived not again until the thousand years were finished. This is the first resurrection. Blessed and holy is he that hath part in the first resurrection: on such the second death hath no power, but they shall be priests of God and of Christ, and shall reign with him a thousand years." (Rev. 20:5-6) For this additional one-thousand-year period the unrighteous in the spirit world will continue their reformation and punishment. Some of them will suffer in hell. But when all accounts have been settled, even hell will be emptied and everyone will come forth for the final judgment. As John says, "And I saw the dead, small and great, stand before God; and the books were opened: and another book was opened, which is the book of life: and the dead were judged out of those things which were written in the books, according to their works. And the sea gave up the dead which were in it; and death and hell delivered up the dead which were in them: and they were judged every man according to their works." (Rev. 20:12-13)

God operates an eternal court room as a part of our third act. But he also has a school room with provision for correction, punishment and education, all designed for the refinement and progress of human souls. Hell itself is a divine institution, where the dross can be eliminated from those who could not get rid of it in any other way. Both here and hereafter there is a purification that can only be brought about by suffering. In the atonement Jesus suffered for our sins, on condition of our obedience. But those who do not repent must do their own suffering. A great modern scripture says "For behold I, God, have suffered these things for all, that they might not suffer if they will repent; but if they will not repent, they must suffer even as I, which suffering caused myself, even God, the greatest of all, to tremble because of pain, and to bleed at every pore, and would that I might not drink the bitter cup, and shrink." Peter tells us that while the body of Jesus lay in the tomb, his spirit was preaching to those "spirits in prison" who had been disobedient during the days of Noah some 2500 years earlier. Paul told the Hebrews about some people who had endured torture in this life that they might obtain a better resurrection. (Heb. 11:35) But the spirit can also be improved beyond this life by the purification of its own suffering. And those who become celestial spirits will then be able to resurrect celestial bodies. A physical body is one of the most important factors in our eternal progress. Without these wonderful physical bodies with their senses and abilities we could never attain a fullness of joy. If a physical body were not necessary it never would have been created in the first place. If it were not necessary for eternity, the resurrection would never have been instituted. If a body of flesh and bones was not necessary for God the Father, then God the Son would never have been resurrected.

God created us in his own image, and with a proper development in these three stages the offspring of God may eventually become like the parent. God does nothing that is superfluous or whimsical, and it was just as necessary for Jesus to be "added upon" with mortality as it was for us. At the crucifixion his 33-year-old body and his eternal spirit were temporarily separated, according to the universal experience of all mankind. During the earth's history we have so covered it with cemeteries that they now contain the vast majority of the bodies of all of God's children.

William Cullen Bryant says, "Those who tread the earth are but a handful to tribes that slumber in its bosom." And all of us are required to leave our earthly joys and employments to share this common destiny. Mr. Bryant says, "and not to this eternal resting place shalt thou retire alone — thou shalt lie down with patriarchs of the infant world, with kings and the powerful of the earth. The wise, the good, fair forms, and hoary seers of ages past all in one mighty sepulchre."

It is interesting to go through a cemetery and read the comments on the tombstones of those who have passed away. The usual epitaph phraseology says, "here lies the body of so and so." This might have been the inscription on the sepulchre of Jesus from that historic Friday night until early the next Sunday morning. But when the women went to the tomb to finish the anointing of his body they were met by an angel who gave them a completely different message. Speaking of Jesus the angel then said, "He is not here: for he is risen as he said. Come, see the place where the Lord lay. And go quickly, and tell his disciples that he is risen from the dead; and, behold, he goeth before you into Galilee; there shall ye see him: lo, I have told you." (Matt. 28:6-7) But by his resurrection Jesus posted a new prospective announcement over every grave. Instead of the old "here he lies" label the new projected sign carries that thrilling future announcement saying, "He is not here, he is risen." The empty tomb of Jesus is not only a symbol but also it is a guarantee of our own eternal life.

Some people complain that they cannot understand the resurrection, and that it is impossible for them to believe in eternal glory and everlasting life. It has never seemed to me that this should be difficult for anyone who can believe in his own birth. That is, if one can believe that two microscopic bits of protoplasm can come together and form a life cell, and then by a process of self-division create other cells completely unlike the original to form this great masterpiece of flesh and blood, bone and tissue, vision and personality, wisdom and love that we call a human being — if we can believe in that, why should we have any difficulty believing that this great creation once in existence could continue throughout eternity?

Edwin Markham put this idea into verse under the title, "The Unbelievable." He said:

Impossible, you say, that man survives the grave,
That there are other lives. More strange, oh friend,
That we should ever rise from out the dark
To walk beneath the skies.

But having risen to life and light,
We need not wonder at our deathless flight.
Life is the unbelievable,
But now that this incredible has taught us how
We can believe that all imagining power
That breathed the cosmos forth as golden flower,
Hath potence in his breath,

And plans us new surprises beyond death,
New spaces and new goals
For the adventure of ascending souls.
Be brave, O heart, be brave,
It is not strange that man survives the grave,
'Twould be a stranger thing were he destroyed,
Than that he ever vaulted from the void.

In anticipating his own death, James M. Barrie's Peter Pan exclaimed, "To die will be an awfully big adventure!" and so it will be for all of us. At this Easter season we anticipate one of our most meaningful experiences when we contemplate the time when it will also be said of us, "He is not here, he is risen." And may God help us to be worthy of that glorious experience he has planned for us.

Heart Trouble

ACH YEAR IN THE United States we set aside the month of February as Heart month. The purpose of this special period is to learn something about our hearts and how we can take better care of them. The heart is a hollow muscle. In human adults it measures about 5 inches long and 3½ inches broad. In the average person it weighs less than one pound. This wonderful little organ serves in many capacities. It is a kind of human engine that occupies the central position in the vast circulation system, distributing life-giving blood throughout the body. Blood itself is one of the wonders of the universe. It contains trillions of red corpuscles manufactured in the marrow of the bones at the rate of some 200 billions per day. They come well trained for their job of carrying nutrition to every part of the body. The blood also contains billions of white corpuscles. These are the body's medical men whose job it is to fight disease, kill infection and keep the body well and strong.

Under ordinary conditions the heart beats 70 times per minute. And in the course of its 24 hours it lifts the equivalent of a hundred and fifty pound man from the ground to the top of the Empire State Building. This amazing organ works without ceasing day and night, and it sometimes lasts for a hundred years, without repairs, lubrication or adjustments. When the individual is asleep the heart slows down accordingly. When extra blood is needed the heart speeds up, and in emergencies it sometimes pounds like a sledgehammer. When one is unconscious or even when one is out of his mind, this faithful little organ continues its work in a miracle that defies our understanding.

Even when a man is born, his tiny heart has perfect connections with thousands of little tubes running in all directions, each functioning perfectly with its proper supply of fluid. All are of proper length and size with automatic equipment for maintenance and repair.

It is interesting to imagine the construction of our circulation machinery. Who determined the size and the connections of our pipes. How were they formed — who was the overseer of construction, and who kept them from being smashed shut, or from making the wrong connections? Imagine if you can the circumstances when this circulation system began to operate, and what keeps it going. If any harmful bacteria gets into the blood, thousands of these little white corpuscle warriors immediately spring into action to fight the disease. How do they distinguish between friend and foe, and where did they get their training, and how does the marrow know the right number of billions that should be manufactured?

A million wonders are taking place every day in our lives that even the wisest medical men cannot understand. We didn't even know that our blood circulated, until Harvey's time a little over 300 years ago. And yet whether we understand it or not this miracle goes on without supervision, assistance or control. The blood runs uphill just as well as downhill, and it doesn't matter whether we are sick or well, asleep or awake. The blood is spread out into thousands of minute pipes which take it to all parts of the body, and when it has done its work it is picked up by other pipes and is returned to the heart to be repurified. It always goes to the right places in the right amounts. For all of this effort the heart seems to supply its own energy. It is its own boss. Without being told, it just took up its work and it continues to function throughout our lives, and yet it has no gadgets, no meters, no measuring tanks, no gauges and no operator.

When more energy is required it knows exactly what to do, and when the body is at rest, it cuts its speed and conserves its strength. When blood is lost more is produced, when the brain has extra work to do a larger amount of blood is supplied. When some other part of the body is in need, blood is automatically dispatched to that area. No wonder the Psalmist sang, "I am fearfully and wonderfully made." (Ps. 139:14) But the heart also has some other important functions. We think of it as the seat of the emotions. It is the center of intuition and feeling. We say that one is honest at heart. The heart is the source of love, courage and enthusiasm. The scripture says that the Lord judges us by looking upon our hearts. (I Kings 8:39)

When the Lord chose David to be the King of Israel the record says that he chose "a man after mine own heart." (Acts 13:22, 1 Sam 16:7) And the Lord gave Solomon a largeness of heart. The scripture speaks of new hearts, and clean hearts, and faithful hearts. The heart can be increased in its ability and size when a greater task is given it to do, and one of our greatest possessions is to have a big heart that is fair and righteous.

The heart is the center of religion. The scriptures say, "Keep thy heart with all diligence, for out of it are the issues of life." (Prov. 4:23) What a great privilege it is to be able to control the health, purity and responsiveness of our hearts! But even the heart itself sometimes has trouble. The fact that most heart trouble is preventable is the reason that the American Heart Association sets aside the month of February to call our attention to those things that we can do to keep our hearts in good health. For example, every pound of excess body weight adds an additional burden on the heart, and the heart is sometimes worked beyond its ability to survive. Some people have had their hearts broken by some severe unhappiness, or great sorrow. A great sin can break a heart or bring on a heart attack, and an improper diet can put substances in the blood that cause various kinds of heart disease.

In January 1964, the Surgeon General of the United States published a report about the various kinds of heart damage that takes place each year in the United States, because we allow nicotine to poison this great little organ that not only forms the center of our lives but also is the core of our success. Alcohol is probably the worst single cause of heart disease. It causes hardening of the arteries and other deterioration, ending in death. And yet a spiritual hardening of the heart causes more serious damage and ages people more quickly than does hardening of the arteries. But there are so many things that can get wrong with our hearts. We sometimes get weak hearts or faint hearts, or broken hearts, or hearts loaded down with feelings of guilt and inferiority. The Lord speaks of those who were slow of heart. Some fail because of the blindness in their hearts. (Eph. 4:18) Some great sin or some sorrow can cause the heart to lose its morale so that it wants to quit, and when that happens, nothing else makes very much difference. Jesus gave us some wonderful heart-month council when he said, "Let not your hearts be troubled." (John

14:1) What a great step forward it would be if we would just get rid of all of our heart trouble!

A roadside oil advertisement says, "a clean engine produces power" and so does clean blood and a happy heart. Solomon said, "A merry heart doeth good like a medicine." (Pro 17:22) Tennyson tells of one of the most famous warrior-knights in the days of King Arthur called Sir Galahad. In accounting for his extraordinary ability Tennyson said, "His strength is of the strength of ten because his heart is pure." A pure heart is one of the greatest of all of the secrets of success. A pure heart is not bothered by conflicts or troublesome foreign matter. One of the most dreadful of all kinds of pain is heart-ache. And the greatest cause of both spiritual and physical death comes from mistreated hearts.

The American Heart Association reports that 53% of all deaths are caused by some kind of cardiovascular disease. That is, of the 1,823,000 people who died in the United States during 1965, 989,130 died of some kind of heart disease. The next greatest physical killer is cancer, with 296,320 deaths; and accidents came third with 106,900. But it is probable that over one-half of our other failures in life also come from some kind of heart trouble. The great field of psychosomatic medicine tells us that most of our physical problems begin as a mental or emotional disturbance. Physical heart disease is not nearly as common among laborers as it is among those who are oppressed with mental burdens and stresses, moral guilt and spiritual conflicts. In diagnosing many failures Jesus pointed out that their hearts were not right in the sight of God. This is the kind of heart trouble that we should spend more than one month a year in trying to prevent.

The Bible makes more than 800 references to the heart. Many of them have to do with the various kinds of heart disease that we ourselves can cure. Other scriptures point out activities that are available to us by way of prevention. The Bible mentions various kinds of heart trouble under the headings of perverse hearts, unbelieving hearts, backsliding hearts, slothful hearts, rebellious hearts, foolish hearts and wicked hearts. Through the prophet Jeremiah, the Lord said, "The heart is deceitful above all other things, and desperately wicked: who can know it?" (Jer. 17:9) In this scripture the Lord was speaking only of certain kinds of hearts. Deceitful and wicked hearts are preventable, as everyone was born with a pure heart. However, just as we can defile our minds, our spirits and our bodies so we can cause our hearts to become diseased.

As Jesus said, "Out of the abundance of the heart, the mouth speaketh." (Matt 12:34) And when we load our hearts up with evil, deceit, crime, atheism, and delinquency, those unprofitable traits will soon manifest themselves in everything that we do. When we saturate our tissues with alcohol, we can easily figure out what the result will be. When we fill our lungs and contaminate our blood stream with nicotine we can expect that the wonderful machinery of the heart will begin having problems.

Many people think of the heart primarily as the seat of love; and just contemplate how many people fall in love with the wrong things. With a little indulgence we fall in love with booze, nicotine, dishonesty, unfairness, and immorality. Usually we can only break our evil habits by an enormous exertion, whereas we can sometimes lose our good things by a mere effortless default, or a contrary interest that at first may be very small. The highest function of the heart is to love such good as God, righteousness and fine people; and we need to be able to tell the difference. Jesus cautioned his disciples by saying "take heed that no man deceive you." (Matt. 24:4) We must not deceive others, and certainly we should not deceive ourselves.

James pointed out that those who were hearers of the word but not doers were deceiving themselves, and those who think they can fill their hearts with evil and avoid heart trouble are deceiving themselves. One of the greatest lines in all of our literature was written by the wise man Solomon, many centuries ago, when he said, "As he thinketh in his heart, so is he." (Prov. 23:7)

But we are given the power of choice. In our own hearts we can develop hate, disloyalty to God and eternal death, or we can develop the greatest blessings of life and health. Every poison that we take into the body tends to tear it down. To store evil emotions and destructive feelings in our hearts causes all kinds of personal malignancies. We even commit the greatest sins like murder and adultery by first permitting anger and lust to get into our hearts.

In this month of February we might include a little thought about the Lord's two cures for heart trouble. One is prevention by the inoculation of good ideas; and the other is a process called repentance. This is an operation of cleaning the heart. The symbol of repentance is baptism by immersion in water. Water is the symbol of life and purity. Through Isaiah the Lord said, "Cease to do evil, wash you, make you clean, put away the evil of your doings from before mine eyes." (Isa. 1:16) That is the best way to cure all heart disease. That is what King David was attempting to do as he cried out, "Have mercy upon me, O God . . . blot out my transgressions. Wash me thoroughly from mine iniquity, and cleanse me from my sin. For I acknowledge my transgressions and my sin is ever before me. . . . Create in me a clean heart, O God; and renew a right spirit within me. Cast me not away from thy presence; and take not thy holy spirit from me. Restore unto me the joy of thy salvation — then will I teach transgressors thy ways; and sinners shall be converted unto thee." (Ps. 51)

When physical heart trouble is sufficiently advanced, it leads to death; and if spiritual heart trouble is allowed to progress far enough, it may exclude us from God's presence in a spiritual death that is far more serious.

It is likely that the greatest opportunity of our lives is bound up in the idea of heart month observance. For with a good heart comes the greatest of all success and happiness. As Jesus himself has said, "Blessed are the pure in heart, for they shall see God," and we can become pure in heart by filling our hearts with good things.

High Notes

ONE OF THE MANY interesting words in our language is the little four-letter word "note." A note may be a memorandum to assist the memory, or we may have notes of explanation, or criticism, or thanks. There are bank notes, people of note, promissory notes, or notes that speakers use. A note may sound a warning or excite a caution or convey a sound of music. In the musical scale there are eight notes with graduated pitches, which are called by the names of do, re, mi, fa, so, la, ti, do. These notes are the elements from which harmonies are composed. Notes are to music what the alphabet is to literature, or what the colors are to beauty, or what chemical elements are to our physical world.

From the twenty-six letters of the alphabet, Shakespeare composed a helpful literature containing great meanings and thought harmonies. The Bible writers made these same individual letters into 773,693 significant words carrying soul-saving messages. Corresponding to our great world of literature we have a wonderful world of music made up of symphonies, harmonies, hymns, carols, war songs and jazz. All of these and other musical combinations are merely different arrangements of these eight simple notes repeated in octaves, reaching up very high and down very low. Many of these notes are too high, and others are too low, to be audible to human ears. We are aware that the atmosphere is filled with inaudible music, some of which can be made usable to our ears by means of a radio.

We have heard of the music of the spheres. It was once supposed that this was music produced by the movements of heavenly bodies. Out on the hills of Judea on a long-ago Christmas night, we heard the songs of some angels singing a refrain of "Glory to God in the highest, and on earth peace, good will toward men." But there are many of these celestial harmonies that are never heard by us. The delight produced by the compositions of Beethoven, Bach and Brahms should help us to anticipate what it will be like when we are able to tune in on heavenly visions and the music of the spheres.

Robert G. Ingersoll once said that there was only one note that he knew anything about, and that was a promissory note. We need to know a lot about some other kinds of notes, including the music of the spheres, and we also need to understand how to develop that divine music within our own souls. The personality, the character, the disposition, and the spirit, have some rhythms of their own, and the fulfillment of these symphonies was intended to give our lives a maximum of benefit.

It has been pointed out that each individual human being is like a many-pieced orchestra. Some lives are famous for their harmonies and some are noted for those flat, sour discords that characterize their existence. In the house of Caiaphas, the servant girl said to Peter, "Thy speech betrayeth thee." (Matt. 26:73) Sometimes under *our* conductor's baton we produce notes of fear, notes of discouragement, notes of sarcasm, notes of irreverence, and notes of disobedience to God. And we make these sounds available for everyone to hear. The harsh, loud, noisy, irreverent sounds called forth by our baser appetites are not as harmonious in our souls as the chorus of the angels, or the inspiring notes of Handel's *Messiah*. Sometimes our lives themselves get off-key and throw us out of harmony with the music of the celestial spheres. Sometimes we distort our symphonies about the way that writers do their literature, when they take the very letters that make up the Holy Scriptures and rearrange them in such a way as to incite lust, stir up violence, cause crime, and develop atheism. A painter with a distorted sense of harmony in nature can take the colors that beautify the sunrise, the ocean, the sky and the landscape, and use them in making pictures of ugliness, depravity and filth. Out of the 102 elements that God has provided, the chemist can create deadly poisons or the most miraculous wonder drugs, anti-toxins and life giving vitamins. It is interesting that the bees get honey from the same flowers from which the spiders extract their poisons. And one of the most thrilling ideas of our world also has one of the most awful responsibilities, and that is that we can put the symphonies of our lives together in any way that we desire. In the very beginning when God said to us, "thou mayest choose for thyself," he was granting us a free hand to use all of life's notes from the top of the scale to the bottom to make ourselves and our environment into anything that we may desire.

In Shakespeare's *Julius Caesar*, Brutus was called the greatest Roman of them all, and it was said of him, "his life was gentle, and the elements so mixed in him that nature might stand up and say to all the world, 'here was a man'." God himself put man together on the grandest scale. He not only created man in his own image but he endowed him with a set of his own attributes and potentialities. But man himself must wield the baton, practice the notes and develop the harmonies of sound, sight, feeling and color for whatever greatness may distinguish his life. It has been said that to help us vitalize ourselves each individual should listen to some inspiring music, read some ennobling literature and fill his soul with some great beauty every day. For built-in virtues life's new cells should be stamped with beauty each day as they are being formed.

Many years ago Elbert Hubbard said, "I am looking out through the library window into the apple orchard, and I see millions of blossoms that will never materialize and become fruit for lack of vitalization. The destiny of an apple blossom is that it should someday become an apple, and the destiny of a human soul is that we should become like God. But neither of these things happens unless the fertilizing pollen gets to the right places at the right time." Mr. Hubbard helped this cross-pollenization process in himself by writing a series of 140 biographies of the world's greatest men and women. Some were living and some were dead. He selected the 10 leaders in each of 14 fields. That is he picked out the 10 greatest teachers, the 10 greatest lovers, and the 10 greatest musicians and tried to make the pollen of their lives negotiable to others. If they were living and available he had a personal interview with them. If they were dead he made an extended research of their lives from every available source and then detailed their virtues on paper. He entitled his fourteen volumes "Little Journeys into Great Lives." From the information thus attained he made many positive suggestions available about how to adjust and to adorn our own lives, but he also made it possible for us to learn much from their mistakes.

Recently a young salesman told about a man who had been his idol. This man called the salesman and asked him to work out a program of costs, benefits, uses, etc. for an intended purchase of a large amount of this salesman's merchandise. But during the negotiations the prospective purchaser proved to be very unreliable. He broke appointments without bothering to notify anyone. He needlessly made the salesman stand around and wait for long periods. He would say one thing, and then do something else. Then after having put the salesman to considerable expense he changed his mind altogether, and without so much as a "thank you" he left the salesman to bear all of the expense that he had incurred. This young man was so disappointed and hurt by the poor quality of the responses of his friend, that he almost went out of business. However, it was pointed out to him that if he would carefully catalog all of this man's wrong behavior, then let them burn themselves deep enough into his own mind so that he would never make any of these mistakes himself, then he would be far better off than if the sale had been made on the most favorable basis. Even the most inconsiderate person playing his lowest notes can help one understand the desirability of frankness, honesty and responsibility under all circumstances, with an authority that can be developed in no other way.

We can learn from the ten grandest, or the ten most humble, or the ten most reprehensible, in any field. A young colored boy once raised his hat to Abraham Lincoln. Mr. Lincoln acknowledged the greeting by raising his own hat in return. Someone questioned the President about it and he replied that he did not intend to let anyone outdo him in courtesy. But Lincoln went much further than that, and was courteous to people even when they were rude to him. A friend once told Mr. Lincoln that an enemy was saying some very uncomplimentary things about him. Lincoln told his friend not to worry about it because he would so conduct himself that no one would believe his accuser anyway. Mr. Lincoln was keeping the sour, hateful, discordant notes out of his life. Sometimes we hear a person referred to as being high-toned. I am not sure just what that means, but it could have reference to someone like Mr. Lincoln who always conducted the symphonies of his life with the highest tones after all of the discords and troubles had been eliminated.

I know of a man who might be called low-toned. He is continually having his feelings hurt even by those who are trying to help him. He frequently becomes angry and sullen when no offense is intended. As he has gone from one emotional depression into another, he has developed a kind of instability that makes everyone afraid to have anything to do with him. This man's sister recently said that she would not have believed that anyone could make life so unpleasant for so many people. And yet, even this man can teach us one of the greatest lessons about how *not* to be unpleasant. He serves as a good example of how unprofitable it can be to travel this low road of disagreeable moods, with all of their discords and unpleasantness.

Even selfishness can contain different degrees of intelligence. Recently a young woman called on the telephone to complain about an employment agency where she had been trying to get a job. She had just moved into the city from a small town and she was very bitter because the employment agency people had wanted to know the address of her parents. The employment seeker thought that this was none of their business as she didn't want her parents or anyone else to know where she was. I tried to make some suggestions over the phone as to how she might change the key in which her negotiations were being conducted, but she was so determined to vent her bitterness that any intelligent solution was impossible. She was out of money and yet she was doing the very things that would prevent her from getting a job. The discords of her attitude would make any employer afraid to hire her and anyone else trying to help her would run the risks of incurring some unpleasant consequences because she was so badly out of tune. In addition to all of these difficulties that she was creating for everyone else, she was also causing her parents needless worry and expense by a kind of stupid selfishness.

After she had hung up the telephone I tried to imagine what her bad attitudes, unjustified accusations, poor judgment, irresponsible threats, and bitter rebellion would sound like if they could be set to music. How unpleasant to live in an atmosphere of the low notes, flat notes, and sour notes of a life that is playing a discord that no one wants to hear, and is itself off-key and out of tune.

Another young lady recently said that a young man had asked her to marry him, and he had said that if she didn't he would commit suicide. Our life's symphony is sometimes made up of threatening notes, disagreeable notes, drunken notes and immoral notes. This kind of music can keep every listener upset and in a state of severe nervous tension, and may result in giving people stomach ulcers, nervous breakdowns, and heart disease. One of the greatest of all human success factors is to be able to get along with our fellowmen. But when we are out of tune we sometimes become profane and rebellious and fight against God. One woman thought that God had let her husband die when he should not have done, and so as a part of her declaration of war against Deity, she quit paying her tithing and saying her prayers. She stopped all religious activities and refused to do her duty or even to let her children go to church. How much better it would have been for everyone if she had lived her life on a little higher level of understanding and had played the notes of faith, trust, repentance, and love.

To develop a higher kind of harmony we might turn on the music of the scriptures and feel the inspiration of Job saying, "Though he slay me, yet will I trust in him," or Joshua saying, "As for me and my house, we will serve the Lord," or Jesus saying, "Father, not my will, but thine be done."

Certainly our greatest opportunities come in developing in our own souls those fundamental symphonies of righteousness. If our lives are properly disciplined, dedicated, focused, motivated, on key and in tune, we may someday hear our Heavenly Father say to us, "Well done, thou good and faithful servant, thou hast been faithful over a few things, I will make thee ruler over many things: enter thou into the joy of thy Lord."

I Walked Today

FOR MANY YEARS walking has been prescribed as an exercise that is very beneficial to our health. This stimulating activity also provides a pleasant way of injecting an extra measure of life into our bodies and minds. And by this process we can also provide some additional arousement for our spirits. I have a good friend who seems to get the maximum benefits out of walking. He gives himself a daily allotment of two miles in going to work and another two miles in returning home. He uses a pace fast enough to open up his sweat glands and get his blood churning. But while all of this physical locomotion is taking place, his mind is employed in memorizing and meditating, and his happy spirit is doing some planning and aspiring.

There is a stimulating uplift involved in feeling the blood pulsating in one's veins, while interesting poetry and ambition-packed ideas are exercising his mind. William James once said, "The mind is made up by what it feeds upon," and with enough mental and spiritual hunger, great satisfactions may be had by feeding one's mind the best food and providing effective exercise for his spirit. Actually the amount of one's personal power can be increased with the right kind of self-administered pep talks to build up the enthusiasm within himself. One's daily experiences will be more interesting if he has a song in his heart as he goes eagerly to meet that part of the work of the world that life has given him to do. It is no small thing to be fully alive and have interesting work to do. It is wonderful to feel strength coursing through one's body, lifting up his mind and putting happiness into his spirit. It is always more stimulating to be active than to be acted upon. It is much more fun to be an athlete winning the game, than to be a mere spectator watching someone else. It is more thrilling to feel a whole-souled song in one's heart than merely to be a listener to some song sung by another.

There is a triple alliance of power that is made up of that very close relationship between the physical, mental and spiritual life departments. A person who is always physically tired and slow moving may also tend to be slow moving mentally and spiritually. Because we are put together all in one piece we should build strength and power into the whole person. Someone has said, "Wherever thou art be wholly there." Fractional devotion, minimum performance and marginal morals slow down life's speed and reduce its volume to a decibel. It has often been said that if you really want a job done get a busy man to do it. A busy man is usually in a hurry, and because all of our faculties seem to operate from the same drive shaft we can strengthen our personality traits and increase our rate of mental response by speeding up our physical activities.

Before a coach sends a football player into the game he sometimes warms him up by having him run up and down the sidelines. When his body is active, his mind and spirit tend to be charging also. My friend does something comparable to this as he walks to work each morning breathing great volumes of fresh morning air, and feasting his eyes upon the beauty of the earth as life goes pulsating through his mind and body. Great satisfaction can come from walking when the weather is fair, but it is also a lot of fun to walk in the rain, and even a first class blizzard can be stimulating.

Dr. Alex Carroll once wrote a book entitled, *Man the Unknown*. In this book it is pointed out that we weaken ourselves and miss many of life's available pleasures and benefits by sleeping in heated bedrooms, riding to work in heated automobiles and eating too much soft food. Creation designed man for struggle. He is at his best when he is lean, hungry and carrying a high spiritual charge. Our ancestors fought with wild beasts, went without food, endured long periods of fatigue, struggled with the elements and learned to overcome many other natural difficulties. We can also tone up our emotions, charge our mental batteries and give more zest to our living by effectively using this wonderful physical equipment with which we have been blessed.

Thre are also a number of interesting things about walking mentioned in the scriptures. The Bible tells us that in the beginning God himself walked in the Garden of Eden in the cool of the day, and we might read an entire volume in between those lines. In telling almost the entire life story of the only man who ever built a city worthy of translation the scripture merely says, "And Enoch walked with God." (Gen. 5:22) But in addition to the physical manifestations of walking, it also has some metaphorical and symbolic functions. In the 23rd Psalm, David sang to his Creator, "Though I walk through the valley of the shadow of death, I will fear no evil, for thou art with me. Thy rod and thy staff, they comfort me."

The dictionary says that to walk is to move on foot. It is to advance step by step. And to reach the greatest objectives of life we are frequently required to take a great many of several kinds of steps. And in one way or another there are a lot of exciting opportunities in walking. Paul speaks of those who were baptized and then walked forth in a newness of life. (Rom. 6:4) And he advises the Ephesians that they should follow Christ by walking in love. (Eph. 5:2) The dictionary goes on to say that to walk means to move around in the performance of one's duty. The scriptures give high praise to those who walk in righteousness. A policeman proves his value by the way he walks his beat while fulfilling his particular responsibilities. The scriptures frequently refer to God's leaders as watchmen who make their regular rounds. But the value of every man is determined by how well he walks life's circuits in fulfilling his earthly duties.

Of course the primary purpose of the gospel is to help us walk at the right speed in the right direction, and the mission of Jesus himself was to guide us in our walk. God also gave us eyes, ears, minds and the ability to reason for this same purpose. But to make our walk happy and profitable, we need to exercise a certain control over our behavior. In our physical environments we have some especially prepared walks to give us profit and satisfaction. Some of these walks are graveled and some are paved. We may take a quiet walk through the woods or walk in the Easter promenade down Fifth Avenue. People take many other kinds of walks. Enoch walked with God and some others walk with Satan.

In speaking of sinners the scriptures say that they walk in the way of the ungodly and sit in the seats of the scornful. Some walk in ignorance and some sit in darkness. The scripture mentions those who "walketh as fools walketh." But in any event, as mentioned by the writer of Ecclesiastes, we must suffer the consequences of what we do. He says, "Rejoice, O young man, in thy youth; and let thy heart cheer thee in the days of thy youth, and walk in the ways of thine heart, and in the sight of thine eyes: but know thou, that for all these things God will bring thee into judgment." (Eccl. 11:9)

The greatest of life's rewards come from walking along the right paths. Jesus recommended the strait and narrow way that leads to eternal life. This is the path that has the greatest of all rewards at its end. This idea reminds us of the sacred song entitled, "I Walked Today Where Jesus Walked." It says:

> I walked today where Jesus walked
> In days of long ago.
> I wandered down each path he knew
> With reverent steps and slow.
>
> Those little lanes they have not changed,
> A sweet peace fills the air,
> I walked today where Jesus walked,
> And felt his presence there.
>
> My pathways led through Bethlehem,
> Ah! memories ever sweet,
> The little hills of Galilee
> That knew those childish feet.
>
> The Mount of Olives hallowed scenes
> That Jesus knew before.
> I saw the mighty Jordan roll
> As in the days of yore.
>
> I knelt today where Jesus knelt,
> Where all alone he prayed,
> In the Garden of Gethsemane
> My heart felt unafraid.
>
> I picked my heavy burden up,
> And with him by my side
> I climbed the hill of Calvary
> Where on the cross he died!
>
> I walked today where Jesus walked
> And felt him close to me.

Wouldn't it be wonderful if on some beautiful day we could go and stand on that spot where Jesus once stood, and feel him so close to us that we could absorb some of the meaning and spirit of his life? It would be a thrilling experience even in imagination to walk by his side from Nazareth up to the capital city of Jerusalem, and enjoy the kind of conversation that would most delight him, as we passed along the way.

Or in our minds we might go with him into the temple that he loved. This temple had been erected on a spot made dear to every Jewish heart by the sacred memories that it enshrined. It was on this spot that at the command of an angel, David, the great ancestor of Jesus, had built an altar to offer sacrifice to Jehovah. At a later date it was on this same spot that Solomon had built his magnificent golden temple for the earthly worship of Jehovah. And while the temple was later desecrated and twice destroyed, yet each time it had been rebuilt for the worship of God. It was to this temple that Jesus himself had come to talk with the wise men when he was 12 years old. During his earthly ministry the temple courts had been the center of his religious activities. And it was here that he had come for the last time during the final week of his life. This was the place where he would finish his mission of teaching the gospel by giving the people their last opportunity for acceptance. Then on that last Tuesday of his life, when they would not accept his message of salvation, he finished his mission and brought his public ministry to an end.

Sometime before this final scene the antagonism of the people had become so severe that he had taken his disciples and had gone into a kind of retirement in the quiet little town of Ephraim some 20 miles north of Jerusalem. Because it was now unsafe for him to walk openly among the people, he used this time to prepare the apostles for the work of the ministry that would soon rest heavily upon their shoulders. But as the Passover Week approached, he startled his followers by saying, "come let us go into Judea again." Then began that long and solemn march toward Jerusalem and the cross.

He arrived back in Bethany on Friday evening just before the beginning of the Sabbath. In just one week, he would hang with outstretched arms above Calvary. We know little of what happened on this last Sabbath, for over this day the gospel writers have drawn a reverent veil of silence. However, early on the first day of the week, he made his triumphant entry into Jerusalem and all day long he taught the people in the temple. On the next day, which was Monday, he cleansed the temple of those who bought and sold; and in driving out the money changers he said, "It is written that my Father's house is a house of prayer, and ye have made it a place of merchandise." Then came Tuesday, which was the last day of the Lord's public ministry. By many acts of unbelief and disobedience he had been rejected and now their time had run out. Therefore at the end of this last Tuesday, he left the sacred courts of his Father's house forever.

As he began the mile and a half walk back to Bethany to the home of Martha, Mary and Lazarus where he was staying, he sat down to rest near the top of the Mount of Olives. His disciples came to him while he discussed with them such important doctrines as the destruction of Jerusalem, his own glorious second coming to the earth, and the end of the world. Then he made his famous speech of farewell to Jerusalem. In imagination we might see him sitting there on the hillside overlooking the temple. We can imagine that the last rays of the declining sun had lighted the western sky with splendor as he said, "O Jerusalem, Jerusalem, thou that killeth the prophets, that stoneth them that are sent unto thee, how oft would I have gathered thy children together even as a hen gathered her chickens underneath her wings, and ye would not. Behold your house is left unto you desolate." But yesterday he had called it "my Father's house." Now that the Father's representative had been rejected, their chance had gone also, and it had become "your house." The people whom he had come to save had spent their time walking along that broad road of disobedience that leads to death, and as a consequence of seeking the wrong objectives they had lost the greatest rewards of their lives.

In a physical sense it may not be practical "to walk today where Jesus walked," but what is practical, and what is a lot more important, we can think today what Jesus thought, we can walk in his mental footprints by memorizing his philosophies, practicing his doctrines, and following his example. We can rerun his sentences through our minds, we can rethink his thoughts, relive his commandments; and walk uprightly before him with his humility and faith.

The song says, "I knelt today where Jesus knelt." And what a thrilling privilege that even today we can kneel again before the King of kings and Lord of lords. His great lessons can still enrich our eternal lives. As of old he still pleads with us saying, "Come ye and let us walk in the light of the Lord." May God help us to continue to the very end of that strait and narrow way that will lead us to eternal life.

The Idea Supermarket

IT HAS ALWAYS been a source of great delight to me to walk through a well ordered supermarket and see the attractive array of fruits and vegetables in every variety and color. While on the farm I learned something about the thrill involved in bringing various kinds of products out of the raw soil. With the right kind of planning, industry, irrigation, fertilizer, cultivation, sunshine and soil, one may literally accomplish miracles in producing beauty, taste and vitamins. It is by this miracle that life is maintained, giving pleasure and strength to the body, the mind, and the personality. I suppose that because my taste buds have been developed above the average, my supermarket appreciation has grown accordingly.

I am confident that these beautiful supermarket products were designed by a Creator who loved color and taste. He also knew how to best pack the nutritious ingredients into them to form strength, vision, personality, love and joy in human beings. Good food also supports the best there is in the mental and spiritual characteristics of people. And if God lacked the ability to manufacture these wonder products out of elements in the sunshine, air, water and soil, everything in human life would wither and die. The light would go out of our eyes, our minds would cease to function, our personalities would no longer operate and the greatest of all of God's creations would come to a halt. As I walk through a giant supermarket literally filled with thousands of God's wonder inventions, I feel as though I was witnessing some kind of an eternal life process. These foods are sent to us from every corner of the globe all beautifully arrayed and packaged for our benefit and pleasure. And as I think about them I am uplifted and made to feel grateful to God.

However, I frequently have a related experience that is even more exciting. Frequently I spend an hour or so in a book store. I see the great volumes that have been wonderfully written and packaged to bring me another kind of nourishment, from the most fertile minds in the universe. I read the challenging titles and imagine their pleasant taste as well as contemplate the faith, strength, personality and vision which they contain. Abraham Lincoln fed on his books as he lay on the cabin floor before the open fire in the evenings. He gained his unusual strength as he digested the Bible and transferred to himself the valuable things that were stored away therein. Young Abe said, "What I want is in books and my best friend is the one who will get me a book that I haven't read." To understand the difficulty Lincoln had in getting books should help us to appreciate our own situation when thousands of excellent volumes are published each year on every conceivable subject by the greatest minds, and they are all made available to us for just a few pennies.

Someone has said that books are among life's most precious possessions. They are the most remarkable creation of man. Nothing else that man builds ever lasts. Monuments fall, civilizations perish, but books continue. The perusal of a great book is, as it were, an interview with the noblest men of past ages who have written it.

Charles Kingsley said, "There is nothing more wonderful than a book. It may be a message to us from the dead, from human souls we never saw, who have lived thousands of miles away, and yet these little sheets of paper speak to us, arouse us, teach us, open our hearts, and in turn open their hearts to us like brothers. Without books God is silent, justice dormant, philosophy lame, and all things are involved in darkness." John Milton said, "books are not dead things, but contain a certain potency of life in them as active as the soul whose progeny they are. They preserve as in a vial, the purest efficacy of the living intellect that bred them."

"A good book is the very essence of a good man wherein his virtues survive while his faults and failings are forgotten." T. G. Cuyler said, "All the goodly company of the excellent and great sit around my table, or look down upon me from my shelves. A precious book can be a kind of foretaste of immortality." In a way books are embalmed minds. "The world's greatest men can put themselves down on paper and give themselves a kind of immortality for our benefit." I never cease to marvel at this great invention where the most delicate or profound meanings can be preserved and conveyed by the marks that are made on paper, parchment, the bark of trees, or even cut into stone buildings. Then, centuries after the buildings have become ruins and the parchment has faded, these magic marks made by those long since dead can still make us weep or laugh or move us to the most profound thoughts.

There is a story told of an early traveler in Africa who sent a written message to an assistant a hundred miles away. The message was carried by a native who knew nothing about writing. At the end of his journey he handed the letter to the one for whom it was intended, and to the wonder of the native the one receiving this flimsy piece of paper with a few marks on it immediately knew exactly where his chief was, how he was dressed, who was with him, what he was thinking and how he fared in every other way. All of this without the messenger himself saying a single word. It so amazed the messenger that he fell down on his face before the reader as though he were a god.

In some primitive places in the past only the priest could read and write, and others have looked upon him as though he were the agent of Deity, the very mouthpiece of God. It was not very long ago that a book was so treasured that sometimes it was bound between oak boards, riveted in bands of iron, locked with a ponderous key and carried with slow steps to the altar by a solemn procession of priests. Then the book was unlocked and opened, and the priest read from it while the people listened in breathless awe to the words that Deity himself had dictated in order that men might save their souls.

And yet even the grandest books don't help us very much unless we are familiar with what they say. Someone recently said that he had never read a single book in the last five years. In the midst of the knowledge explosion which makes us the beneficiaries of the greatest miracles of enlightenment that the world has ever known, this man is still living in the mental and spiritual dark ages. As a consequence of such an unfortunate situation the Lord once said about another group of people, "They have sinned a very grievous sin in that they are walking in darkness at noon-day." (D&C 95:6) It is this darkness in human souls that makes our world sick. Woodrow Wilson was referring to this general problem when he said, "The greatest ability of the American people is their ability to resist instruction." And I suppose that most of us have our share of that unfortunate talent. Sometimes even the most significant happenings leave us unchanged. A prophet speaks, or the gospel is restored, or even the Savior visits the earth, but like the antediluvians to whom

Jesus compared us, we frequently go along relatively unconcerned, insisting upon our puny business affairs proceeding as usual.

Thomas A. Edison indicated a related difficulty when he said, "There is no limit to which a man will go to avoid thinking." Thinking is often the most disagreeable, unpleasant exercise that most of us ever undertake, and yet as Solomon said, "As a man thinketh in his heart, so is he." Now I don't know exactly where that leaves us, if we are what we think — and if we don't think — but it indicates that we have a problem. One man once said that there were only two books in the world that had ever done him any good — one was his mother's cook book, and the other was his father's checkbook.

It might help us to remind ourselves of the experience that Goliath had when he met David with his slingshot. After the whole affair was over someone commented that such a thing had never entered Goliath's head before. In a little different way, the experiences that most of us need more than about anything else is to get more things into our heads, and into our hearts, and into our activities.

Upon the cross, Jesus said, "Father forgive them, for they know not what they do." The people referred to were committing the greatest possible sin but didn't even know what they were doing. But almost all of the sins in our world are the sins of ignorance. The people who involve themselves wth alcohol, nicotine, and caffeine, don't realize what they are doing. Those who absent themselves from church, or engage in the various kinds of evil, don't understand that they are changing themselves and that in some degree they are destroying their own eternal possibilities.

The scriptures say that no man can be saved in ignorance. But neither can anyone make himself happy or successful in ignorance, and even most of our satisfactions in life come from the way that we ourselves think. People with negative minds think negative thoughts. Depraved, unhappy thoughts are produced in depraved unhappy minds. When we feed our minds out of poison books we produce poisoned minds. There is a deadly "fall out" that comes from the violence, hate, and immorality of certain movies, newspapers, and magazines. But some good treatments from the right kinds of books can build minds capable of thinking the most pleasant, happy, constructive thoughts. Someone has asked this question: "How would you like to create your own mind?" But isn't that exactly what we do!

William James said, "The mind is made up by what it feeds upon." The mind, like the dyer's hand, is colored by what it holds. If I hold in my hands a sponge full of purple dye, my hands become purple, and if I hold in my mind and heart great ideas of faith, industry, and obedience to God, my whole personality is colored accordingly. Edwin Dyer says:

> My mind to me a kingdom is.
> Such pleasant joys therein I find
> That it excells all other bliss
> The earth affords or grows by kind.

There is a physician in Birmingham, Alabama who goes around writing prescriptions for people to get filled, not at drugstores, but at bookstores. He believes that almost all cures must first be made in the mind. Even our physical health is largely governed by what and how we think. Someone has pointed out that very few of us ever get stomach ulcers because of what we eat. We get stomach ulcers because of what is eating us, and that is how we get heart disease, nervous breakdowns and social infirmities.

In times of old, many books had an influence almost equal to divine authority. But as the number of books has been increased the appreciation of their value has diminished in the minds of some people to where they have little importance. However, suppose that we go into one of these great supermarkets of the mind and think about their various titles. We will find books of poetry that can start feelings of love, and metered rhythm moving through our hearts. There are many books of useful fiction, books of history, books of biography and books of religion.

Charles Lamb said, "I love to lose myself in other men's minds." Through books we may enjoy with Shakespeare, and think with Emerson, and pray with Jesus. We can see into the mind of Moses, feel the faith of the Apostle Paul, and live the visions of John the Revelator. It is much easier to make our lives productive if we have some good books to help us. Erasmus said, "When I get a little money I buy books and if any is left over, I buy food and clothes." Fenlon said, "If all of the crowns of Europe were placed at my disposal on condition that I should abandon my books and studies, I should turn away from the crowns and stand by my books."

But books are only waste paper unless we can translate into action the wisdom that their thought stimulates. We make a serious mistake when we spend more money for beer than for books, and life's most critical danger comes from full stomachs and empty minds. Empty minds are like deserted houses that attract the haunting stay of base spirits, whereas the love of knowledge is a warrant for the excitement of superior passions and virtues. We learn to read in the presence of books and the love of knowledge not only comes from reading but grows upon it.

May God help us to eat wholeheartedly from those great books growing on the tree of knowledge.

Incompatibility

ELBERT HUBBARD once said that so far as he knew the unpardonable sin was incompatibility. There is a serious religious offense where one sins against great knowledge that has been said to be "unforgivable." Those who commit it are referred to as the Sons of Perdition. The term Perdition was first applied to Satan and carries with it the idea of a complete loss. It indicates a total destruction, or an eternal death. Satan was once a personage of great intelligence and power, and his sin was unpardonable because it was committed in the face of superior knowledge. As a consequence of leading the antemortal rebellion against God, Satan drew away one-third of heaven's population after him, and was cast out of heaven. Since that time those who have followed Satan beyond the point of no return have been called the Sons of Satan or the Sons of Perdition. They commit the sin that is unforgivable.

We don't know how much Mr. Hubbard knew about the unpardonable sin, nor what extremes of incompatibility he was familiar with. The punishment imposed upon the Sons of Perdition is so severe that the Lord has said that no one will ever know very much about it except those consigned to suffer its eternal misery. And it is also likely that no one will ever fully comprehend the torments of incompatibility except those who endure its awful pain. Usually loneliness does not consist of being alone. More frequently it comes from being involved with some highly incompatible human beings. There are so many ways that people can be offensive and disagreeable with themselves.

Some boys once caught a rattlesnake. They put it in a big box where it couldn't hurt them. Then to hear it hiss and rattle and to see it strike, they hit it and poked at it with sticks and otherwise tormented it. The snake generated extreme anger. Its useless striking and hissing added to its frustration and rage. Apparently rattlesnakes are capable of a violent temper, and they can become so angry that they will sometimes bite themselves to death. Most people would not get much satisfaction from a close association with the angry rattlesnake. But as people we can sometimes be about that unpleasant and poisonous.

Someone recently told of a small group of business partners with whom he was connected some years ago. All were very agreeable and easy to get along with except one. But he just seemed to try to be offensive. He was always misquoting someone, or was laying on them the blame for his mistakes. He was frequently hissing and striking, and sometimes it seemed that he was about to bite himself. His vote was necessary for the conduct of the organization's business and even though the others almost wore themselves out trying to handle him with kid gloves, yet he was always causing some unpleasant scene. But even at his best, he kept everyone under an unpleasant tension worrying about where the next outbreak would take place.

There are many things that can cause incompatibility. It is often partially made up of hate, scorn, untruth, and unnecessary arguments. Its ingredients are in direct contrast to the great principles of the gospel which teach love, soft answers, cheerful hearts, merry countenances and genuine good will. Jesus said, "Peace I leave with you; my peace I give unto you." Incompatibility is much more than an occasional isolated problem. The world itself is a hotbed of strife, anger, jealousy, and a kind of rattlesnake hate instead of the "peace on earth, good will toward men," that the angels sang about. Jesus taught compatibility. He said, "Love one another." He went around among people saying such things as "Why are ye troubled?", "Why do thoughts arise in your hearts?", "Rejoice and be exceedingly glad."

When Jesus visited in ancient America after his resurrection he learned of some contention existing among the people. He said, "There shall be no disputations among you . . . for verily I say unto you the spirit of contention is not of me, but is of the devil, who is the father of contention." (III Nephi 11:28-29) The two greatest commandments have to do with compatibility. They teach us to love God and love our fellow men. We should also love our employment, love righteousness, and even love our enemies. We should put incompatibility as far from us as possible. Strife, bickering, and bitterness probably ruin more lives than almost any other thing. When extreme incompatibility gets into our homes, our businesses, or our churches, it can cause a near total loss, and it can even make life itself seem unprofitable. Over one-fourth of all marriages are broken up, mostly because of

incompatibility. Out of 1641 divorces recently granted, 1537 were
based on grounds of mental or physical cruelty. Translated into
understandable terms that probably means incompatibility. But
all the other divorces seemed to be for about the same reason
although they were listed under different headings. Fifty three
divorces were on the grounds of non-support, 31 for desertion, 15
were for the conviction of some crime, 3 were for drunkenness,
and 2 were for adultery.

Fortunately not very many people ever become Sons of Perdition. And while Perdition is the greatest sin in "enormity,"
yet in any contest to produce misery, incompatibility would win
hands down so far as "frequency" and total suffering is concerned. Incompatibility gets much of its destructiveness because
it is so common and infects so many people. But at the same
time it also generates in people such a large posterity of other
sins. Incompatibility frequently is the father of boredom, contention, distrust, hate, nervous breakdowns, communication failure, stomach ulcer, frigidity, disillusioned parents and neurotic
children. And while the Lord himself has said that only a few
will become Sons of Perdition, yet millions will have their blessings wiped out by incompatibility.

I know of a middle-aged woman who is the mother of four
children. On the surface she seems reserved and even shy, but
underneath she has a vein of absolute ruthlessness, and cruelty
so far as her husband is concerned. He makes mistakes and yet
in the best way he knows how he has tried to make a happy
home for his family; and the price that she demands for any
cooperation is to be served and waited upon. Of course she
herself is not happy. Happiness comes to us only when we give
it to someone else. She has a kind of sadistic streak comparable
to the little boy who delights in pulling the legs off of grasshoppers. She is not even congenial with herself, as she has often
wished that she could die. The cause of her unhappinness is that
she breaks the law of love and does not support her husband.
She doesn't love her husband, nor her parents, nor herself. She
could get all excited about living if she vigorously tried to make
the lives of others beautiful and happy. Satan is miserable because he makes other people that way, and most of our unhappiness comes from that same cause. A long time ago someone
coined a phrase meaning incompatibility. They called it a "hell
on earth." Probably better than any other this phrase describes

the situation where husbands, wives and children are afflicted with a serious case of incompatibility. Someone has said that it takes two to have an argument, but that is not so and incompatibility on the part of one often multiplies itself into those harmful emotions of hopelessness, discouragement, despair, and desperation that it sets in motion in other lives.

The most famous and far reaching example of incompatibility is Satan himself. Even though God is the author of righteousness and fairness Satan couldn't get along with him. Satan was once very highly favored in heaven. He was extremely intellectual and was called the Light Bearer, the brilliant Son of the Morning. In the Grand Council he proposed that the free agency of man should be done away with, and that he should be put in charge of saving everyone by compulsion. When his proposal was rejected by God and a two-thirds majority of heaven he became angry and started hissing and biting people. And ever since that date he has continued to foster evil as the world's chief trouble maker.

When we follow Satan in fostering unhappiness and destroying harmony we are committing one of the most destructive of the sins. And that is also what we are doing when we take marriage vows agreeing to show love, honor and consideration, and then become agitators, dictators, sinners and trouble makers. When everything doesn't go right some people get angry, or sulk, or go on a sit-down strike. Some become moody and contentious and begin invoking sanctions. Incompatibility has some of the repelling qualities of the negative pole of a magnet. A magnet's chief function is to attract, but it also has a pole that repels. Last year at Christmas time I saw a magnetized toy made up of three flat circular disks on a stick. Each of these disks was about the size of a silver dollar. A hole through the center enabled them to slide freely up and down a stick about the size of a long pencil. When they were put on the stick with their drawing powers facing each other, they developed such a strong attraction that all three clung together so tightly that they could hardly be pried apart. But when their incompatible faces were placed together they repelled each other with an equally violent force. Then by their repulsion they pushed apart from each other on the stick so that each was suspended in the air, with three or four inches separating it from the others. If you forced them together there would be a violent rebound as soon as they were released. They resembled people who just couldn't stand each other. But that is the way some people respond to life. Some people are repelled by their parents, their parents-in-law, and particularly their mates. They resent almost everything that others do. God said to the woman, "Thy desires shall be to thy husband." (Gen. 3:16) And he gave directions that husbands should love their wives. However, this magnetism of attraction and the sportsmanship of give-and-take are almost completely unknown to some people. They pick out the faults of others but are unable to recognize them in themselves.

To be most compatible one must learn to think clearly, reason effectively, and be able to see the point of view of others. Some people discard their reason and respond to life and to other people by how they feel at the moment, and their feelings today may be completely different from their feelings of yesterday. Incompatibility becomes a more serious problem when it is also unpredictable. Some people imagine that it will relieve their own hurt feelings to hurt someone else. Nothing could be further from the truth. Even a constructive suggestion made to a touchy person is often interpreted as an unfriendly criticism and causes serious offense. The inability to get along with others may indicate a stunted affection, but it also frequently indicates a lack of good sportsmanship.

To live the gospel of Jesus Christ is the best guarantee that we will be compatible with all good things. Just suppose that we religiously kept all of the Ten Commandments. Then so far as we were concerned there would be no lying, no stealing, no profanity, no immorality, no coveting, no deception and no false witness. We would honor our parents, and we would always obey God. We would keep the Sabbath day holy, and work effectively during the balance of the week. Under these conditions how could we have any problems? Think how our favorable public relations would increase. What a lot of fun we would have if we practiced the Golden Rule, and treated other people as we would have them treat us. What great spiritual, social, mental and financial progress we would make if we loved everyone and always did good things for people.

How we treat others also determines our own feelings of peace, happiness, and success. There is an old story about two families seeking a new home. Both stopped in the same community and made inquiry of the same man as to the kind of people living in this new community. In answer the local man asked each inquirer "What kind of people lived in the place that you just left?" One thought *his* former neighbors were wonderful and the other thought that *his* were terrible. To both inquirers, the man said, "That is the same kind of people that live here." Wherever we live those who love their neighbors and families are happy. And those who love God have a much better standing with him.

Inoculations

SOMETIME AGO WHILE making preparations to travel abroad, we were told that the nations we expected to visit would require us to be vaccinated to safeguard them against any contagious diseases. Our doctor also recommended that we take additional shots for our own protection. Whether we are at home or abroad this idea of being inoculated against disease is a very good one. It lengthens life, eliminates suffering, decreases expense and saves time. As late as 1924 there were 1,270 deaths from smallpox in the United States. But because of the immunity that we have now produced within ourselves, we have not had a single smallpox death in the last 17 years. Millions of people have been spared from ugly disfiguring pox marks and other by-products of this once dreaded disease. Some good anti-toxins can also decrease the intensity and duration of some diseases after they have already begun.

In the days before vaccine, the body was required to manufacture its own anti-toxins and the disease frequently killed the patient before the anti-toxin was strong enough to kill the disease. Now science can assist the body, or through an inoculation in advance it can prevent the disease altogether. Certainly the use of vaccines represents one of our most valuable scientific advances. But this idea can also be applied in the religious, moral, and occupational fields. If one desires to enter a new business it is not now necessary for him to proceed by the former wasteful processes of trial and error. And just as no one is strong enough to withstand the ravages of every disease, so no one can afford to make all of the business or moral mistakes personally. Because of good books and the training courses that are available, instances of failure in others can be used to make us immune to their errors, and by building up our own resistance to failure we can give ourselves strength with the know-how skills and attitudes of success. We have a powerful literature that can put almost any variety of success corpuscles into our bloodstream. To be effectively inoculated against mistakes can greatly reduce those self-defeating activities that are causing our high occupational failure rate, and at the same time they will give us greater strength when we are successful. A few of the right kind of thoughts properly placed in the mind can build a roadway on which any desired success can travel in safety.

A good imagination has the power to visualize success in advance. It is a manifestation of that mental ability which is able to decompose its conceptions and recombine their elements in whatever success combinations are desired. Its scouting skills can also recruit the most worthwhile abilities. In the imagination we can go back into the past and reabsorb the original good of every experience, or we can go up into the future and establish almost any success pattern in advance.

In his great book *Gospel Ideals,* President David O. McKay said, "Last night I dreamed about my mother." Then he said, "I would like to dream about my mother more often." In his dream he went back and relived those important lessons learned at his mother's knee that have guided him to his present high place. Then, when he awakened in the morning, these stimulating experiences had been re-established and re-vitalized in full power in his life. Of course it is unnecessary for one to go to sleep in order to dream. One who is wide awake has a much better selection of success possibilities. And through this wonderful mental vehicle one may have any experience without becoming involved in its risks or expense. As we make our bodies immune to disease by the right kind of injections into our bloodstream, so we can ward off evil and make success more vigorous by using the many emotional stimulants and vitamins that are so easily available to us.

Sometime ago a young man was taken into the army where he was very unsuccessful in making the proper adjustments. He didn't like the food, and he was homesick and lonesome. When he received word that his girl friend was becoming very friendly with someone else, he began entertaining the idea of deserting the army. Then one night he had a dream. In his mind he left his army post and went home. But when he arrived conditions were not as pleasant as he had anticipated.

Now that he was a deserter his parents were ashamed of him. Instead of welcoming him with open arms, his girl was disgusted and would have nothing to do with him. Everywhere he went, he was the object of criticism and scorn, and he knew that it would only be a matter of hours until he would be placed under military arrest. Life in the army had not been very pleasant, but he now discovered that desertion was worse. Now it occurred to him that he had made a terrible mistake, and he was very sorry that he had not stuck with his job like a loyal soldier. As his remorse was reaching its pinnacle, he awoke.

At first he just couldn't believe that he was still in camp. As the truth began to dawn upon him, he quickly put on his trousers and rushed outside to make sure that his good fortune was real. When he was finally convinced that he was not a deserter he could hardly contain his joy. What a difference it made to him to have this shot of desertion anti-toxin circulating around in his system. Now a little poor food or a touch of homesickness was of little consequence. And no matter who married whom, from this moment on he would be the best soldier in the army. This emotional experience made him so immune to desertion that he would never get the real disease. To be a dishonorable quitter in anything, was now unthinkable for him. And in the future he would outwork, outtrain, and outappreciate everyone else in the army.

But the teachings of Jesus were also intended to serve us as a valuable collection of helpful inoculations, to be used to prevent us from getting some of life's most serious diseases. For example, we remember the story of the prodigal son. This young man left his home and spent his time and his inheritance in riotous living with undesirable companions. What made this experience so wasteful was that the prodigal had to have the actual experience of losing his wealth, ruining his good name, hurting his family and eating husks with the swine before he could cure the diseases that were causing his trouble. And by the time he had built up enough strength in himself to say, "I will arise and go to my father," most of the damage had already been done. The difficulty of this kind of personal experience is that many people never survive long enough to regain their original health. Therefore Jesus made some disease-killing emotional medicine out of the prodigal's experiences so that we could immunize ourselves. By taking these inoculations as needed, we can make it unnecessary to personally suffer from all of the actual diseases. In fact, one of the reasons why God permits evil in our world is that we may use it to inoculate ourselves against it.

In applying this idea, the ancient Greeks set apart a special day to immunize their young men against drunkenness. They poured an overdose of raw wine down the throats of some, so that others could see how people behaved when their bodies were drugged with alcohol and their minds inflamed with booze. By this process the Greeks made a benefit for all from the drunkenness of a few.

In pointing out the advantages of opposites Jesus said that a taste of the bitter should help us to appreciate the sweet. But we do not need to have all of these experiences personally. A close-up view of a bloated, mentally unbalanced, bleary-eyed drunkard should help us to understand the pleasure of clear eyes, straight thinking, a logical mind, a steady hand and a guilt-free soul. And one of our greatest opportunities is to become so expert in the use of life's anti-toxins that we can make ourselves immune to all of the diseases, so that we will not need to agonize with them personally.

The problem is that the patient himself is usually not aware of his danger until the disease has such a headstart that is too hard to overcome. When an intelligent man gets physically ill he seeks help. But moral diseases can so deaden the will that the patient actually resists help. Frequently we put off vaccinating ourselves gainst such things as dishonesty, alcohol, dope, nicotine, laziness, negative thinking, atheism, and immorality until it is too late. If we could become more expert in this skill of inoculation, we could do with the dread moral diseases what physical medicine has already done with diphtheria, tuberculosis, leprosy, and smallpox. It was for such an immunity that Jesus was praying when he said, "Thy kingdom come; thy will be done, on earth as it is in heaven." But this will be a difficult prayer to answer as long as we are glamorizing the very things that are making us sick. When we hold liquor, immorality, dope and weakness up before our minds as something to be sought after, none of their anti-toxins are very effective. Of course, we know that no disease produces happiness. And it would be just as reasonable for us to argue that lung cancer is good for us, or that everyone should have a good case of polio or that it is fun to be mentally retarded as it would be to entice ourselves with any wrong.

It is not only true that an alcoholic is sick, but so is the nicotine addict, the thief, the liar, the atheist, and everyone else who disobeys the divine laws. We often get cancer, or diabetes, or heart trouble through no fault of our own; but the moral counterparts of these dread diseases are all self-induced and can be cured or prevented if we take the right treatment early enough. Then, by proper mental diet and spiritual exercise, one can keep himself in such excellent good health that he will have very few weaknesses and very little sickness. Of course, we ourselves should know something about the practice of medicine. Jesus said, "Physician, heal thyself." But not even the best doctor can cure a moral depression while he continues to drink the alcohol that causes it. And all of the best doctors put together can't stamp out lung cancer while the patient is continually filling his lungs with nicotine. However, through the power of prevention, the most unskilled among us can keep ourselves in glowing good health and so immunize ourselves that the dread disease will never develop in the first place, whereas if we cultivate spiritual malnutrition and allow the moral diseases to go unchecked, they can carry us a long way down that broad road that leads to eternal death. What we need is a spiritual medicine cabinet filled with such anti-toxins as faith, obedience to God, courage and straight thinking. Then we could free ourselves from all of the aches and pains that are persistently making us so miserable. There is a wonder drug called repentance that is one of our most effective means of fighting disease. In fact if we are to be saved at all, we must either repent or suffer. Hell itself is a kind of hospital. It is a divine institution established by God as a place where the ravages of disease can be burned out of the lives of those who have been unable to repent by themselves.

But if our unchecked sins are allowed to go too far, then even the fires of hell won't cleanse us. About those who have passed this point of no return the Lord has said, "These are they who are the Sons of Perdition, concerning whom I have said there is no forgiveness in this world nor in the world to come." (D&C 176:32-34) Of this group John the Revelator said, "Then they who are filthy shall be filthy still." Apparently these will never be able to clean themselves up and get well, but they will be forced to endure their self-imposed moral cancers and painful heartaches forever. Even a bad sore throat can cause a lot of suffering, make conversation unpleasant, prevent sleep and make us miserable and unhappy.

An alcoholic or a dope addict may actually go insane if he is unable to satisfy the evil appetites that he has brought upon himself. But try to imagine one who can never repent. Think how he would feel dragging his addled brain, his foul liquor smells, his shaky hands and unsteady legs into the presence of God. The scriptures say that God is such a glorious personage that no mortal in his natural state is fitted to endure his presence. Even the best people have some changing to do to prepare for God's glory. And certainly it would not be very pleasant for one to enter his presence loaded down with the sores, the decays and the pains of a lot of moral diseases that he had brought upon himself.

God will help us to clean up our lives; and then, by absorbing his righteousness, we can immunize ourselves against those evils that otherwise might destroy us.

The Last Days of Pompeii

ONE OF THE MOST unusual cities of the world is the ancient city of Pompeii. It is a Roman city that died during an eruption of Mount Vesuvius on August 24, in the year 79 A.D. It was literally buried alive by the rain of pumice and volcanic ash that was spewed over the city by the exploding volcano. After the 48-hour eruption, Pompeii lay under 20 feet of ashes and lava chunks, and the next 17 centuries added another twenty feet of dirt covering. The volcano had changed the shore line and Pompeii was all but forgotten until 1748, when a peasant digging a well over Pompeii made some valuable finds which stimulated excavation attempts. In 1755 Charles III dug into some public buildings. And Pompeii sprang to life as the most famous archaeological site in the world. It was soon famous for its buried treasures, its historical data, its life-like reality, and a kind of immortal uniqueness unknown to any other city.

In the 19th Century, Lord Lytton stimulated general interest by writing his classic *The Last Days of Pompeii*. He pictured Pompeii in her final hours before the eruption as a town of some 20,000 inhabitants, located across the bay from the great Roman naval base at Naples. It was a favorite resort town for the wealthy people of Rome. Many famous Romans built villas here by the sea in the glamor of Greek elegance.

The people of Pompeii built low single-family houses of stone, brick and stucco. They turned blank walls to the streets and each house looked in on an interior open court called an atrium. This airy atrium was the heart of the Pompeiian home, and it was usually guarded by the graceful little statue of their household God. He was saluted with a morning prayer, and an offering was made from the table to encourage him to keep the family healthy, prosperous and fruitful. Treasures and jewelry were highly prized and were often taken with their owners to their tombs. Pear trees, cypresses, pomegranates, and oleanders grew in profusion in the gardens, and householders planted rose bushes and violets beside their fountains.

A man too poor to afford a large domestic establishment usually hired a painter to portray an imitation garden on the walls of his smaller house. But frescoes of one kind or another were everywhere in Pompeii, and some 3500 of them can still be seen. The rich people commissioned artists to paint hundreds of elaborate scenes, many of which are now found in our own museums of art. More paintings have survived from this ancient city of Pompeii than from all the rest of the classic world put together.

The main street led to the forum, which was the center of the city's life. Merchants thrived from their various trades, and the citizens ate and drank well as they reclined on the sloping shelves around movable tables. They rose at dawn and went to bed shortly after sunset, and about half of their days were holidays, on which they patronized gladitorial contests or went to the theater or to the temple.

The women of Pompeii were very fond of jewelry and collected rings and brooches, gold bracelets, pins and jeweled buttons. But on that fateful day of August 24, 79 A.D. everything in Pompeii was changed by the 4,000-foot mountain that stood brooding behind them, preparing to explode. The eruptions were preceded by tremors and muted roarings. Horses and cattle became uneasy, birds fell silent and some flew away. Then just before noon it happened — an ominous shudder shook the ground and ashes and smoke came billowing forth from the throat of the mountain. Some people ran screaming toward the sea, but most of them stayed to be buried and preserved in their own homes, and the better class of homes were scarcely injured by the ashes and pumice that preserved them for our day.

At the time Vesuvius blew up, Pliny the younger was visiting his uncle across the bay of Naples, and recorded the scene in his famous letter to Tacitus. He wrote, "There was a cloud like an umbrella pine which rose to a great height on a sort of trunk and then split off into branches. When night fell, broad sheets of fire and leaping flames blazed at several points."

Few things in our world are more common than the deaths of cities. Almost all of the great civilizations of history have now passed away, and many of them have left no trace of ever having lived. The Bible mentions the great civilization of Noah's day that was overcome by the flood. But outside the Bible

nothing is left to tell us about it. A rainstorm of fire and brim-
stone wiped out Sodom and Gomorrah. The once mighty nation
of Babylon has also disappeared from the earth. The great nations that have lived and died upon our own land have left
only some crumbling ruins and a few hieroglyphics to tell us of
their civilization. But in the dead city of Pompeii most of its
people are still in their homes, as though they were still going
on with their work. Some cook stoves were found with loaves of
bread still in the ovens. Half-eaten meals preserved in the ashes
were still on the tables.

Last days are always very important. The last days are the
key days. The last days judge all of the other days. You could
never judge a civilization or a life without knowing of their last
days. The life of Judas Iscariot, or Jesus of Nazareth, would lack
much of their significance without their last days. Our own
last days will also stand out as our most important days. That
will be true of the earth itself. It is interesting that everyone
wants to know about how things are finished. At any of the
races of life the largest congregation always assembles as near
as possible to the finish line. In many sporting events they
record the finish on television so that it can be rerun occasionally
and let everyone know how the contestants finished.

There is an interesting scriptural account of the last days of
a man who spent his life accumulating wealth. Finally when
he had no space left to store his goods, he said to himself, "I will
pull down my barns, and build greater; and there will I bestow
my fruits and my goods. And I will say to my soul, Soul, thou
hast much goods laid up for many years; take thine ease, eat,
drink and be merry." But God said unto him, "Thou fool, this
night thy soul shall be required of thee; then whose shall those
things be which thou hast provided?" (Luke 12:18-20) It doesn't
matter very much how big our barns are, if we are poor toward
God when we reach the finish line. But no one will ask us what
kind of starts we make, the only thing that most people are
interested in is how we finish. This interest gives an added
importance to our own last days.

Lord Lytton has aroused our concern over the *Last Days of
Pompeii*. But there is every indication that we are now on the
threshold of the greatest of all sets of last days as they apply
to our own earth. Our earth is already groaning and trembling
with trouble. We are already aware of the tremors and muted

roarings taking place beneath our feet. All nature is uneasy with its wars, its earthquakes and its great tribulations. All of the earth's people have a sense of danger, fear, and foreboding. The signs of the times indicate that some shocking devastation is about to take place. We feel sorry for the people of Pompeii, who have remained packed in volcanic ashes for 1,888 years, and we can imagine how helpful it might have been if they had known in advance about the future plans of the great Mount Vesuvius, with its insides filled with lava and fire, ready to belch out upon them. However, a clear warning did not seem to help the people of Noah's day very much. And only Lot and his family were willing to leave Sodom when the angels told them that everything would be destroyed. But our most important question is, What about ourselves? Our own last days have not only been foretold, but almost every detail has been written down for us to read about in advance.

In speaking of our time, Paul said to Timothy, "This know also, that in the last days, perilous times shall come. For men shall be lovers of their own selves, covetous, boasters, proud, blasphemers, disobedient to parents, unthankful, unholy, without natural affection, truce-breakers, false accusers, incontinent, fierce, despisers of those that are good, traitors, heady, high-minded, lovers of pleasures more than lovers of God, having a form of godliness, but denying the power thereof." Paul says, "from such turn way." And no wonder, for this in itself ought to be enough to cause an explosion.

Peter also talks about those things that have always trig-gered explosions when he says, "knowing this first, that there shall come in the last days scoffers, walking after their own lusts." (II Peter 3:3) Jesus himself looked down to our day and told of the wars and troubles that should immediately precede his second coming to the earth. The last days of the earth as we have known it are upon us, and they are our most important days. All of the prophets seem to have been given divine knowl-edge concerning our day. One of the most widely discussed sub-jects in all of the scriptures is that great event when Christ shall come with his holy angels in flaming fire, to cleanse the world of its sin, and take care of its unfinished business. This is when most of our important events will take place. At the second coming a main part of the resurrection will take place, and Christ will inaugurate his own millenial reign upon the earth.

This will be followed by the final judgment and the glorification of the earth. This wouldn't be a very good time to be packed in ashes.

Almost every prophet has had his vision focused on the earth's finish line. Jacob predicted what would happen to his own posterity in the last days. (Gen. 49:10) The scattered children of Israel will be gathered in the last days. The lost ten tribes will be restored. The gospel of Christ will be preached as a witness unto all nations. (Matt. 24:14) Isaiah almost lived in our day. And the Lord even showed to King Nebuchadnezzar what would happen in the last days. Daniel calls it "the time of the end" and he predicted our great knowledge explosion. He also foresaw the time when all earthly thrones would be thrown down; and Adam, the ancient of days, or the oldest man would, under Christ, be the leader of his posterity. (Dan. 7:9-10) The Apostle Peter quoted the words of Joel saying, "And it shall come to pass in the last days, saith God, I will pour out of my Spirit upon all flesh: and your sons and your daughters shall prophesy, and your young men shall see visions, and your old men shall dream dreams: . . . and I will shew wonders in heaven above, and signs in the earth beneath; blood, and fire, and vapor of smoke: the sun shall be turned into darkness, and the moon into blood, before that great and notable day of the Lord come: and it shall come to pass, that whosoever shall call on the name of the Lord shall be saved." (Acts 2:17-21)

If anyone thinks it would have been exciting to be living in Pompeii at noon on August 24, 79 A.D., he has something even more exciting to look forward to when the Lord shall come to fulfill his prophecy made through Malachi, saying, "For, behold, the day cometh, that shall burn as an oven; and all the proud, yea, and all that do wickedly, shall be stubble: and the day that cometh shall burn them up, saith the Lord of hosts, that it shall leave them neither root nor branch." (Mal. 4:1)

John the Revelator gives us a preview of our own last days that makes the last days of Pompeii look like a summer picnic. John says, "And I beheld when he had opened the sixth seal, and, lo, there was a great earthquake; and the sun became black as sackcloth of hair, and the moon became as blood; and the stars of heaven fell unto the earth, even as a fig tree casteth her untimely figs, when she is shaken of a mighty wind. And the heaven departed as a scroll when it is rolled together; and every mountain and island were moved out of their places. And the kings of the earth, and the great men, and the rich men, and the chief captains, and the mighty men, and every bondsman, and every free man, hid themselves in the dens and in the rocks of the mountains; and said to the mountains and the rocks, Fall on us, and hide us from the face of him that sitteth on the throne, and from the wrath of the Lamb: For the great day of his wrath is come; and who shall be able to stand?" (Rev. 6:12-17)

In the excavations of Pompeii her people are found in different situations. Some were in the streets attempting to escape, some were found in deep vaults where they had gone seeking security. But where do you think they found the Roman sentinel? They found him standing at the city gate where he had been placed by his captain, and his hands were still grasping the arms which had been given him to protect Pompeii from any possible outside enemy. And there, while the heavens threatened him; there while the earth shook beneath him; there while the lava stream rolled around him, there he stood at his post doing his duty; and there after the centuries have passed away he was found. So let us stand to do our duty in the posts in which our captain has placed us, and may God help us that when the explosion comes we will be ready.

The Law

EACH YEAR IN THE United States we set aside the first day of May as Law Day. An annual presidential proclamation encourages us to be aware of the important part that the law and the courts play, in the spiritual and social values so highly prized in this country. The national commemoration of this day began in 1958. President Eisenhower and President Kennedy both felt that an annual reaffirmation of our faith in the rule of law would greatly improve the daily lives of all Americans. And it has been strongly urged that appropriate recognition be given to this idea in the churches, schools, courts and various other meetings of public and private organizations. In his message to congress in 1904 President Theodore Roosevelt said, "No man is above the law, and no man is below it."

Of course, the big problem of nations and individuals is not alone in understanding the law, for we frequently have difficulty in obeying those laws that we understand perfectly and that were made exclusively in our interests. What a challenging idea to think of developing a discipline and a love of order that would enable us to always obey every detail of the law! What would it be like to live in an America where we had no lawbreakers? Then there would be no crime, no sin, and very few other problems. Everyone would then have complete confidence in everyone else. Our taxes, medical bills, court costs, and other expenses would be drastically reduced and we would have sufficient wealth to supply ourselves with every possible luxury and convenience.

If such an attitude were held in every nation, we would soon have God's paradise in operation upon this earth. On the other hand if our lawlessness increased substantially, then anarchy would take over the government as well as our individual lives. One of our greatest blessings is that God believes in law. The universe itself was created and is operating according to law. We can depend upon the orderly movements of the planets and the return of the seasons. In our own interests, we can utilize the important laws of gravity, electricity, light, health, morality, heredity, growth and faith. God has given us certain rules called the laws of health by which our minds, bodies, and spirits are kept at their maximum of effectiveness. The laws of happiness are to the effect that when we do our best we feel a spirit of joy and enthusiasm, but when we violate our conscience, injure others, or allow hate and evil to grow in our hearts, then we are depressed and miserable. Heaven itself is a place of joy because it is a place of law, order and righteousness.

The scriptures tell us that "sin is the transgression of law" and that no sin is permitted in the presence of God. Consequently there is nothing there that can cause unhappiness. We might give ourselves a boost in the right direction in our imaginations by putting ourselves in God's shoes on Law Day, and then try to understand what it would be like to carry the responsibility for bringing success and happiness to lots of people if they were law breakers.

Long before Law Day was established the great Creator had ordained many wonderful laws which, if followed, would make us great, good, capable and happy, both here and hereafter. Sin is the most foolish, shortsighted and unprofitable of all activities. The Lawgiver of the universe is all wise; he can see every end from its beginning. He sees the fruit in the seed, the chicken in the egg, the oak in the acorn. He sees in advance the misery that awaits in our sins as well as the joy that is inherent in our righteousness. One of our primary law-day developments might come in training our vision to see the misery and death that lies at the end of the broad road of evil mentioned by Jesus. We need to be able to see the lung cancer in the cigarette, the alcoholism in the liquor bottle, the misery in the immorality, the failure in our bad habits as well as the eternal glory in our godliness. It was to give us every advantage that God established the great laws of the gospel. Nothing so profoundly influences human success and happiness as to be in harmony with the right principles. And the most valuable principles are the principles of the gospel of Christ.

Of course the most important part of law observance is that which is done voluntarily. Very little virtue comes because a handcuffed criminal in solitary confinement obeys the law. In the interests of our own training God has made us free and placed us in a world where the extremes of good and evil are easily available to us.

In one of the most inspiring statements of Jesus he said, "I call you no more servants but friends." But it is difficult to be friends of God while we are acting like criminals and delinquents. There are millions of forms of life that are governed by the limitations of instinct. The animals are given specific metes and bounds beyond which they cannot go. Cows or honey bees or grasshoppers behave today exactly as they have always behaved because they have no choice. And only to his children did God give the great law of freedom saying, "Thou mayest choose for thyself." We remember the proposal of Lucifer in the Council of heaven, that human salvation should be brought about under his direction by compulsion. But then our success would have belonged to our master and not to us. We learn to do by doing, and God has made it possible for us to assist in bringing about our own salvation. However, going hand in hand with this law of free agency, is its companion law of consequences. One difference between a cow and a child of God is that we are accountable for what we do. If I should decide to dive head first out of the window, I cannot logically ask someone to endure the pain that may be generated when I hit the sidewalk. The farmer who plants his corn in the chill of a December blizzard, is not entitled to the same kind of harvest as the one who does his planting during the warmth of the May sunshine. A great lesson for Law Day is that there is no growth without responsibility.

It is interesting to contemplate that in the face of the tremendous natural rewards for obedience to the law, our most serious problems arise because of our violations. When Adam partook of the forbidden fruit, he also partook of the consequences. When Cain destroyed his brother Abel, he started a long chain of events working against him. The transgressions of Noah's day brought a devastating flood upon the world. And it is still the law that everyone must settle his own accounts. One cannot be untruthful or dishonest and expect to maintain his prestige in the minds of other people. One can quickly lose the confidence of his family, his business associates or God by violating this law of responsibility. So far as I know, no one has ever yet discovered a way of running a million volts of electricity through his body without suffering the consequences. Neither can one become an alcoholic without incurring the mental incompetence, moral decay, financial expense, nervous disorders, and delirium tremens that are contained in the liquor bottle. May 1st has been set apart to help us to get these ideas so clearly in our minds that a determination to obey the law will grow in our hearts.

We remember that Law Day of 3,400 years ago when God himself came down onto the top of Mount Sinai, and to the accompaniment of lightnings and thunders gave ancient Israel Ten Commandments which, if kept, would make them the chosen people of the Lord. But just think how many millions have suffered in this life and will also suffer eternally because they have violated these important laws saying, "Thou shalt not kill; Thou shalt not steal; Thou shalt not commit adultery; Thou shalt not bear false witness; Thou shalt have no other gods before me." And I suppose that even the Creator himself could not make a godly, well-favored person out of one who insisted on acting like a criminal. No one can go up and down at the same time. And failure and success are located in opposite directions.

In one of his greatest laws of success Jesus said, "All things are possible to him that believeth." Faith has been established by God as the first principle of the gospel. It is also the first law of success. Belief must always precede and underlie every accomplishment. Faith is the foundation on which every success rests: The life of the greatest oak tree depends upon someone having enough faith to plant an acorn. On the other hand, we can avoid all failures if we refuse those activities that lead to them.

As soon as it was discovered that strychnine would kill, it became forever unnecessary for people to keep on performing that experiment for themselves. And when someone tells us not to sit on a red hot stove our interests will be best served by following directions. And yet one of the greatest weaknesses in human nature is that we deliberately disobey an all-wise, all-powerful, all-righteous God. The most serious kind of irresponsibility is where we don't care one way or the other whether a thing is right or not. So frequently when we are confronted with one of God's great truths we merely say, "So what," or we might respond by saying, "I don't believe it."

A tourist traveling in a country with which he was not familiar might have some problems if he didn't believe in maps or road signs. And if we put ourselves in God's shoes we might understand how difficult it would be to get atheists and confirmed sinners into the celestial kingdom. An attitude of disobedience and contrariness can make the easiest success impossible. Like spoiled children we sometimes put our hands on the red hot stove merely because someone told us it was the wrong thing to do. Jesus pointed out the distressing fact that many people love darkness rather than light, and frequently we are more attracted to evil than to good. To some people there is more satisfaction in loving Satan than in loving God. And it doesn't take very much perverseness to lead us to hell. Even normal doubts improperly handled may bring failure upon us. There is an interesting account of unbelief mentioned in the Bible. Before the death of Jesus he had taught his followers that he would rise again, the third day. Then after his resurrection he appeared to ten of the apostles and some others who were gathered together at Jerusalem.

Even now for them to believe that Jesus was alive, after they had seen him crucified, was a little bit difficult. Jesus tried to reassure them by saying, "Why are ye troubled and why do thoughts arise in your hearts. Behold my hands and my feet, that it is I myself. Handle me and see, for a spirit hath not flesh and bones as ye see me have." And when he had thus spoken he shewed them his hands and his feet. Then the scripture says that while they yet believed not for joy and wondered, Jesus said unto them, "have ye here any meat. And they gave him a piece of broiled fish and of a honeycomb. And he took it and did eat before them."

But Thomas, one of the twelve, was not with them when Jesus came, and when the other disciples told him that they had seen the Lord, he would not believe them. He said, "Except I shall see for myself, I will not believe." He said, "Except I shall . . . put my finger into the print of the nails and thrust my hand into his side, I will not believe." Eight days later the Lord appeared to them again and this time Thomas was present. Then the Lord said to Thomas, "Reach hither thy finger, and behold my hands; and reach hither thy hand and thrust it into my side, and be not faithless but believing." (John 20:24-27)

Because of Thomas's problem we call him "Doubting Thomas," and yet our own doubts also cause many of our problems. After Thomas had been convinced Jesus said to him, "Thomas, because thou hast seen, thou hast believed: blessed are they that have *not* seen and yet have believed." This ability for greater believing is one that we should try diligently to acquire.

After telling of the experience of Thomas, John's Gospel says, "And many other signs truly did Jesus in the presence of his disciples, which are not written in this book: But *these* are written, that ye might believe that Jesus is the Christ, the Son of God; and that believing ye might have life through his name." (John 20:28-31) This kind of faith puts us well on our way towards eternal life. Over the centuries our biggest problem has been that men and women have traditionally disbelieved. We have disbelieved in God, we have disbelieved in law, we have disbelieved in consequences; and we have disbelieved in ourselves. To suffer the consequences later on is not a very good substitute for obedience now. Every sin that we commit incarnates itself and becomes a part of us. Some of the penalty imposed on one who tells lies is that he eventually becomes a liar. We are not only punished *for* our sins, but we are also punished *by* our sins, and we are punished over and over again. God will judge everyone according to his works. Jesus said, "for every idle word that man shall speak he shall give an account thereof in the day of judgment."

I pray that God may help us to obey his law and I know that our lives will be improved accordingly.

The Law of Witnesses

ABOVE ALMOST ALL other things God has commited himself to man's free agency. He always maintains a democratic relationship in dealing with his children. In spite of his superior wisdom God never uses force, and he has promised to make kings and priests of those who obey his laws. These will rule and reign with him during the millenium and throughout eternity. The scriptures indicate that God has already exalted many of his children now living in his presence to positions of great trust and responsibility. Paul speaks of the "mighty angels that will come with Christ to cleanse the earth of sin." In heaven as well as here, God works through his children. It is very important for us to understand that God, angels and men are all the same species in different conditions of excellence and stages of development. All of God's angels and messengers are members of his family who either have lived or who will yet live upon the earth. Michael the Archangel whom the scripture called the "ancient of days" is Adam, the oldest man. Under the direction of the antemortal Christ, Michael or Adam led God's forces against Lucifer, (Rev. 12:7) and he will officiate in sounding the trump announcing that part of the resurrection that will take place at Christ's second coming. (D&C 29::26)

Gabriel, who announced to Mary that she would become the mother of the Son of God, (Luke 1:19) was one of the great prophets who had lived in mortality approximately 2,500 years previously. There are many other prominent angels mentioned in the scripture having great authority, and God has a wonderful future planned for all of his obedient children. He has created us in his image, endowed us with his attributes, redeemed us from death, and made us heirs to his glory. Then as far as possible his program of salvation is carried on primarily by those who will be the beneficiaries. In some measure it is another program "of the people, by the people, and for the people." He has apostles, prophets, and other constituted servants to carry on the work of his Church here, and they will also be a part of his government hereafter, as he has said that they will rule and reign with him forever.

Many centuries ago it was said through the prophet Amos, "surely the Lord God will do nothing, but he revealeth his secret unto his servants the prophets." (Amos 3:7) He teaches us correct principles so that we can govern ourselves. As a help-ful means of getting his messages over to us he has established what has been called the "Law of Witnesses." People have not always read very extensively, and most of the teaching has been done by witnesses on a person to person basis. Speaking of the earthly ministry of Jesus, Luke says, "He called unto him his disciples, and of them he chose twelve, whom he . . . named apostles." (Luke 6:13) Then with these specially selected men, Jesus organized his Church, established its ordinances, created its offices, appointed its officers, and announced the required doc-trines of salvation. He not only performed many miracles him-self, but he also allowed his apostles to share in his power. After his own work had been finished and he was about to ascend into heaven, he said to the eleven, "Ye shall be witnesses unto me, both in Jerusalem and in all of Judea, and in Samaria, and unto the uttermost parts of the earth." (Acts 1:8)

Paul was referring to this law when he said to the Corin-thians, "In the mouth of two of three witnesses shall every word be established." Witnesses are called to teach, warn and encourage the people. And we to whom the word comes are obligated to listen, believe and obey. Under the law of Moses, more than one witness was required before anyone could be con-victed of a capital offense. And the witnesses themselves carried an important responsibility. For example, when someone was con-denmed to death by stoning, it was the job of the witnesses to cast the first stones. However, if anyone should bear a false witness, the law condemned him to suffer the same punishment which would have been imposed upon the accused. (Deut. 19:16-19) The bearing of false witness has always been one of the most serious sins; and one of the Ten Commandments that was thun-dered from Mount Sinai said "Thou shalt not bear false witness."

On four separate occasions God the Father has served as witness for his Son, and the Holy Ghost whispers a divine wit-ness to the hearts of all of those who will prepare and listen. As Jesus taught people how to live during his mortality, he was not only his own chief witness, but he was his own example as well. To help people understand the immortality of the soul, he showed his own resurrected body to many witnesses. Then the apostles wrote down what they had seen and heard and also bore their personal testimonies.

One of the most common means for people losing their blessings is their inability to believe God's witnesses. One man said that he would never believe anything that he couldn't understand. Anyone with that kind of philosophy would be severely limited, as even the wisest among us don't understand very much about anything. We don't understand light or heat or sunshine, or how our hearts beat, or how our minds work, or how the grass grows. We should be grateful that we don't have to understand electricity, refrigeration, heat, light, transportation, and communication before we can receive their benefits. We could not eat, breathe, pray or even be born if we first had to understand these processes. To disbelieve in the resurrection or our divine destiny merely because we didn't understand them would not make very good sense.

Anyone who trusts in his own reason, instead of the wisdom of God, is exposing himself to dangerous risks. And many Christian ministers have become false witnesses by trusting too much in their own opinions. One is a false teacher who follows his own supposition and says that God is dead or that revelation from him has ceased. The scriptures themselves enumerate many of God's greatest revelations that are yet to come. With his "mighty angels" Christ is scheduled to return to earth again to usher in the millennial reign of a thousand years when he will rule personally over the earth, and restore its paradisiacal glory. The biggest part of the resurrection, including our own, is also yet in the future. The scripture tells us that in order to get the earth ready for its winding-up scene, many important heavenly messengers must first come to the earth to bring about a restoration of all things promised by the holy prophets since the earth began. Through Malachi the Lord said, "Behold I will send you Elijah the prophet before the coming of the great and dreadful day of the Lord." (Mal. 4:5)

Just before Jesus was crucified he looked beyond the black night of the apostasy and the dark ages, to the time when the gospel would be restored. After telling of the wars and troubles that would characterize the last days he said, "And this gospel of the kingdom shall be preached in all the world as a witness unto all nations, and then shall the end come." (Matt. 24:14)

John the Revelator also foretold this restoration saying, "And I saw another angel flying in the midst of heaven, having the everlasting gospel to preach unto them that dwell on the earth, and to every nation, and kindred, and tongue, and people, saying with a loud voice, fear God and give glory to him, for the hour of his judgment is come." (Rev. 14:6-7)

In our own day many duly qualified witnesses are testifying of the fulfillment of these and many other prophecies. It is the testimony of The Church of Jesus Christ of Latter-day Saints that in the early spring of 1820, God the Father, and his Son, Jesus Christ, reappeared upon this earth to establish among men a belief in the God of Genesis, the God of Calvary, and the God of the latter days. A young man by the name of Joseph Smith was divinely called to be the instrument through whom the priesthood would be restored and the Church of Jesus Christ again organized upon the earth. In the restoration process a series of heavenly messengers — including Elijah, Peter, James and John, Moses, John the Baptist, and others, — have revisited the earth to confer upon men the particular authority which had been held by them. Paul refers to our days as the "dispensation of the fullness of times," when Christ would gather together in one, all things in Christ both which are in heaven and which are on the earth. (Eph. 1:10)

The angel foreseen by John the Revelator came on September 21, 1823. He was the last of a long line of prophets who had lived in pre-Columbus America. Among other things he made known the hiding place of an ancient record containing a fullness of the Gospel of Christ, as it had been revealed to the ancient inhabitants of this continent. This message was engraved on metallic plates having the appearance of gold. It was translated by the power of God and is now known to us as the Book of Mormon. In following this ancient law of witnesses, eleven men were selected by God and directed to bear their testimony concerning the truth of the important message contained in this inspired book. They were also commanded to sign their names as God's witnesses, and their written testimony is now included as a frontispiece in every copy of this great book.

They say, "And we declare with words of soberness, that an angel of God came down from heaven, and he brought and laid before our eyes, that we beheld and saw the plates, and the engravings thereon; and we know that it is by the grace of God the Father, and our Lord Jesus Christ, that we beheld and bear record that these things are true. And it is marvelous in our eyes. Nevertheless, the voice of the Lord commanded us that we should bear record of it; wherefore, to be obedient unto the commandments of God, we bear testimony of these things." Certainly such a testimony should at least be thoroughly investigated as these men were appointed by God and their witness is fully binding upon us.

There is also an interesting testimony in the book itself, in which the great prophet Moroni says, "And when ye shall receive these things, I would exhort you that ye would ask God, the Eternal Father, in the name of Christ, if these things are not true; and if ye shall ask with a sincere heart, with real intent, having faith in Christ, he will manifest the truth of it unto you, by the power of the Holy Ghost." There are thousands of people testifying that this tremendous promise has been literally fulfilled to them personally. If we understood these testimonies and their eternal consequences, we would not dare to disbelieve them. Certainly not before putting the prophet's promise to the test.

The entire Book of Mormon is itself a new witness for God which has the familiar spirit of truth. It bears a divine testimony concerning the Holy Bible. It assures us that God lives and that many important events are about to take place. The Book of Mormon contains an account of the appearance of the resurrected Jesus to a large group of people gathered upon the western continent after his ministry in the east had been finished. Jesus taught these pre-Columbus Americans the gospel, and organized his Church among them just as he had done in Jerusalem. The Book of III Nephi in the Book of Mormon contains the informative account of his visit here. The traditions of the Indians themselves and the inscriptions on their ancient ruins give testimony that they had a knowledge of Christian doctrines learned from a great white God who visited them and promised them that he would return at a later date.

There is in existence another witness for Christ in a modern volume of scripture called the *Doctrine and Covenants*. This book contains over a hundred sections with many revelations given specifically for our day.

In many parts of the world a hassle is going on about whether or not God is dead. Some believe that he is, some half-believe that he is, and some don't care whether he is or not. But if God lived once, he is still alive. Moses saw God face to face, and so did Joseph Smith, and so did Sidney Rigdon, and the last two mentioned publish their witness to everyone in the world in our own day. They say:

"And now, after the many testimonies which have been given of him, this is the testimony, last of all, which we give of him: That he lives! For we saw him, even on the right hand of God; and we heard the voice bearing record that he is the Only Begotten of the Father — that by him, and through him, and of him, the worlds are and were created, and the inhabitants thereof are begotten sons and daughters unto God." (D&C 76:22)

It is my prayer that God will help us to so conduct our lives that we may also qualify as his witnesses and the beneficiaries of all his blessings.

The Little Match Girl

ONE OF THE GREAT story tellers of our time was Hans Christian Andersen. Mr. Andersen loved people, and he particularly loved children. He also tried to help us understand that all lives do not automatically have a happy ending. Recently I reread Mr. Andersen's story about the Little Match Girl. As I admired Gretchen, the youthful heroine, I thought about the futures of my granddaughters. Gretchen was very young and had no mother. A wonderful grandmother with whom she had previously lived had just passed away. With a thoughtless, uncaring father, Gretchen now lived in a cold desolate house on a scanty ration of food, and even smaller portions of love and happiness. She contributed to their meager living by selling matches on the streets, and her father became angry and unpleasant when she didn't do well. Mr. Andersen effectively describes the final scene in Gretchen's life that took place on the last day of the old year.

All day Gretchen had walked the streets, but the attention of people was centered on other things and she had sold nothing. Gretchen's head was bare. That morning when she had left home the slippers that had previously belonged to her mother had been on her feet, but because they were much too large she had lost them while hurrying to avoid being run over by a carriage. Her feet were blue with cold and she was tired and hungry. Her little heart ached for love and companionship, but no one had given her a kind word or bought any matches, and we wonder how much misery can sometimes exist in a world of happiness. Gretchen thought how pleasant it would be to feel warm and comfortable again with her grandmother's arms around her. She dared not go home to her father, and anyway their house would not be much better than the street as it also lacked food, fire and friendship. And even at this late hour she still hoped that someone might buy her matches or give her something to eat. Although she was downcast with fear, and faint with hunger and cold, she continued to walk the street.

The snowflakes fell on the long golden hair that curled so prettily over her neck, and she was aware of the lights shining from the windows of happy homes and the fragrance of cooking suppers was filtering out into the street. Gretchen seemed to be warmed somewhat as she looked up at the stars and imagined them to be little fires burning in the sky. The time of year also reminded her of the Christmas stories that her grandmother used to tell. Then they had sung beautiful Christmas carols together around the fire, and she had gone to her warm comfortable bed, thinking about the angels and the holy child that was born in Bethlehem.

Thoughts of him gave little Gretchen a feeling of comfort and kinship as she remembered that the Christ-Child had also been poor. She thought of that long-ago night when he was born in a stable and cradled in a manger. He had also known what it was like to be hungry, and forsaken, with no place to lay his head. Then she wondered if it was warm in heaven where Jesus now lived, and if there was enough food there for everyone.

It was now very late. Gretchen heard the clock in the church tower strike the midnight hour. Hoping to get some rest she found a partially sheltered place between two buildings. Somehow she felt that Jesus was near her, and she struck a match upon one of the walls, and looked around hoping to find him there. Then Mr. Andersen says:

> The single match was kindled,
> And by the light it threw,
> It seemed to little Gretchen
> That the wall was rent in two.
>
> And she could see folks seated,
> At a table richly spread
> With heaps of goodly viands,
> Red wine and pleasant bread.
>
> She could smell the fragrant savor
> She could hear what they did say,
> Then all again was darkness,
> For the match had burned away.

In trying to make herself comfortable Gretchen sat down and drew her feet up under her, but she then seemed colder than ever. She thought that if she could light another match, it might serve as a little candle, enabling her to warm her stiff, blue hands around it. Accordingly she struck a second match against the wall. At first it sputtered uncertainly, and then it burned with a clear bright flame.

> And now she seemed to see,
> Within the same warm chamber,
> A glorious Christmas tree.
>
> The branches were heavily laden
> With things that children prize,
> Bright gifts for boys and maidens
> And she saw them with her eyes.
>
> And she almost seemed to touch them,
> And join the welcome shout,
> When the darkness again fell 'round her
> For the match had been burned out.

One by one Gretchen lighted her matches. As each one cast its light upon the wall, it seemed that she was looking through a transparent curtain into a room filled with the most wonderful things to eat, wear, keep her warm, and make her happy. She was particularly aware of a savor of roast goose in the air and many pleasant friends were near, with enough love, comfort and happiness for all.

Then she lighted several matches all together and a great flame burst around her. Then she stretched out her hands into the air, for the matches seemed to become tall Christmas candles that rose higher and higher until they merged with the stars. At that instant one of the stars fell, and made a long streak of fire across the sky. Gretchen said, "Someone is dying now." Her kind, thoughtful grandmother had told her that when a star falls, a soul is going up to God. She struck one more match against the wall — and in its wonderful light she saw her grandmother. "Grandmother," she cried, "take me with you, for I know that, like the warm fire, the delicious roast goose and the beautiful Christmas tree, you will also go away when the match has burned out." In order to prolong her grandmother's stay she hastily struck all of her matches at once. They blazed with a glow that seemd brighter than day. Her grandmother had never before seemed so beautiful, so gracious and so loving. Then she lifted little Gretchen into her arms, and in the warm brightness and supreme joy of being together, they flew far away to a beautiful place where there was no cold, or hunger, or fear. There everyone was warm, happy, comfortable and well provided for, for they were with God.

When the cold morning of the New Year dawned, neighbors found the little match girl in her scant and tattered garments between the buildings. She sat there facing the wall. Her cheeks were filled with roses and a beautiful smile was on her face. They saw her burned-out matches and said, "She tried to warm herself." As they lifted her up they shuddered and exclaimed, "It was a bitter, bitter night." However, they could not know what beauty she had seen, and in what brightness she had gone with her grandmother into the joys of the New Year. Neither did they know how much happiness there can sometimes be, in a world of misery.

Mr. Andersen's story might well remind us that in more ways than one each of us is a kind of poor little match girl, as we make our individual ways through the fears and difficulties of life. Each of us has his own bundle of matches made up of the words and deeds that we may strike into a flame along life's way. Then in their light and warmth we see the visions of our own happier, better world. It may have been with these life possibilities in mind that Jesus said, "Ye are the light of the world. Therefore, let your light so shine before men that others, seeing your good works, may glorify your Father which is in heaven." This reminds us to keep our matches burning as brightly as possible.

Recently as I visited with my three little granddaughters who are just learning to talk, I wondered how I might best use my matches to light and warm their lives. I thought about the light of love, faith, industry and righteousness that they might find along their eternal pathway. I shuddered a little bit as I remembered the darkness and bitter cold in which many lives are lived. One of my most heart-warming experiences is to see these little girls chattering and laughing as that magic emotion of love and joy bubbles up into their faces. Their eyes sparkle and their countenances beam with a radiance greater than if a whole box of matches were burning in their hearts. Only recently they were in the presence of God and, as they put their arms around my neck, I feel a radar beam of joy kindling the most pleasant responses in my own soul.

My life has already been moderately long, and satisfactorily eventful. I have known many pleasures and some successes.

But what satisfaction can excel that which comes from the pure love of little children! It was of them that Jesus said, "Of such is the Kingdom of Heaven." God centered the primary focus of children's love in their parents. And sometimes when these particular parents are about to leave their little girls even for a short time, they sob and cry as if their hearts were breaking. Their eyes get red, and their faces fill up with an intense and visible sadness. Recently as I watched tears run in rivulets down their cheeks, I was aware that some parents leave their children exposed to a spiritual frost and a darkness of evil because the fires of faith and righteousness are not lighted in the children's youthful lives. I think I can partially understand what Jesus meant when he said, "He that offends one of these little ones that believes in me, it had been better if a millstone had been hanged about his neck, and he had been drowned in the depths of the sea."

It is sometimes difficult for loved ones to endure even that temporary suffering that children feel when they are threatened with the short-term loss of their security and happiness by the absence of their parents. Then what might it be like to some day discover that our neglect or bad example has led them into that bitter cold of outer darkness that lies at the end of that broad road leading toward death. The weeping, wailing and gnashing of teeth that characterizes eternal evil may not be so temporary.

Gretchen was more afraid of her father than of the cold, and in more than one way we often share in this father's sins. From the top of Mount Sinai God indicated that the sins of the fathers would be visited upon their children. And Jesus pointed out the strange fact that frequently a man's foes are they of his own household. Isn't it startling that we often pick up our worst habits from our best friends, whereas our greatest need is for more kindness and more righteousness? With a personal application someone has said that, "We need more mistletoe and less missile talk." Love and righteousness are the two greatest powers in the world. Children have better health when they are loved. A mother's kiss can stop pain, dispel the clouds of gloom, and make the sun shine and the flowers bloom. And with godliness in one's heart he always grows stronger and more productive.

We might imagine what a great pleasure it would have been to have befriended little Gretchen on that long-ago New Year's eve, and yet many of God's children are presently suffering from a cold that is far more severe. Love, kindness and righteousness are not just the health requirements for children. Their importance is frequently increased as we advance through youth and maturity and into old age. There is nothing quite so important to mothers, fathers, children, neighbors, or friends as a genuine love that is fully returned, and a sincere righteousness that is easy to follow.

Sometime ago a husband expressed some annoyance that his wife needed a daily assurance of his love. He understood that people sometimes get sick and die if they don't get food, water, air and exercise every day. However, it was more difficult for him to understand that if we want to be happy and successful we also need a ration of love, appreciation, kindness and righteousness every day.

In his famous 13th chapter of I Corinthians, the Apostle Paul wrote a description of love that everyone should reread frequently, and then attempt to make as many applications as possible. We might ask ourselves how much of a part do we have in fulfilling the prophecy of Jesus when he said, "And because iniquity shall abound, the love of many shall wax cold." When iniquity abounds in people, their love always waxes cold and lifeless. All family problems, personal difficulties and international disputes would be quickly solved if we followed the simple directions of love and righteousness given to us in the religion of Christ. Certainly one of our greatest opportunities has to do with lighting those matches that will keep our love and righteousness radiant and warm as we make our way through this wonderful great New Year that lies immediately ahead.

Mightier Than the Sword

EDWARD BULWER LYTTON once made a famous statement saying, "The pen is mightier than the sword." Of course, the pen by itself actually has no power. It gets its importance as one of the instruments with which we form the tools of thought known as words. And words can become mighty when they are fashioned into speech. But whether words are written or spoken or thought their influence for good or evil can be very great. It is with words that we instruct, persuade and inspire. Words can build faith, sharpen integrity and motivate ambition. Even our ideals, our religion and the other elements involved in our eternal welfare are largely shaped by our words. If words are used carelessly, ignorantly or maliciously, they can help to tear the world down instead of building it up. The wrong use of words in our own day is destroying more people than all the swords in the history of the world put together.

Some nations are using these tools of thought to stir up hate, build prejudice and cause conflicts. All of the wars could be stopped, and peace and happiness permanently established upon the earth, if everyone always used the right kind of words, supported with the mental attitudes that makes them effective.

The enormous consequences that can come from inaccurate communication was dramatized by an incident that occurred at the end of World War II. After the atomic bomb had been prepared the allies sent an ultimatum to Japan demanding that she surrender or be destroyed. It is reported that the Japanese Cabinet was ready to agree to the ultimatum but wanted some time to consider the proposal. In the Japanese reply the word *mokusatu* was used to convey the meaning that they wanted to withhold comment temporarily. But this same Japanese word can also mean to "ignore." Because of the mix-up in translation the allies interpreted the message to mean that the Japanese Cabinet was ignoring the demand to surrender. No one can say for sure, but if this one word had been understood, it may have been unnecessary to destroy the thousands of lives at Hiroshima and Nagasaki.

But far greater damage is now being done in the world because individuals misunderstand each other, than because we misinterpreted the intent of the Japanese Cabinet.

There are millions of people in our world who are presently throwing around some verbal atomic bombs that are causing nervous breakdown, death, and emotional distortions that are far more serious than those more material bombs dropped on Hiroshima and Nagasaki. There is an old nursery rhyme that says, "Sticks and stones may break my bones, but words can never hurt me." Nothing could be further from the truth, for in exploding the wrong words we cause more deformities than any atomic radiation, fallout or concussion could possibly do.

Another source of word damage comes because language itself is often so inexact that we lose control of the intended effect. If we get a large dictionary, we will find that in some cases there are as many as forty different meanings for the same word. The word wreckless can mean without any wrecks. But if you leave out one letter, reckless then means a lack of caution and may indicate one so heedless of danger that many wrecks may result. In addition to the words themselves being ineffective in conveying accurate meanings, the spirit in which they are used often adds to the confusion. As words are used they are colored, polished, poisoned, and sharpened until their very identity is all but destroyed. It is also true that with every spoken word there are always some hidden non-verbal communications. The pitch of one's voice, the look on his face, his accent, his body gestures, the speed with which he speaks, the quality of his expression and even the way he pauses, all change the meaning of what is said.

Winston Churchill had powerful, driving, convincing words. Someone else uses mostly nagging, tiresome, offensive words. Some people specialize in cynical, critical, discouraging words. Some have words loaded with faith, encouragement and good cheer. It also makes a great difference when the background of understanding in the speaker varies from that of the hearer. All of these differences so distort the meaning that the message seldom arrives at the heart of the hearer in the form it had when it left the mind of the speaker.

Another interesting thing about human beings is that we all have subconscious garbling devices in our communication systems that we ourselves may not be aware of. And no matter what message is sent we frequently hear about what we want to hear. The same set of word combinations striking the ear drums of a thousand people at the same time would be interpreted by each one differently. The Democrat and the Republican, the labor leader and the capitalist, the drunkard and the teetotaller all use a different mental dictionary for their definitions. Some people may think that a particular lecture is wonderful, whereas others may think the same lecture is terrible. In some conversations the people concerned never discover that they are talking about completely different things. And sometimes the intended message never gets over at all. We say that actions speak louder than words but even actions are sometimes misleading. We frequently do not even understand why we ourselves do as we do. Words are mightier than swords and they can do far more damage.

Many people are in mental hospitals because their emotional balance has been destroyed by the poisoned ideas, or the confused or evil meanings of words. There are also many unstable and unhappy people outside of institutions who live in a kind of mental twilight caused by conflicting emotions or confused ideals, brought about because the wrong words have gotten into their minds.

Often we respond to a word as though it were actually the object that it represents. Many people automatically recoil from a snake and the mere mention of that word puts an image in the mind that causes the recoil. To hear the word "cancer" may cause some people to react with serious fear and apprehension. When some people are having a physical examination they show a highly elevated blood pressure and other physical and mental irregularities while the examination is in progress. While this attitude is in their hearts the most genuine reassurance from competent medical authorities cannot change the situation.

In our daily living we often acquire some mental allergies which cause harmful reactions. Our own spiritual prejudices and personal imaginations also cause us serious problems. Surveys show that a very large percentage of people are sometimes bothered by a degree of mental ill health. In fact, most of the time all of us probably have some problem festering below the level of our consciousness and doing us harm that has been put there with words. It is so easy to misunderstand or to be misunderstood, and we are often thrown from that straight and narrow way leading to success by our mental blind spots, our inattention, our word inaccuracies, our misuse of meanings, our negative attitudes, our differences in backgrounds and our general lack of understanding. There are millions of messages that go astray either in the sending or in the receiving, or because of the static they pick up along the way. When we half close our eyes, or half shut our ears or half turn off our hearts, we are bound to miss much of the meaning contained in those great messages concerning our eternal exaltation that come from God himself. One's judgment is no better than his information and we usually need a lot more information in a lot clearer form if we are to live most effectively. Even if we wished to know why a person lost his job, we would have to have many questions answered, as usually there is not just one reason for a thing, but several.

If we are going to understand Mr. Jones, we must realize that he is not the same Mr. Jones today that he was yesterday, and we can be sure he will change again before tomorrow. Even on the same day Mr. Jones is not the same man in his office that he is at his home or on the golf course. Some people are completely different people in business situations than they are in the area of social activities. One person sometimes feels great competence, freedom and prestige in one situation, while he feels inferior and depressed in another.

The story is told of one little boy who said to his friend, "Why does your father wear a coat that is so much too big for him?" The boy said, "Oh, that's the coat he bought in St. Louis." His friend said, "What difference does that make?" And the son replied, "Oh, my dad is a big man in St. Louis."

To some degree we all change our size and our attitudes and even what we think as our conditions change and these communications from our environments bear in upon us. Isn't it interesting that one of the things that we can be absolutely certain about is that the one receiving our communication will never get exactly the same message that we are attempting to send? It is one of the greatest of abilities to be able to communicate with any other person with anywhere near complete accuracy. Think how many wives misunderstand their husbands and how many husbands misunderstand their wives. Or think how many people even misunderstand themselves. We load ourselves down with complexes or our imagination presents material to us that only faintly resembles the facts. One of our most serious mistakes is to misunderstand God. Jesus taught the necessity of baptism by saying, "Verily, verily I say unto thee, Except a man be born of water and of the Spirit, he cannot enter into the kingdom of God." (John 3:5) To some Bible translators the word *baptize* means to be buried in the water. But some believe it means to be sprinkled. Some say that it should be done by one having authority from God, and some think that authority doesn't matter. Some feel that Jesus didn't mean what he said; some feel that this command is out of date; and some think that it just shouldn't concern us very much one way or the other.

In about the same way we misconstrue the meaning of life, and what our relations with God should be. In spite of the fact that many of the greatest revelations are still to be fulfilled, many say that God has gone out of business and that all revelations from him have ceased. Because of these many inaccuracies of thought we sometimes get all mixed up and frequently lose even our eternal directions.

We all have the holy scriptures available, but if we don't even understand the word of the Lord our salvation itself is placed in serious jeopardy. Solomon was trying to prescribe a remedy for these problems when he said, "With all thy getting, get understanding." This is especially good counsel in religion, as here we are particularly vulnerable to mistakes, because religion is the area that we frequently pay the least attention to. In this zone particularly ideas are mightier than swords. Swords can only cause physical destruction, but a few wrong ideas can bring eternal death upon our souls. And on the other hand we do not think of swords as performing a constructive function, whereas words can also take us to heaven.

Our eternal Heavenly Father has caused some of the most powerful words to be written down in the sacred scriptures which, if understood and followed, we could help to bring about our own eternal exaltation. We should not try to argue with the idea that "except a man be born of water and of the Spirit he cannot enter into the kingdom of God," nor should we try to rationalize ourselves out of it or think that Jesus didn't know what he was talking about. Rather, we should try to understand this important message, believe it and live accordingly. We should have that same spirit when we read the Ten Commandments, and the Sermon on the Mount. Or we might also take those two great commandments about loving God and loving our fellow men and try to get them into operation in the form in which they were intended. We can greatly increase our understanding if we make a little greater effort in that direction and then put our understanding into operation. But when we add a little hate, or a little doubt, or a little suspicion, or a little uncertainty, or a little insincerity, or a little sin into the mixture, it changes meanings and makes the right accomplishment impossible.

When chemists mix substances, they change the nature of the total. For example, common table salt is necessary to maintain life, but if its elements of sodium and chlorine are taken separately they can destroy us. It is also true that when the wrong elements are added to certain thoughts or when some necessary element is left out, we can produce a poisonous situation that works against our best interests. Because words are mightier than swords we should first learn word meanings and then use them carefully, because they can cut us down to death or build us up to eternal life.

The scripture says that on one occasion some of the disciples took offense at what Jesus had said, and they turned back and walked no more with him. Then said Jesus to the twelve, "Will ye also go away?" But Simon Peter had received a different meaning; he answered him and said, "Lord, to whom shall we go? Thou hast the words of eternal life." We ought to remember that if we can understand these words and if we live by their precepts, we can become like God and live forever in that order to which God himself belongs. Peter said, "We believe and are sure that thou art that Christ, the Son of the living God." What powerful uplifting words and what a tremendous message! If we can understand this one fact alone we can make our lives eternally successful.

Mother's Day

ONCE AGAIN WE come to Mother's Day. This is one of those important days that we mark on the calendar in red letters. There is an old Jewish saying that "God could not be everywhere present, and therefore he made mothers." And as we honor our mothers, we uplift ourselves. For —

> When the high heart we magnify
> And the sure vision celebrate,
> And worship greatness passing by,
> Ourselves are great.

Certainly if we were going to make an appraisal of our blessings we would put our mothers at the very top of the list. Charles Dickens once said, "I think it must be somewhere written that the virtues of the mothers shall be visited upon the children, as well as the sins of the fathers."

I would like to pay my tribute to the spirit of this day by relating a personal experience. For a number of years I have followed with great interest the activities of a certain couple that now have three young children. Because of the sickness of the mother I recently became a visitor in their home. And even though they live in modest circumstances, their family life is a joy to behold. They have circulating in their midst a more or less mysterious quality called love. There are some things that cannot easily be described because they cannot be seen or heard, and therefore they can only be partially understood. For example, it is difficult to see electricity, or feel the flowers grow, or hear sunshine enter a room.

As I visited in this home, I was aware that many miracles were taking place all around me. Powerful electric currents were running into the house along copper wires at inconceivable speeds. They came from a power plant many miles away in the form of energy, but when they reached the glass bulb in the living room they immediately turned into light. Human voices were also traveling back and forth through the house on telephone wires, and the entire room was filled with dozens of choirs and television shows that could be immediately picked out of the air by merely turning the knob of a receiver set. To add to the wonder, freezing temperatures were forming in the refrigerator, and life-giving heat was being supplied from the furnace. We can only understand these things by applying the formula of Jesus who said, "By their fruits ye shall know them."

But the miracle that gave me the greatest thrill and caused the most awe and wonder to form in my heart was the radiations of love that were passing around among the family members. The mother's sudden sickness had caused something of a crisis to develop. And as the father was driving me toward their home he told me of his love for his wife and children in such a way, that a lump formed in my throat and tears gathered in my eyes.

He told me how each night his wife sang wonderful songs to the children and how the entire family would sing, laugh and talk together about interesting and important things. Everyone received a lot of fun and inspiration from their family membership. To relieve the sick mother, the children had lived with relatives for the two days of her sickness. While they were away they had had more luxurious accommodations, but how happy they were to be back in their own home with their own parents and each other. You could also feel their gratitude to know that their mother was now going to be all right. I couldn't see the electricity running along the power company's wires, or feel the lines of force by which gravity was drawing everything downward, but as I watched the little three-year-old daughter standing at the bedside of her mother, I could see a miracle in her eyes and hear a holy gratitude in her voice. In addition I could feel the power of a great love passing between the daughter and her mother, which was making the child happy and the mother well. It occurred to me again that God did not perfect his greatest inventions to run along telephone wires or come out of transistors. He put his greatest powers and most worthwhile gifts into human lives. We classify these great benefits under the titles of love, faith, hope, happiness, and righteousness. And these godly traits are manufactured in abundance in the lives of noble mothers from whence they are transmitted into the characters of their children.

When Napoleon was asked what was the greatest need of France, his one-word answer was "mothers." That is also the greatest need of this little three-year-old now standing at her mother's bedside. Abraham Lincoln was one of the greatest men who ever lived, and in explaining his excellence he said, "All that I am or ever hope to be I owe to my angel mother." As I watched this little three-year-old girl standing by the sick bed of her mother I felt that for the first time I understood what Mr. Lincoln meant about the debt he owed to his mother. While this little girl is with her mother their spirits are merging with each other, and as she grows and new life cells are being formed each day, they are being stamped with the impress of her mother's love, faith, virtue and happiness and they will determine the quality of the daughter's character, religion and personality. Women and girls acting on their own make some mistakes, but as mothers they seem to be acting under a higher power that greatly reduces the likelihood of error. Whatever wrong things this young mother might be tempted to do as an individual is largely eliminated while she is bound in the magic spell of her family's love and confidence.

Macaulay said, "Children, look into those beautiful eyes, listen to that dear voice, feel the gentle touch bestowed upon you by that loving hand, and make as much of it as you can while yet you have that most precious of all good gifts, a loving mother." It may be that in heaven we will have better associates, but until then we never know more inspiring love and never have a more tender gentleness lavished upon us than that which is bestowed by our mothers.

This Mother's Day is saddened by the wars and sins that presently desolate our lands and tend to make many homes seem barren and lonely. During the second World War, Edwin McNeill Poteat wrote a poem in which he said:

And Mary stood beside the cross! Her soul
Pierced with the self-same wound that rent his side
Who hung thereon. She watched Him as He died . . .

Her Son! Saw Him paying the cruel toll
Exacted by the law, and unbelief,
Since He their evil will had dared defy.
There stood the mother helpless in her grief
Beside the cross, and saw her firstborn die!

> How many mothers in how many lands
> Have bowed with Mary in her agony,
> In silence borne the wrath of war's commands
> When every hill is made a Calvary!
>
> O pity, Lord, these mothers of the slain
> And grant their dead shall not have died in vain.

The problems, heartaches, and loves of this life teach us that God is building us for eternity. And it is the job of mothers to provide the rallying point around which affection, obedience, and a thousand tender endeavors to please and grow are concentrated. Mrs. Segourney has said to mothers, "What a holy charge is yours, and with what kingly power your love can rule the foundations of a new-born mind." Mrs. White says:

> Oh wonderous power, how little understood
> Entrusted to the mother's mind alone,
> To fashion genius in the soul for good,
> Inspire a Lincoln or train a Washington.

Henry Ward Beecher once said, "The babe at first feeds upon the mother's bosom and then upon her heart." And I suppose that the most appropriate way that we can honor our mothers is by adopting their teachings. As Nancy Hanks lay on her death bed she said to her nine-year-old son, "Abe — go out there and amount to something." And we are still being benefited by his obedience. This same thrilling hope that *we* will also amount to something is still the greatest prayer of our mothers. One mother said to her son:

> Do you know that your soul is of my soul such a part
> That you seem to be fiber and core of my heart.
> None other can please me as you dear can do,
> None other can please me or grieve me as you.
>
> Remember the world will be quick with its blame
> If sorrow or shame ever cover your name.
> Like mother, like son, is the saying so true,
> The world will judge largely of mother by you.
>
> Be yours then the task, if task it must be,
> To force the proud world to do homage to me.
> Be sure it will say when its verdict you've won,
> She reaped as she sowed, lo this is her son.

God is also suggesting that his children amount to something. And he has given us the program as to how our excellence may be brought about. The word *gospel* means "the good news" or "the God story." And one of its most significant chapters is written around the operation of the family unit. The family organization and the family relationship was intended to last forever. In the very beginning God said, "It is not good for man to be alone," neither is it good for woman to be alone, and it is not good for children to be alone, either in time or in eternity. The first family upon this earth was established by God himself before death had entered the world, and it was planned to be eternal. And anything that tends to bring about a dissolution of the family organization or a lessening of the family's welfare should not be permitted. Jesus had family permanence in mind when he said, "What therefore God hath joined together, let not man put asunder." (Matt. 19:6)

We sometimes take a short-sighted view of things and imagine that there is more difference between this life and the next than there actually is. The same body that Jesus had here was resurrected and taken with him into the hereafter. And so will ours be. Our minds and personalities will also go with us. The body functions continue. After his resurrection Jesus walked and talked, loved and was loved, much as he did here. After his resurrection he moved about and talked with his disciples, and showed them his hands and his feet. He said, "Have ye here any meat? And they give him a piece of broiled fish, and of an honeycomb, and he took it, and did eat before them." (Luke 24:41-43) He also cooked breakfast for his disciples on the Sea of Tiberius. Certainly it would be the height of foolishness to suppose that his own family relationship with his Father would be discontinued after his death. As we are aware, the spirit of Jesus was begotten of God in heaven, and so were ours. Our family relationship with God runs through all three spheres of our existence.

In the Garden of Gethsemane Jesus said, "And now, O Father, glorify thou me with thine own self with the glory which I had with thee before the world was." We might also pray this same prayer. Paul said, "We have had fathers of our flesh which corrected us, and we gave them reverence: shall we not much rather be in subjection unto the Father of spirits, and live." (Heb. 12:9)

The scriptures speak a great deal about men, and not very much about women. The Bible Concordance has many times more references to fathers than to mothers. But women are not the less important merely because they are not as prominently mentioned in the Bible. There are mothers here, and there will be mothers in eternity. God mentioned both "male and female" in heaven. We speak of an eternal Heavenly Father. And no one either in heaven or upon the earth ever had a father without also having a mother. And just as we have one in heaven who is the Father of our spirits, so we also have one in heaven who is the Mother of our spirits.

An inspired poet once said, "Truth is reason, truth eternal tells me I've a mother there." The family is as much the basic unit in the Celestial Kingdom as it is here. And far more children have been born in heaven than have been born upon the earth. As we contemplate the love we have for our families here, think what that love might become hereafter when we will have quickened senses, amplified powers of perception, and vastly increased capacity for love, righteousness and happiness. And as we worship our eternal Heavenly Father we might also think a little more about our eternal heavenly Mother. On this Mother's Day we might try to imagine the kind of a person she must be to have been selected the companion of God, and to preside with him over that glorious heavenly home.

There is much more pleasure and happiness in heaven than we are capable of understanding here, and much of it will come from the joys of the family; and to bring this about may God help us to make the most of our Mother's Day.

The New Year

THE CHALLENGING idea of a new year can be very inspirational and constructive. By the time January first has arrived, the old year has been finished. Our books have been closed, our scores have been added up, and the decks are being cleared for some more worthwhile accomplishment. It is an exciting and significant fact that these particular 365 days lying immediately before us will constitute the most important year that has ever been known since creation. More progress will be made, more new things will be invented, more babies will be born, more people will die, more good things will be done, and more sins will be committed than in any previous year. But the new year also represents that wonderful idea of beginning again. And we should use this idea in the most effective and profitable way possible. In an interesting New Year's philosophy Thomas Wearing says:

> Upon the threshold of another year we stand again.
> We know not what of gladness and good cheer, of grief or pain,
> May visit us while journeying to its close — in this we rest,
> God dealeth out in wisdom, what He knows for us is best.

The start of any undertaking is usually the most important part of it. The beginning often gives the whole project its character. But any enterprise conducted in time is always particularly important because time is the material out of which this most valuable commodity of life itself is made. Perhaps our most important New Year's thought is that of raising our own sights and more effectively motivating our own ambitions. Certainly each new year should be greater than the one preceding it. From this particular New Year just now being born, should come our greatest challenges and our most thrilling opportunities. Annie Flint Johnson suggests that both of these should be accepted enthusiastically, when she says:

> God hath not promised skies always blue,
> Or flower-strewn pathways, all our lives through;

God hath not promised sun without rain,
Joy without sorrow, or peace without pain.

But God *hath* promised His help for the day,
Strength for the labor, light for the way,

Grace for the trials, faith from above,
With unfailing sympathy, and undying love.

And God has also granted us that inestimable opportunity of always doing our best under every circumstance. What a tremendous privilege it is to be free, to be free to work, to win, to love, to laugh, and to live interestingly and successfully! It was not intended that we should be cowards, or sinners, or idiots, or weaklings. We are men formed in God's image and endowed with his attributes. It is not desirable for us to be protected from every difficult problem or to know in advance everything that lies ahead. It might help us to more courageously live each day as it comes if in our hearts we applied the philosophy of George Croly's hymn which says:

I ask no dream, no prophet's ecstasies,
No sudden rending of this veil of clay,
No angel visitant, no opening skies,
But take the dimness of my soul away.

It is God's program that we should learn to effectively walk a little way by faith. With a little extra New Year's courage, a little more thoughtfulness, a little more of the power of believing, a little stronger ambition, and a little more solid obedience, we can get most of the dimness out of our souls and make ourselves a little more worthy of our divine destiny. Life was never intended to be merely a pleasure trip: it is a testing, a contest, a time when we demonstrate the kind of stuff we're made of. In Edwin Markham's poem he says:

When, in the dim beginning of the years,
God mixed in man the raptures and the tears,
And scattered through his brain the starry stuff,
He said, "Behold! yet this is not enough
For I must test his spirit and make sure
That he can dare the vision and endure."

"I will withdraw My face,
Veil Me in shadow for a certain space
Leaving behind me only a broken clue —
A crevice where the glory glimmers through,
Some whisper from the sky,
Some footprint in the road to track me by.

I will leave man to make the fateful guess;
Will leave him torn between the No and Yes,
Leave him unresting 'til he rests in Me,
Drawn upward by the choice that makes him free —
Leave him in tragic loneliness to choose,
With all in life to win or all to lose."

Inasmuch as we usually count our successes and mistakes by the year, the first of the year is the logical time for preparation. It has been said that "planning" is the place where man shows himself most like God. Nothing is more Godlike than the ability to think ahead, to organize thoughtfully, to make a definite program of good quality and then to carry it out faithfully. This is also the time when we should think about God and plan for the eternal welfare of our own souls.

Some clearly worded, strongly held objectives might well be written down on this new page that life has granted for our use. To put our goals down in black and white not only gives our program definiteness, but also it gives us a greater power to achieve. The total time allotment of this new year is meted out to us one day at a time in order that we may make the most of each one separately. We never have to worry about any two days coming at once, but we do have the responsibility of living each one as well as it can possibly be lived. We might join with Sybil F. Partridge in singing her constructive prayer:

Lord, for tomorrow and its needs, I do not pray,
Keep me, my God, from stain and sin, Just for today,
Let me no wrong or idle word unthinking say,
Set thou a seal upon my lips, Just for today.

Let me both diligently work and duly pray:
Let me be kind in word and deed, Just for today;
Let me in season, Lord, be grave, in season, gay,
Let me be faithful to Thy grace, Just for today.

In the cleansing fires of pain and grief, brief be my stay;
And bid me if today I die, Come home today;
So for tomorrow and its needs, I do not pray;
But keep me, guide me, love me, Lord, Just for today.

By daily thoughtfulnes, daily obedience, and daily worship, we may perfect our communication with the divine and build a stronger fellowship with God. Under the title of "Anchored to the Infinite," Edwin Markham suggests a procedure for linking our lives with the divine. He says:

The builder who first bridged Niagara's gorge,
Before he swung his cable, shore to shore,
Sent out across the gulf a venturing kite,
Bearing a slender cord for unseen hands
To grasp upon the further cliff and draw
A greater cord and then a greater yet;
Until at last across the chasm swung
The cable — then the mighty bridge in air!

So we may send our little timid thoughts
Across the void, to God's outreaching hands —
Send out our love and faith to thread the deep —
Thought after thought until the little cord
Has greatened to a chain no chance can break,
And we are anchored to the Infinite!

We might borrow some of the great New Year's prayers to serve our need. Here is one from Max Ehrmann. He said:

Let me do my work each day;
And if the darkened hours of despair overcome me,
May I not forget the strength that comforted me,
In the desolation of other times.

May I still remember the bright hours that found me
Walking over the silent hills of my childhood
Or dreaming on the margin of the quiet river,
When a light glowed within me,
And I promised my early God to have courage
Amid the tempests of the changing years.

Spare me from bitterness
And from the sharp passions of unguarded moments.
May I not forget that poverty and riches alike are largely of the
    spirit.

Though the world know me not,
May my thoughts and actions be such
As shall keep me friendly with myself.

Lift up my eyes from the earth,
And let me not forget the uses of the stars.
Forbid that I should judge others
Lest I condemn myself.

Let me not follow the clamor of the world
But walk calmly in my path,
Give me a few friends who will love me for what I am!
And keep ever burning before my vagrant steps
The kindly light of hope.

And though age and infirmity overtake me,
And I come not within sight of the castle of my dreams,
Teach me still to be thankful for life,
And for time's golden memories that are good and sweet;
And may the evening's twilight find me gentle still.

The first day of this New Year is the time for New Year's
plans and New Year's resolutions, but it is also the time for
some New Year's dedication and some New Year's industry.
Then we have the 364 other wonderful days to bring our program
to its completion. On January 1st we should also remember that
another December 31st is just around the corner. The year's
end will bring with it an inevitable need to add up the score.
Then we must figure out our gains and mark down our losses.
Then is when we compare our performance with our previously
set goals. Then is the time when we discover the ratio of our
actual to our potential accomplishment. There are two very
interesting emotions that come into operation in connection with
this year-end settling-up process. If we have met our goals we
feel that wonderful emotion of joy. If we have missed the mark,
we suffer the awful pain of regret. The end of the year is like
the end of a basketball contest. That is when we learn the score,
telling us how well we have performed. It is only when the final
whistle blows that we discover whether we are winners or losers.
The *score* is what everyone remembers, and whenever we start
a new game we should be aware that we are also arranging for
a new score.

Many years ago, Grantland Rice, the late dean of sports-writers, wrote some stimulating lines around this "year end" or "end of the game" idea. He said:

> When the game is done,
> And the players creep
> One by one to the league to sleep,
> Deep in the night they may not know
> The way of the fight
> Or the fate of the foe,
> The cheer that passed and applauding hands
> Are still at last, but the record stands.
>
> The errors made and the base hits wrought —
> Here the race was run,
> There the fight was fought,
> But the game is done when the sun sinks low
> And one by one from the field they go,
> Their day has passed through the twilight gates
> But the scroll is cast and the record waits.
> So take, my lad, what the great game gives:
> For all men die, but the record lives.

Each game, and each year, and even life itself will someday have its December 31st, its last whistle and its final score. Then the supreme referee will add up our credits and mark down our debits in his permanent record. It is on *his* scorecard of our deeds that *our* lives will be judged — winners or losers. Rudyard Kipling once wrote a poem entitled "L'Envoi," which means "to bid farewell." To bid farewell to the old year is a kind of symbol for what we will someday do to life. In trying to center our minds on the future last whistle, Mr. Kipling says,

> When earth's last picture is painted, and the tubes are twisted
>   and dried,
> When the oldest colors have faded, and the youngest critic has
>   died,
> We shall rest, and faith, we shall need to — lie down for an
>   aeon or two,
> 'Till the Master of All Good Workmen shall put us to work anew.
>
> And those that were good shall be happy: They shall sit in a
>   golden chair,
> They shall splash at a ten-league canvas with brushes of comet's
>   hair;

They shall find real saints to draw from — Magdalene, Peter
and Paul,
They shall work for an age at a sitting, and never be tired at all.

And only the Master shall praise us, and only the Master shall
blame,
And no one shall work for money, and no one shall work for
fame;
But each for the joy of the working, and each, in his separate
star,
Shall draw the thing as he sees it, for the God of Things as
They Are!

Mr. Kipling's picture reminds us that with each new beginning we should keep one eye on the end. God must have had
something like this in mind when he referred to himself as
Alpha and Omega. He has often called himself the first and
the last, the beginning and the end. He sees the end from the
beginning. He sees the fruit in the seed, the bird in the egg, the
consequences in the deed. But like him we should also learn to
see the finish more clearly from the start. To be adequately
successful we must have a great beginning, we should have a
strong finish and we should make sure that all of those wonderful
days in between are lived at their maximum. Because every
experience will go into that rich fabric of life exactly as it is
fashioned, then each day should be its own masterpiece. We
should have some great beginnings; and may God grant us the
victory, happiness and success of some glorious ends.

Not Understood

MANY YEARS AGO I read a poem written by Thomas Bracken entitled "Not Understood." Since that time frequently it has seemed that the problem expressed lies at the root of much of the failure and misery that presently flourishes in our world. We bear the unbearable burdens of war because some nations refuse to understand other nations. Our racial strife, damaging labor disputes, destructive family feuds, and bitter personal differences, are largely because we fail to tolerate those whose situation differs from our own. And it therefore becomes impossible for us to live harmoniously together.

Someone has indicated this personal difference of viewpoint when he said, "I looked at my brother through the microscope of hate and said, 'How small my brother is.' I looked at my brother through the telescope of scorn and said, 'How low my brother is.' Then I looked at my brother in the mirror of truth and I said, 'How like me my brother is.'"

We even have such serious misunderstandings with ourselves that we frequently bring on major internal conflicts, and cause severe emotional instability and damage. Elbert Hubbard once said that in his opinion the unpardonable sin was incompatibility. But incompatibility is often just the beginning of many more serious problems. As individuals we do not have much direct personal liability for our international affairs, but everyone has a great challenge in solving those problems of understanding others and of being understood. Some of these problems are pointed out in Mr. Bracken's poem. He says:

> Not understood. We move along asunder;
> Our paths grow wider as the seasons creep
> Along the years; we marvel and we wonder
> Why life is life, and then we fall asleep —
> Not understood.
>
> Not understood. We gather false impressions,
> And hug them closer as the years go by.

'Till virtues often seem to us transgressions;
And thus men rise and fall and live and die —
Not understood.

Not understood. Poor souls with stunted visions
Oft measure giants by their narrow gauge;
The poisoned shafts of falsehood and derision
Are oft' impelled 'gainst those who mould the age —
Not understood.

Not understood. The secret springs of action
Which lie beneath the surface and the show
Are disregarded; with self satisfaction,
We judge our neighbors, and they often go —
Not understood.

Not understood. How trifles often change us!
The thoughtless sentence or the fancied slight
Destroys long years of friendship and estrange us
And on our souls there falls a freezing blight —
Not understood.

Not understood. How many breasts are aching,
For lack of sympathy! Ah, day to day
How many cheerless, lonely hearts are breaking;
How many noble spirits pass away —
Not understood.

Oh God! That men would see a little clearer,
Or judge less harshly where they cannot see;
Oh God! That men would draw a little nearer
To one another; and they'd be nearer thee —
And understood.

One thoughtless or false judgment can sometimes ruin a person's entire life. I know of a man serving in a public capacity who spent a great deal of time without any thought of reward trying as best he could to help solve the problems of other people. But one who had a different make-up and an opposite point of view misunderstood his purpose, and such a severe censure was brought upon him that it almost destroyed all of his future ability to do good.

Our expressions about others, and even our attitudes, can cause blighting guilt and inferiority complexes in people that may last a lifetime. A little misinterpretation, a few rumors and the disapproval of certain people has often deformed a life. And sometimes we are willing to disregard long years of merit and faithful service to jump at some ill-founded conclusion. It is said that when one member of a wolf pack is wounded, his former companions jump on their bleeding member and finish the job of destruction. We sometimes do about the same thing when some human being makes a real or imagined mistake. Or, we build up secret resentments about people and more or less unconsciously carry on this unpardonable sin of incompatibility by some degree of misunderstanding, lack of confidence or even hate. This damaging process works against our families, our friends, our own selves, and even God.

Many husbands don't understand their wives, and some wives resent their husbands; parents don't know very much about their children, and children fail to appreciate their parents. Thus we lose many of the benefits of God's two greatest laws indicating that we should love God and each other. Not only do we misunderstand people, we also misunderstand ideas and words and situations. It is very common for us to misunderstand the value of honesty, the need for courtesy and the importance of fairness. The people of Noah's day didn't understand their situation — neither did those who lived in the days of Jesus and neither do we.

So frequently we don't understand the meaning of death or the purpose of life, or the need for disciplining ourselves. It is likely that the most misunderstood individual in the universe is God himself. Many people are not quite certain whether he is alive or dead, or whether or not he is still interested in his creations. Many people insist on depriving God of his body, and then they take away his personality, his right of communication, and his authority. In downgrading God we often make him a "thing," or change him from a "thou" to an "it" because we don't understand. We tell ourselves that we don't need him any more, and that what we think or do is not important anyway. Some half believe that God is dead and some don't care one way or another. One of our biggest problems in all of these departments of misunderstanding and being misunderstood is that we don't take enough time or make sufficient effort to reach a more favorable objective.

Theologians used to say that God made the world out of nothing. We now understand that that is not possible, as matter cannot be created or annihilated — it can only be changed in form. However, we still seem to imagine that we can get success and faith out of life without putting anything in. No one can ever make something out of nothing. We often fail to understand because we fall into one of the categories mentioned by Jesus, who said that we have eyes that don't see, and ears that don't hear, and minds that don't believe, and hearts that fail to understand. We become so accustomed to seeing things through our prejudices, our hates, our jealousies, our appetites and our impulses that our eyes go blind. To avoid using our senses we often accept the ready-made opinions of others, or recognize only those meanings that seem most advantageous to us.

In America there are some 250 Christian churches with thousands of times that many members, who all claim the Bible as their infallible source of religious authority and doctrine. And yet there is little unity. From this one set of directions we come up with hundreds of antagonistic beliefs and procedures.

The Lord himself said to his apostles "Go ye into all the world and preach the gospel unto every creature. He that believeth and is baptized shall be saved: but he that believeth not shall be damned." (Mark 16:15) That should be clear enough. And yet most present-day people do not believe this statement or they only believe it in some minor fraction. But in one way or another we get a hundred points of view instead of one.

It seems to be human nature for us to be less impressed with truth than we are in holding our opinions in common with those people who have standing with us. I know of one man who, when opinions are being expressed, always likes to be the last to respond. When every point of view is known, then he can identify himself with the viewpoint of whoever has the best chance to win. This may be a pleasant procedure for some people, but it doesn't contribute very much to an understanding of the facts. Regardless of right or wrong, it is so easy for Republicans to side with Republicans, or members of labor unions to think alike on matters involving pay increases.

In the mob that went before Pilate there were not very many who could understand the other side of the argument, or see the virtue in the cause of the lonely and rejected Nazarene. But when the tide of popular opinion shifts to the other side, it always carries a lot of people with it.

When the idea of assassinating Julius Caesar was being built up to its fever's pitch, the would-be assassins sought Brutus to be their leader. Brutus had great prestige among the people and they said, "That which would appear amiss in us, his countenance, like richest alchemy, shall change to virtue and to nobleness." They knew that they were doing wrong, but if Brutus was leading them it would make the deed seem right to many people. When Brutus finally took over, one of the conspirators by the name of Ligarius said in substance "lead on, my lord, and with a heart new-fired I'll follow thee. To do, I know not what, but it sufficeth that Brutus leads me on." (Act II Scene I) This tendency to let the influence of a person be more important than the righteousness of the cause is still operating in one way or another to kill our understanding and destroy people. Caesar was stabbed with swords, but we can kill others just as effectively by breaking their hearts, or worrying them to death, or destroying their morale, or ruining their reputation, or in some other way subjecting them to the distortion of a wrong point of view.

People engaged in aviation speak of "the degree of visibility." We can develop a greater "degree of understanding" if we always insist on the facts and look at things from the point of view of truth. A great scientist was once asked to comment on the conflict between science and religion. He said he didn't think that there was any conflict in God's mind. God is the God of truth; there are no inharmonies in his mind. He has only one point of view and that is truth. We sometimes get confused and can't tell right from wrong because we have so many conflicts going on inside ourselves. If 250 churches look at the gospel principles with their own interests in mind, each may get a different answer; or if several people were reporting an automobile accident their reports might differ if one represented the insurance company, one the injured party and one had no interest at all. So frequently our misunderstanding is in ourselves and in our own point of view.

If one tells a joke to 10 people some may think the joke is funny, some may be unimpressed, and some may be actually bored by hearing it. Yet it was the same joke heard by everyone in the same tone of voice, under the same *external* circumstances. But the internal circumstances are never quite the same. As has been pointed out "the jest is in the ear of the hearer, not on the tongue of the teller."

It is also true that understanding, righteousness and faith cannot help us very much until they are internalized. Someone has said that most Christians are merely Bible Christians — that is when the Christianity is mostly in the Bible and not very much in us. It has been said that it doesn't help us very much to go through college unless the college goes through us. Great benefits may accrue to us when "we get into the church," but it isn't until the "church gets into us" that things really begin to happen.

The dictionary says that the word enthusiasm means "God in us." It is God's program for our growth to get his Spirit into us. The third member of the Godhead has the assignment to inspire and direct our lives according to God's wisdom, and only as we adopt this program of getting "God in us" will we see things from his point of view. With "God in us" we will not look at people through the microscope of hate or the telescope of scorn, nor will we see through the distortion of indifference or the clouds of ignorance. Then we will see everything in the mirror of truth. Then we will see as we are seen, and we will understand as well as be understood.

One of the greatest keys of understanding was mentioned by Jesus when he said, "If any man shall do his will he shall know of the doctrine." To do God's will creates the kind of climate inside of us wherein to understand his doctrine becomes comparatively simple.

Emerson mentioned this same principle when he said, "do the thing and you shall have the power." Andrew Carnegie once said that as he grew older he paid less attention to what men said and more to what they did. I suppose that this is also God's philosophy, as the Bible frequently reminds us that faith without works is of little value. And God himself has decreed that as we do the right things we will not only have the right judgment but we will also have sufficient power to put our understanding into operation. Actions always speak louder than words, and so we pray with Thomas Bracken:

> Oh God! That we may see a little clearer,
> Or judge less harshly where we cannot see;
> Oh God! That we will draw a little nearer
> To one another, and we'll be nearer to thee —
> And understood.

Our Midget Suits

ONE OF THE IMPORTANT facts of our existence is that we live in a world of opposites. Everything has something working against it, and everyone has someone else disputing the passage with him. Some of these pairs of opposites are made up of God and Satan, life and death, up and down, north and south, good and bad, failure and success, day and night, ignorance and knowledge, damnation and exaltation. One of the most important of our competing pairs is growth and decay. In one of his great parables Jesus compared the Kingdom of Heaven to the growth of a mustard seed. The mustard seed starts out as the least of the seeds, but when it is planted in the field it becomes the greatest of all the herbs, and the birds of the air are able to lodge in its branches. (Matt. 13:32)

If heaven can be properly compared to growth, then stagnation and death must most effectively represent hell. But if we are to be successful, both of these processes, as well as the places they lead us to, should be well known to us. However, growth is pretty difficult to understand. It is hard for us to figure out how a giant redwood with enough timber to build houses for forty families, can come from such a tiny seed that it takes five thousand of them to weigh an ounce. However, it is by this growth process that we get our houses, our food, our clothing and even ourselves. The growing root of a tree can break the concrete foundation of your home, and it can split open the granite wall of a canyon. A growing tree root three inches in diameter and ten feet long produces fifty tons of pressure. But the greatest of all power comes from growing men. And we think what has happened in the world because such men as Thomas A. Edison, Abraham Lincoln, Christopher Columbus, and the Apostle Paul lived in it.

But, like everything else, human growth processes also have their opposites. All around us we are opposed by the manifestation of those powerful forces of decay, death, decrease, shrinkage, and failure. There are a lot of belittling sins that make us less than we were. But God has set our human goals as "up," and not down. The ultimate objective was pointed out by Jesus when he said, "Be ye therefore perfect, even as your Father which is in heaven is perfect." That requires some substantial growing. It was one of the Master's most profound teachings that, under certain conditions, the offspring of God may eventually hope to become like the eternal parents. But these belittling influences are also very strong in us and we put our growth in reverse and commit the most serious sins when we foster sloth, negative thinking, disbelief and other forms of godlessness in ourselves. And thereby we fight against the purpose of God.

It has been pointed out that the most widespread disease in the world is the inferiority complex. We stunt our own growth and bring a condition of failure upon ourselves when we believe in inferiority strong enough. When we think, talk, and perform like mental pygmies, drunkards, sinners, and ne'er-do-wells a worsening process is set in motion that brings these conditions about. Doubt can kill faith and make us less. Sloth can wipe out industry, fear can destroy courage, and sin can make eternal progress and make happiness impossible. One of the conditions that most incites our pity is to see someone whose body doesn't grow, or whose mind always remains infantile. These are accidents and come through no fault of the one concerned. But what about those who are permanently stunted in their eternal prospects? Human beings can grow backwards even after a substantial progress has already been achieved, if they permit these belittling sins to reverse their growth processes. Even after having walked a substantial distance along the straight and narrow way, some people change to the broad road and finish the journey walking toward death. It is pointed out that all forms of success deaths are suicide. Every sin first takes place in our own minds. And our growth is never destroyed all at once by some kind of a blowout. Our virtues usually go flat because of a series of slow leaks. A little thoughtlessness, a little indifference, a little ignorance, a little disobedience, and before we are aware these belittling sins have made us into midgets.

Recently a man was released from a Church assignment after having been ten years in office. When he was called upon to speak he began by saying, "I am just as frightened to stand up before you today as I was when I stood up here to accept this position 10 years ago." Then for the next fifteen minutes he breathed out over 2,000 people the most negative, depreciating, belittling, almost profane kind of attitudes. In substance he said, "I am just as frightened, and just as lazy, and just as ignorant, and just as weak, and just as sinful, and just as worthless, and just as undependable, and just as unbelieving as I was ten years ago." And everyone could tell that he was not exaggerating. It seemed as though he had taken every possible kind of shrinking powder and was profaning the great being in whose image he had been created. We were not given this great gift of life and the power of growth to trifle with. Actually we have no business being just as frightened or just as sinful as we were ten years ago. The scriptures say that no one can be saved in ignorance, but neither can anyone be saved in indifference, and no one can be saved in indecision, and no one can think little and be big at the same time. The difference comes in the way we choose between our opposites.

Winston Churchill was once accused of being partial. He said that no charge against him could have been more accurate. Then he enumerated a large number of things he was partial about. For example, he said that he could not be impartial as between the fire brigade and the fire.

Jesus was also known for his strong partialities. He was partial as between heaven and hell, success and failure, truth and error, right and wrong. When the unprofitable servant said to him, "I was afraid so I hid my talent in the ground," the Lord said, "Thou wicked and slothful servant." Jesus was kind to the repentant adulteress. He had a sympathetic interest in the thief on the cross who wanted to do better. But about the man who wasn't improving himself, the Lord said, "Take the talent from him and give it to him who has 10 talents, and cast the unprofitable servant into outer darkness, where there shall be weeping and wailing and gnashing of teeth." Jesus was partial to growth and good works. He cursed the unproductive fig tree, and gave us the general law that "every tree that bringeth not forth good fruit is hewn down and cast into the fire." (Matt. 7:19)

The Master's attitude toward the unprofitable servant indicated that the disuse of our talents can be as serious a sin as the misuse of our talents. And the punishment for neglect is often as severe as it is for abuse. When the mole stopped using his eyes, nature took away his eyesight. When we don't use the muscles in our arms, nature takes the muscles away. When we discontinue our works our faith dies. Then on the other hand the greatest of all the miracles are performed under the heading of growth. Acorns become oak trees, and the most delicious foods in the greatest varieties of taste, color, and vitamin content, can be brought out of the raw soil through the instrumentality of a few unimpressive looking seeds. We can get five thousand giant redwoods from an ounce of redwood seed. However, the most serious concern of Jesus was not about redwoods. His greatest interest was centered in bringing growth about in people. He made it possible for us to build muscles on our bodies and in our minds, and in our personalities, and in our spirits if we are willing to exercise them effectively. And we would all be moral, spiritual, social, physical, and financial giants if for a lifetime we followed the simple teachings of Jesus. But for some mysterious reason most human beings have usually rejected his direction and resisted their own growth. We have forsaken right principles, refused to believe his truth, and disobeyed his programs for progress. It seems that we have a partiality for being various kinds of mental and spiritual pygmies. The large number of people traveling the broad road indicate that we have a stronger inclination for misery and death than for happiness and life.

When Jesus told the people that he was the Son of God, and tried to help them to understand their own divine destiny that as the children of God they might also hope to become like their eternal parent, they refused to listen and straightway accused him of blasphemy. (John 10:32-39) Isn't it strange how vigorously we oppose our own welfare and happiness by our refusal to grow? Ancient mythology tells us of some races of dwarfs and pygmies. These diminutive human beings are not only described as being small, but they were frequently mis-shapen, ugly, and caused a great deal of trouble for everyone. But in several ways pygmy stories are much more than myths. Some groups of these very small people presently live in Central Africa. They have dark skins and are poorly developed physically and mentally. They have no language of their own, and live as crude hunters under very primitive conditions. But the word *pygmy* is not limited to its physical meaning. And some people who are small physically are mental and spiritual giants. But this general term is sometimes used to describe other undersized insignificant persons. There are so many ways in which we can be small, ugly and misshapen. The significant fact is that we usually bring this undesirable stunted condition upon ourselves. And even self-murder may not be any more serious than the self-mutilation which makes us mentally, spiritually, and socially weak and sick.

In writing to the Ephesians the Apostle Paul said, "Be strong in the Lord and in the power of his might." To win in their battle of life he counseled them to put on the whole armor of God, that they might be able to stand against the wiles of the devil. And as a part of their battle-dress the great apostle mentions the girdle of truth, the breastplate of righteousness, the shield of faith, the helmet of salvation and the sword of the spirit which is the word of God. But instead of putting on the whole armor of God we frequently just dress ourselves up in the midget suits of our belittling sins. We put on a girdle of grumbling, a breastplate of disbelief and a shield of sin. There is small chance that we can overcome the wiles of the devil by rationalizing, alibiing, and procrastinating. We are playing into the devil's hand when we feed our spirits on the feelings of guilt and inferiority that come from low-grade past performances, or a misunderstanding of God's purposes or a disbelief in ourselves. When our minds are filled with doubt and error we can only shrivel and fail. When we believe that God is dead our hope also dies. When we lack faith in ourselves our effort loses its power. And when we are bound down in our midget suits, we develop midget deformities and restrictions. Certainly we will never reach our divine destiny as God's children while we are thinking like a tribe of twisted and deformed pygmies. We may not be aware of all of the problems responsible for making our mini-skirts shorter and tighter, but even mini-skirts may have some advantages over the growing and distressing scantiness of our mental, spiritual and social midget suits.

The growth formula of Jesus says that we should be born again. But we must be born bigger and better, not smaller and worse. When Saul was appointed King he was a giant in the sight of the Lord. The Lord referred to him as the goodliest person in Israel. But by the time Saul finally took his own life a few years later he had become a pygmy. Somewhere along the way Saul had made himself a midget suit out of his wrong thinking. He got some ideas that he was too important to obey the word of the Lord.

The scripture says that the Spirit of the Lord departed from Saul, and then Saul began to shrivel. As Saul grew smaller the evil spirit that troubled him grew larger, until it became a dangerous giant. But each time that Saul was reborn he was reborn smaller and worse. His belittling decisions and his deforming acts gave him a spirit of melancholia and hate, and by the time he died he was a small, misshapen pygmy. And how terrible it is when all that one has for his burial dress is a midget suit!

Many people are presently replacing the armor of God with the small pieces of pygmy clothing. When we discard our honesty we become smaller. When we break any commandment a worsening process sets in that makes us weaker. When we leave any gospel principle undeveloped in our lives we stunt our own growth. Ignorance, disbelief, disobedience, indecision and indifference all belittle us and make success more difficult and our spiritual mini-skirts shorter and tighter. It was not intended that we should conduct ourselves like cowards, weaklings and sinners, but rather like men formed in God's own image and endowed with his attributes and potentialities. The offspring of God are expected to become like their eternal parents. And any deformed midgets found in the family group are bound to embarrass the other members. The devil is not a pleasant adversary for weak people, and we need to take off our midget suits and redress ourselves in the whole armor of God where we can make a better showing. We need to cling to our inheritance by having a daily record of righteous accomplishment. And we should constantly reaffirm our belief in our destiny by our daily growth.

What a thrilling part of our faith to believe that foreheads can get broader, and hearts can get bigger, and faith can become stronger, and understanding can be increased! We can be born again as frequently as we desire, and each time we can be born better. But we ourselves must work at it. The Master said, "Follow me." That is a great idea. Suppose that we follow him in his belief in God. We need to follow him in his righteousness and in his faith and in the vision of his destiny. May we live as his children dressed in the shining armour of his clothing.

Our Friendly Enemies

Sometime ago Paul Harvey wrote an interesting newspaper article about our giant tobacco industry. He called it "our friendly enemy." This article pointed out that in America tobacco is "big business" in any sense of the term. Each year it surpasses 8 billions in dollar volume. Of all the money spent by Americans for consumer goods, some 2% goes for tobacco. Then much of this money is re-spent several times, and many such industries as advertising, transportation, radio and retailing are benefited. Tobacco also supports 520,000 farms, and 700,000 farm families, living in sixteen American states. In addition, tobacco taxes pour into our Federal and State treasuries at the rate of 3¼ billion dollars per year, supporting all forms of government, besides giving a generous boost to our general economy.

Tobacco also makes necessary the manufacture of the matches and lighters required to set ablaze the 563 billion, 164 million cigarettes, and the 8 billion, 883 million cigars that are used every year. In addition, it is necessary to set on fire the other 169,000,000 pounds of pipe and bulk smoking tobacco. This might be called a grand-scale arson where the product, as well as the effort to produce it, all goes up in smoke. However, this giant, friendly industry now stands indicted before our public tribunals as one of our most deadly enemies. It is accused of placing in jeopardy the health of the very people that it attempts to please. Aside from the many criminal charges against it, tobacco is also accused of monopolizing some of our richest American soils, and absorbing the efforts and resources of many able farmers, manufacturers, advertisers, transportation facilities and merchandisers in its destructive purposes, at a very time when many people in the world are starving for bread. Tobacco also disturbs the peace and comfort of many non-smokers. It fills airplanes and other public places with clouds of secondhand tobacco smoke. It saturates the clothing and fills the lungs of many people who, if given a choice, would prefer to avoid the secondhand indulgence. Even some unwilling homes must endure the air pollution caused by this foul, unclean, friendly enemy.

It is an interesting fact that in an age noted for its scientific health-research, and in our greatest Christian nation, we should assign some of our most resourceful advertising agencies to expertly entice other people to take this dangerous enemy into their bosoms, knowing that many will be impoverished and destroyed by it. And through all of this process many of us sit back comfortably and count the money that is paid to doctors, nurses, medicine-dispensers, hospitals and undertakers to repair this enemy damage in the living, and to bury those victims that don't survive.

Our attitude toward our friendly enemies furnishes substantial proof for the oft-repeated claim that the people of our earth have always seemed determined to destroy themselves. Our society was not very old before the very man that God had created in his own image brought forth a divine pronouncement from God saying "cursed be the ground for thy sake," and each generation seems to have added something to the curse.

The people of Noah's day brought a watery destruction upon themselves. The people of the meridian dispensation brought on the dark ages, and by their apostasy from God they covered the earth with spiritual night. In our own time, we are contributing some crime waves, dope addiction, alcoholism, tobacco diseases and the curse of atheism. By one means or another we keep our evil programs going so effectively that we continue to live in a state of darkness. The cancer in our lungs, the gloomy, spiritual clouds in our minds, and the miserable consequences of sin in our souls, make our lives so much less than they ought to be. And many of these problems started when Columbus discovered a group of near-naked, half-savage Indians going around inhaling the fumes of rolls of tobacco leaves that they were burning in their mouths. Tobacco originated in America, and with our usual American ingenuity we have made it into one of the world's most flourishing industries. In spite of our Christianity, our educational standards, and our desire for scientific progress, we are now pushing tobacco to new heights by inducing our women and children to smoke it. This evil-smelling agent of destruction consumes our time, uses up our family resources, and puts stains on our hands as well as on our minds and souls.

Tobacco addiction has probably caused a more serious condition of bondage in this great free land of America than ever existed here because of Negro slavery. Yet we continue to smack our lips over the dirty money paid to us for corrupting ourselves. We use about as much logic in our smoking as we do in our glue-sniffing and other forms of dope addiction. We light these bonfires in our faces and blow poisonous clouds of tobacco smoke onto each other as we jeopardize the general health and contaminate our free American air.

I imagine that the logic of our tobacco television programs might compare favorably to those reasons that the antediluvians gave for fostering the evils that brought on the flood. The arguments of those who lived in the days of Jesus brought about the crucifixion. But we may come nearest to winning the prize for inconsistency when in our period of greatest opportunity we keep a dangerous enemy in our bosoms at great expense, who is constantly nibbling away at our vital organs.

One of the primary indictments against tobacco came on February 27, 1833 when God himself gave a revelation to the world through the Prophet Joseph Smith at Kirtland, Ohio, known as the "Word of Wisdom." In part it says "to be sent . . . by revelation and the word of wisdom, showing forth the order and will of God in the temporal salvation of all saints in the last days — given for a principle with promise, adapted to the capacity of the weak and the weakest of all saints, who are or can be called saints." Then the Lord pointed out that wine and other alcoholic drinks should not be taken internally.

He particularly emphasized that tobacco was not good for man. He also pointed out the danger in such harmful habit-forming stimulants as tea and coffee, and said that they should *not* be used as beverages. However, this command presents no problem to many people as it is so easy to reject the word of the Lord by merely saying, "I don't believe." And yet we *must* believe, as God has given us an ability to reason, and our reason tells us that God could not possibly favor our destructive tobacco habits. However, in January 1964, the Surgeon General of the United States published a report verifying what the Lord had said about the detrimental effects of tobacco. This was accompanied by scientific proof of the great damages that it is causing. We haven't paid much more attention to the testimony of the Surgeon General than we have to the word of the Lord.

In our disregard, we go on each year reaching new highs in our tobacco sales. And every month we bring thousands of new addicts under its dominion. We might try to estimate the misery, waste, suffering and death that will be caused by this enemy between now and the time when the judgment of God finally cuts off all of our programs of destruction. But in the meantime families continue to be broken up, our useless expenses are going higher, and our physical weakness and enslavement will continue to take much of the profit from our lives that otherwise could have been ours. It seems that the pride we have in ourselves as free men able to discipline ourselves is not strong enough to save us. And even our vaunted *knowledge* doesn't seem to give us much protection, as we have known for a long time of the high correlation existing between the consumption of liquor and the degeneration of the physical, mental and moral qualities in human beings. But because we have fallen in love with our enemies our liquor sales continue to mount. Our physical problems continue to increase, our moral sicknesses become more severe and our spiritual decay continues to get worse.

Many of the crimes, auto accidents, work absenteeism, labor inefficiencies, broken homes and soul diseases that threaten our civilization are caused by these unfortunate liquor and nicotine appetites. And as we *use* these things that God has forbidden, we decrease our value to ourselves and others both as citizens and as human beings, and we also place an additional curse upon the earth.

In the past few years the coffee break has placed a great burden on our time and mental and material resources. And our American cocktail party and social hour has become a giant national disgrace. Some great American corporations that ordinarily devote themselves to doing the most worthwhile work of the world, are now also engaged in doing serious harm with the great reservoirs of free liquor that are placed under their control. These rivers of alcohol are poured down the throats of those very people whose betterment these corporations are pledged to foster. In these so-called "social hours" some of our finest corporations get their people together under a sociability pretext, and train them in the arts and attitudes of liquor drinking. Then this custom is passed down from the national leaders to those who govern in the regions. From there they reach the local leaders and from this level these swollen streams of booze are subdivided and trickled out to the company's individual representatives, who in turn drink with their customers so that every level is victimized.

However, no one can violate God's laws with impunity. The scriptures say that God cannot look upon sin with the least degree of allowance. Someday even the great corporation leaders must answer to God for their misdirected influence, even though it is carried on under the cloak of friendship. The situation described by Jesus of wolves masquerading in sheep's clothing is still one of our most serious problems and we are frequently unaware of our own disguises.

God was speaking on this subject when from the top of Mount Sinai he said that, "The sins of the fathers would be visited upon the children." And whether one may be aware of it or not a liquor-drinking, cigarette-smoking, negative-thinking, immoral-acting father can do great damage to his children by a misuse of their God-given, parent-loving instincts. That is, God has given parents a special significance in the eyes of their offspring, and Jesus emphasized the penalty for abusing this power when he said, "But whoso shall offend one of these little ones which believe in me, it were better for him that a millstone were hanged about his neck, and that he were drowned in the depth of the sea." (Matt. 18:6) The Lord pointed to one of our most destructive situations when he said "A man's foes will be those of his own household." Isn't it interesting that we usually acquire most of our bad habits from those closest to us, including our best friends, our companies, and the members of our own families.

It is pretty difficult to overcome the effect of the early home-teaching, or to counteract the evil sociability of friends and employers. Jesus said that we should love our enemies. There are several reasons why we should love our unfriendly enemies. Reason number one is that loving these enemies is a good way to keep unnecessary hate and ill-will out of our hearts. Reason number two is that the bad habits of our unfriendly enemies are more likely to repel us than those same bad habits when practiced by our friends and family members. Reason number three why we should love our unfriendly enemies is that frequently it is their opposition that stings us into action and keeps us awake and on our toes. Someone has pointed out still another reason why we should love our enemies, and that is that we made them ourselves. But some of our biggest problems arise when we fall too much in love with our friendly enemies. And one of our biggest problems comes in distinguishing our real friends from our real enemies. For just as most of our blessings come in disguise, so most of our enemies come in disguise also. Too frequently we think of discipline and labor and the people who make us toe the line as our enemies. Yet far more often it is the soft life and the friendly attitudes of appeasing our appetites and allowing ourselves to do as we please that do the most serious damage. We often learn dishonesty, irreverence and church absenteeism in our own homes. And our best friends join hands with those forces that are seeking to destroy us by influencing us to smoke, drink, be dishonest and be immoral.

We frequently say that whether or not we use liquor or tobacco or do other evil things should be left to our individual choice. And so it is. But in a little more realistic sense most of us are not our own masters. The greatest power in the world is the power of example. Example is stronger than discipline or willpower, and everyone must be responsible for the influence that he exerts upon others.

Thomas Carlyle once said, "We reform others when we walk uprightly." The best way to reform someone is to set him a good example. And the best way to destroy someone is to set him a bad example. When Lucifer walked out of the Council of Heaven, one-third of all the children of God walked out behind him. And Cain lost the argument with God when he inferred that he was *not* his brother's keeper, and some of our most serious evil pressures emanate from the *families* we love, the *friends* that we associate with, and the companies that we serve.

Someone has said, "God protect me from my friends; I can handle my enemies myself."

Paradise Lost

ONE OF THE GREAT authors of all time was John Milton. His narrative poem *Paradise Lost* is rated among the first ten of the world's great books. Very early in his life Milton developed an insatiable love of learning. And from the time he was a child he had an ambition to write a world-moving epic poem. He once told a friend that he was pluming his wings for a flight, and he intended that its influence would reach to the highest heaven and to the lowest hell. However, for many years he was plagued by poverty and disturbed by political difficulties. He suffered seriously from family problems, and was finally engulfed by blindness at age 44. However, Milton believed that no man could do his best, "until he has suffered much." And after some fifteen years of blindness his great masterpiece was published. Certainly no one could accuse him of picking a subject that was small or unimportant.

Milton's story is centered in "the war in heaven" and its results. Satan's revolt from God not only emptied heaven of one-third of its inhabitants, but it has radically changed the history of this world and the welfare of everybody in it. Most of our life's problems have always involved the influence of Satan. He caused the expulsion of our first parents from their paradise in Eden, and he has also had a hand in most of our difficulties since. It is interesting to imagine what our world would have been like if we had always effectively resisted the devil. The Bible, supplemented by modern revelation, tells us a great deal about Satan and the events that cast him in his present role as the enemy of God and the promoter of evil. To our scriptural information about the war in heaven, Milton has added generously from his own imagination. And while Milton makes some mistakes in theology, our mental powers are greatly stimulated as we become familiar with his tremendous war scenes and the eternal consequences of the enterprises of Satan.

Trying to make a comparison with Milton's theme, I recently looked up the world's ten top news stories for the last several years. But the most important events of this most important age all pale into insignificance when placed alongside the war in heaven. Even our most important present-day events have Satan as one of their chief participants. Among the most important news stories of recent years are the Negro riots, the war in Vietnam, the assassination of President Kennedy, the Kennecott and Ford labor strikes, the disposal of Khrushchev, the U. S. Surgeon General's report of the health hazard of cigarettes, and the Chinese Communist nuclear explosions. These and all other events are important or unimportant, depending upon the effect they have on the lives of people. In each of the above listed events someone got hurt. But because of Lucifer's rebellion, one-third of all of God's spirit children were forever denied the privileges of mortality and eternal progress. It has been estimated that of the two-thirds of God's children who did *not* rebel, some 80 billion have already lived upon this earth. This would mean that the corresponding one-third who *did* rebel would number over 40 billion. But the welfare of the entire 120 billion has been seriously influenced by Satan.

Milton begins his poem with a prayer to God for guidance. He says:

> I hence invoke thy aid to my adventurous song
> That with no middle flight intends to soar
> Above the Aonian mount, while its pursues
> Things unattempted yet in prose or rhyme,
> And chiefly thou, O spirit, that dost prefer
> Before all earthly temples the upright heart and pure,
> Instruct me, for thou knowest. Thou from the first
> Wast present, and with mighty wings outspread,
> Sat dove-like, brooding o'er the vast abyss,
> And made it pregnant. What in me is dark,
> Illumine; what is low, raise and support;
> That to the height of this great argument,
> I may assert eternal providence,
> And justify the ways of God to men.

The scriptures make it plain that Satan was once Lucifer the light-bearer, the brilliant Son of the Morning. (Isa. 14:12) And he, with all of those who followed him, were the literal spirit children of God. One of our important religious problems is that we frequently think of eternal beings, including God, as foggy, mysterious influences, whereas Milton shows these spirit participants as the real, tangible people that they are. He makes a kind of catalog of the great generals, statesmen, and warriors on both sides of the war in heaven so that we understand them as real people.

Some of the generals assisting Satan in leading the rebellion are listed as Beelzebub, Molock, Mammon, and Belial. Milton describes Beelzebub as having shoulders like Atlas, capable of bearing the responsibility-weight of the mightiest monarchies. He seemed like a pillar of state, and even after his ruin his princely face revealed an unmistakable majesty. But dominating the rebellion was Satan himself. And Milton gives us a stimulating picture of this proud and once noble spirit so highly favored of heaven. He had stood very close to God until his unrighteous ambition had caused him to defy the Almighty. Isaiah quotes him as saying, "I will be like the most High." Satan's program was highly offensive to God as it was characterized by force. Even Satan himself resorted to arms in challenging the Omnipotent. The forces opposing the rebellion were led by Michael, God's Archangel. According to Milton he was assisted by Gabriel, Raphael and other powerful spirits under the general direction of Jehovah. Jehovah is the eldest and most capable son of Elohim, the Eternal Father. The scriptures refer to Jehovah as a man of war. (Exo. 15:3) That is, before he was the Prince of Peace, he was Jehovah the Warrior.

Milton knew nothing of nuclear warheads and guided missiles. But even then God had all knowledge, and the most powerful weapons were available to him. However, Milton talked of "sulphurous hail," "winged thunder," and "red lightning." But because the rebels sought to thwart the work of God and would not repent, and because they could not stand against the superior intelligence and greater power of the Almighty, Satan and his forces were expelled from heaven. What a significant vacancy of emptiness must have been indicated by the statement of John the Revelator when he said, "Neither was their place found any more in heaven"! (Rev. 12:8)

Milton tries to have us feel the importance of this expulsion by having Satan and his followers falling for nine days and nights. Then, for a similar period, their vanquished crew lay rolling on the fiery gulf of hell. And although they were immortal spirits, the confusion and bewilderment of their fall so dulled their minds that for a time they were only partially conscious of their fate. As their senses began to revive they felt the full torment of their lost happiness, their everlasting humiliation and their awful suffering. Their horrible dungeon was aflame on every side, and yet the only light was a thick, visible darkness by which they discovered their dismal, wild, and wasted doom. Hell was full of sights of woe, regions of sorrow, and doleful shades, where neither peace, nor rest, nor love could ever dwell. This fiery deluge causing torture and misery without end was fed by ever-burning sulphur unconsumed. How unlike was hell to that magnificent place from whence they fell! In Milton's story, as Satan's mind began to clear, the baleful eyes he cast around him were still filled with obdurate pride and steadfast hate. As they became accustomed to the scenes of awful affliction and terrible dismay, he discovered that Beelzebub was weltering by his side. This great spirit was Satan's second in command, next only to himself in crime and power. Breaking the horrid silence Satan said, "If thou beest he — but oh, how fallen, how changed from him who in the happy realms of light was clothed with transcendent brightness. Yet *we* with mutual consent, united thoughts and equal hazards did join in that tremendous enterprise to contend against the most-high. And now we have been joined by misery and defeat in equal ruin." Then Satan began to think about how the results of their expulsion could be repaired; and with great speeches, Milton puts into the mouths of Satan and his vanquished generals sentiments that under more godly circumstances might have done credit to the grandest enterprises. In spite of being cast out of heaven Satan was still defiant and unrepentant. He said:

> What though the field be lost?
> All is not lost; the unconquerable will,
> And study of revenge, immortal hate,
> And courage never to submit or yield —
> And what is else not to be overcome?

Beelzebub suggested that maybe God had permitted them to retain their mental strength and physical vigor that he might use them in hell for his own purposes.

> Then the archfiend said to Beelzebub —
> "Fallen cherub! To be weak is miserable whether
> Doing or suffering; but of this be sure,

To do good, never will be our task,
But always to do ill our sole delight,
If then out of our evil,
His providence seeks to bring forth good,
Our purposes must always be to pervert that end.

Satan then decided to reassemble his afflicted warriors and
plan how to make the most of their situation and to most seriously offend God. He indicated his own attitude when he said:

"If this be the seat that we must change for heaven,
This mournful gloom for that celestial light,
Then be it so!
Infernal world! Receive thy new possessor!
One who brings a mind not to be changed by place or time.
The mind is its own place, and of itself
Can make a heaven of hell, or a hell of heaven.
What matter *where*, if *I* be still the same,
Better to reign in hell, than serve in heaven.

Satan wondered what the reaction of his other followers
would be, and Beelzebub paid a great compliment to Satan's
leadership when he said that they would need only to hear his
voice to fully revive and regain their oldtime courage and united
effort. Then Milton says of Satan:

On the beach of that inflamed sea he stood,
And called his legions, these angel forms, who still lay entranced
Under the amazement of their hideous change.
He called so loud that all the hollow deep
Of hell resounded: — Princes, Potentates,
Warriors, the flower of the heaven once yours; now lost,
How can such astonishment as this, seize eternal spirits!
Or have ye chosen this place
After the toil of battle to repose your wearied virtue?
Awake, arise, or be forever fallen!
They heard, they were abashed, and up they sprung
As when men, wont to stand watch,
Are found sleeping on duty by one whom they dread.
And ere they were well awake
They did vigorously bestir themselves.
And though they did perceive their evil plight
And felt the fiercest pains of hell,
Yet their general's voice, did that innumerable company
     promptly obey.

In their council it was decided that someone must get out of hell and make his way through the almost impassable chaotic darkness and prepare to take over the earth, and destroy those who had helped to banish them from heaven. In making free agency the underlying principle with his children, God is quoted as saying, "I formed men free and free they must remain till they enthrall themselves. I will not change their natures nor revoke the high decree that hath ordained their freedom. They themselves ordained their fall."

But Satan would still use force, hate, war, and deception. By means fair or foul he would still try to overthrow the work of God. One said:

> How wearisome to spend eternity
> In worship, paid to him whom we hate.

Milton tries to indicate the vast power and great ability of Satan by saying:

> He above the rest
> In shape and gesture proudly eminent,
> Stood like a tower. His form had not yet lost
> All of its original brightness.
> On his face deep scars of thunder had entrenched themselves
> And care sat on his faded cheek, under brows of dauntless
>   courage.
> Cruel was his eye, yet showed
> Signs of remorse and passion, to behold
> The fellows of his crime, . . .
> Now condemned forever to a Hell of pain;
> Millions of spirits, for his fault deprived of heaven
> And from eternal splendors flung for his revolt,
> Yet with withered glory
> Faithful to their chief they dauntless stood.

Satan was the only one capable of making this necessary trip to the earth. Milton says:

> Into this wild abyss the wary fiend
> Stood on the brink of Hell and looked a while
> Pondering his voyage.

Then Milton describes that persistence that has always characterized Satan's evil accomplishment by saying:

So eagerly the fiend
O'er bog, or steep through strait, rough, dense or rare
With head, hands, wings, or feet, pursues his way,
And swims, or sinks, or wades, or crawls, or flies.

And when Adam and Eve were placed in the Garden of Eden, Satan was already there waiting, and since that time the battle between good and evil has continued unabated. Satan has had some defeats, and many victories. He is now working desperately, with his accomplishment at its zenith, as he knows that the time is near when he will be bound. But in the meantime we should be aware of the ability of our enemy, and the many things that we might do in being valiant soldiers for righteousness to make the cause of our great King victorious.

The Passover

ONE OF THE IMPORTANT occasions in our world's history is known as the "Passover." This interesting event took place when God intervened with Pharaoh and released the ancient Israelites from their Egyptian bondage. While the Israelites were serving in Egyptian slavery for some 215 years, they had become a great multitude numbering over three million people. The Lord wanted them to be free and he desired to establish a great nation from the seed of Abraham. Accordingly, he sent Moses, and his brother, Aaron, into Egypt to entreat the Pharaoh to let the Israelites return to their promised land. They had left their homeland when they were few in number while Canaan was being ravished by famine. As might have been expected, Pharaoh was very reluctant to release this vast, well trained, and profitable labor force. It therefore became necessary for Jehovah to apply enough pressure on the Pharaoh to change his mind, and it required 10 plagues to convince him that he should do as God commanded. However, it so happens that obedience to God has always been a very difficult lesson for human beings to learn, and many nations have been wholly or partially destroyed before they have gotten the point.

The Egyptians had some exciting experiences while God was trying to get the idea over that he governs in the affairs of men. In plague number one the water of the rivers, lakes and pools of Egypt was turned into blood. This was followed by a plague of frogs, then a plague of lice, a plague of flies, a plague of murrain among the cattle, a plague of boils and blains, a plague of fire and hail, a plague of locusts, a plague of thick darkness, and finally as plague number ten, the first born among all of the families of Egypt, beginning with that of Pharaoh, was slain. We can well picture the misery and unhappiness existing among the Egyptians as one after another the Lord sent these devastating punishments upon them.

Not only were they individually tormented by lice and boils and blains, but they had no water to drink, their crops were destroyed by hail, fire and locusts, and their cattle died of this contagious disease called murrain. Then for three days they were overcome with such a severe darkness that no light could be kindled in their dwellings. This unusual darkness was so intense that it could be felt. After each plague Pharaoh relented temporarily, and then as the plague was abated he would change his mind and withdraw his promise.

On several occasions the scriptures say that the Lord hardened Pharaoh's heart, but Bible experts tell us that this is an incorrect translation. Like most of us Pharaoh didn't need any help in hardening his heart. Actually the Lord was trying to get Pharaoh to *soften* his heart and become obedient so that he could win God's blessings, instead of having so much trouble. But because Pharaoh himself was in a cloud of darkness so far as God was concerned, it was necessary for him and his people to be humbled by suffering. Even then Pharaoh did not let the people go until the most severe of all plagues — when the first born of every Egyptian family was slain.

To make sure that the Israelites were spared, the Lord made a special "passover" arrangement with them. Before the 10th plague began, he advised the Israelites to be ready to leave Egypt immediately after Pharaoh had given his permission. If they had to prepare for their journey after they had been released, the Lord knew that Pharaoh would again change his mind. The Lord provided for their last meal in Egypt by instructing them that each family should kill a specially selected lamb that was without blemish. This lamb was to be roasted with fire and then eaten with unleavened bread and bitter herbs. In slaying the passover lamb special precaution was taken that no bones were broken. And the blood was to be used on the doors of their houses as a token of the passover. The Lord had said to Moses, "And they shall take of the blood (of the lamb) and strike it on the two side posts . . . of their houses." He said, "For I will pass through the land of Egypt this night, and will smite the first born . . . of both man and beasts . . . and when I see the blood, I will pass over you, and the plague shall not be upon you to destroy you." (Exo. 12:7-13)

The Lord indicated that this last meal should also be a ceremonial called the "Feast of the Passover," and that it should be commemorated thereafter as an annual rite among the Israelites.

It was intended that this ritual would forever hold their attention on this great event when the Lord had preserved their lives, led them out of bondage and established them in their promised land as the chosen people of the Lord. But it would also focus their devotion on a still greater event that was to come in the future. It was through their lineage that the Savior of the world would come, and the perfect Passover lamb would serve as a symbol of the coming Messiah. The slaying of the lamb was to typify that far greater event when the Son of God would be slain for the sins of the world. As with the Passover lamb, no bone would be broken in the crucifixion, and the blood of the Son of God would save the obedient inhabitants of the earth from death.

For over 1,500 years the faithful followers of Jehovah commemorated their last supper in Egypt, and they also looked forward to the atonement on Calvary. It was the feast of the Passover that Jesus commemorated with his apostles just prior to his crucifixion, and in *this* last earthly meal eaten by Jesus he fulfilled the feast of the Passover and instituted the sacrament of the Lord's supper as a memorial to be kept by us until he comes again to cleanse the earth of its sin. This we do as we look forward to our redemption from death through his promise that if we will always remember him and keep his commandments that he has given us we will always have his Spirit to direct our lives. Our obedience to his laws symbolizes that we are headed for a far more glorious promised land than the one in which the Israelites lived in Palestine. As the Israelites looked back upon their deliverance from bondage, so we look ahead to our deliverance from death through our obedience to God's laws. In the upper room with his disciples Jesus blessed the emblems of his flesh and blood, and gave instructions that his followers should meet together often and partake of these emblems in remembrance of him, to keep us free from the bondage of sin until he comes to the earth again. However, the Passover also still serves as a symbol of man's universal struggle against tyranny and wrong. It was not intended that any Pharaoh or other oppressor should take away our God-given gift of freedom. It is a serious denial of God's will when *any* child of God is held in *any* kind of bondage.

The Passover effectively represents many other events in history when people have been freed of oppression. Lucifer was banished from heaven and the Egyptians were drowned in the Red Sea because they insisted on ruling by force. At Runnymede King John, the British monarch, was forced to sign the Magna Carta granting greater freedom to many human beings. The American Revolution was also a battle against oppression. But the struggle for freedom and righteousness is still going on. And it will finally be won at the glorious second coming of Christ when he will cleanse the earth of its sin. Then, in great power and glory, he will again pass through the land, and the disobedient and those who fight against freedom and righteousness will be destroyed. This memorial might help us to remember that disobedience to divine laws always brings plagues upon the offenders. Plagues were sent upon the Egyptians but they were also sent upon the Babylonians, the Sodomites and the people of Noah's day. And it was not just the first born that were destroyed by their sins. Many nations and many individuals have fallen when they have been unwilling to obey God's commands. And many of our present difficulties are coming upon us because we keep hardening our hearts and refusing to obey God. At the present moment there are more than ten plagues that we are compelled to wrestle with.

On February 7, 1833, the Lord gave a revelation to the world through the Prophet Joseph Smith, advising all people to abstain from alcohol, tobacco, tea, coffee, and other substances that are harmful to the body. In this, as in everything else, a blessing was promised for obedience, and some kind of plague always follows disobedience. This Word of Wisdom was not intended to apply only to the members of one church. It applies to every individual person upon the face of the earth. To those who obey this law the Lord gave an interesting promise saying, "And all saints who remember to keep and do these sayings, walking in obedience to the commandments, shall receive health in their navel and marrow to their bones; and shall find wisdom and great treasures of knowledge, even hidden treasures; and shall run and not be weary, and shall walk and not faint. And I, the Lord, give unto them a promise, that the destroying angel shall pass by them, as the children of Israel, and not slay them." (D&C 89:18-21)

We ought to make sure that the sign of obedience is clearly marked upon the doorposts of our activities. Over a hundred and thirty years after this commandment was given, the Surgeon General of the United States published a report giving some statistics about the amount of sickness and death caused in the United States because we are not following the Lord's instructions. The Egyptians had the plagues of frogs, and lice, and darkness, and boils, and blains. While these were all unpleasant, they didn't last very long. And certainly there was no way in which they could compare with the torment of the lung cancer, heart deterioration and the other diseases coming upon us in conection with our present day tobacco plague. The Egyptians had another advantage in that *their* plagues were limited to ten, whereas the hardening of our hearts have already taken us far beyond that number. We have a plague called alcoholism that by comparison would make all of the Egyptian plagues combined seem insignificant. We have a coffee plague, a plague of vandalism, a plague of draft-card burners, a plague of slogan-carriers and protest-marchers, wherein special groups try to force their beliefs onto others by appealing to subreasonable means.

We have a plague of beatniks with uncut hair, sloppy dress, distorted minds, and unclean bodies. The Egyptian plague of darkness lasted for only three days, and even then it was only a physical darkness; but we have a far more serious plague of darkness. About our modern variety the prophet said, "For, behold, the darkness shall cover the earth, and gross darkness the people." (Isa. 60:2) He said, "The earth also is defiled under the inhabitants thereof, because they have transgressed the laws, changed the ordinance, and broken the everlasting covenant." (Isa. 24:5) In our own day the Lord has said, "They walk in darkness as at noonday." We have a plague of atheism, as a result of which people are saying that God is dead or that he never existed, and that all divine revelation has ceased. There is a plague of criticism and a plague of the "New Morality," and a plague of rebellion.

The plague of murrain among the Egyptian cattle was less contagious than many of our present day moral and spiritual diseases. The thought of the black plague in the Middle Ages struck terror into the hearts of people, and yet its damage doesn't compare with the trouble caused by the present heavy traffic on that broad road leading to eternal death which doesn't seem to arouse much concern in us. The bubonic plague was characterized by fevers and chills, great prostration, and the swelling and enlargement of the glands. But we are also buboed with those lumps and growths that crime, sin, atheism and disobedience are forming in our lives. Some people even say that because of our new scientific know-how we no longer have any use for God or righteousness.

The most serious of all Egyptian plagues hit Egypt in that long, last, awful night when the angel of death passed through the land at midnight, and smote the first born of every family in Egypt. But again this was a physical death and only one per family was affected. Compare this with the plague of indifference, disobedience and immorality that brings a fate worse than death upon entire families. The scripture makes an interesting point when it says, "Fear not them which kill the body, but are not able to kill the soul: but rather fear him which is able to destroy both soul and body in hell." When the soul has passed the point of no return, it gets sick enough to be cast into hell. Each individual must be responsible for his own spiritual sickness. And what great opportunities we have when we erect our own memorial to put this great passover idea in force in our own minds! Then we will be able to mark the door posts of our own houses with God's righteousness, so that his angel of death and condemnation will pass over our houses.

Phantom Pains

SOMETIME AGO A friend of mine had an amputation performed on the lower ten inches of one leg. Since that time he has been going around the country trying to find some artificial limb manufacturer to supply him with some reasonable substitute for this important part of himself. But it is not easy to satisfactorily replace any part of the human machinery. And I am sure that as the resurrection approaches, one of the anticipations in which my friend will find greatest pleasure will be the expectation of getting his leg back into service.

Everyone has a very interesting relationship with himself. Because each of us is a duality, we all have a kind of double exposure of life. The spirit is an architect which fashions the body into its own likeness. Our spiritual bodies are constructed of a finer substance than that part which is flesh and bones. But flesh and bones can also become pretty important, especially if we have to walk around for a few years on a combination of cork, straps and springs that now serve some people as legs.

However, my friend also associates with his lost leg in a kind of phantom relationship. The dictionary says that a phantom is a specter or an immaterial semblance of something. It is an illusion which may be more imaginary than real, and my friend frequently imagines that he is wiggling his missing toes. He also gets pains in this foot that he doesn't have. Occasionally he feels that his leg is itching, and yet he has nothing there to scratch. When his missing foot gets tired, there isn't anything that he can do about it, as he has nothing to rest. These strange disturbances that keep coming from a foot that isn't there are sometimes called phantom pains. The nerve communications running to his brain are so stimulated that the pain seems to be originating in the amputated foot. Therefore my friend lives his life with one real foot and one phantom foot. It sometimes seems a little unfair that the phantom should give him so much pain while giving him so little actual service.

But this is not our only illusion in life. We have many other experiences with various kinds of phantoms, and we sometimes entertain a whole group of these immaterial specters that are not related to foot amputations.

Many of us are continually accosted by phantom fears, we are pursued by phantom memories, plagued by phantom ambitions, and stimulated by phantom anticipations. Severe pain sometimes comes from phantom feelings of guilt, although the sin that caused the suffering has long since been repented of so that the conscious mind has forgotten it. We have many destructive inferiority complexes and attitudes of belittling self-depreciation that cause trouble even though they are often more imaginary than real. In America each year we pay millions of dollars to get psychiatrists to dig down into the dark regions of our subconscious minds and ferret out those hidden, ghost-like forms of our past experiences that have lodged there causing a depression in our feelings and an uncomfortable sense of failure and misery. After an amputation the nerves that have been carrying the messages may lose their ability to tell us where the pains being reported are actually coming from. But our mistakes, our misdeeds, and even our imaginations create a host of ghostly specters causing confusion and distortion. And even though they may be immaterial, ghost-like resemblances of something that does not exist in actual being, they mix up our attitudes and activities. In fact, those ghosts that arise from our fears, our fancies, and our imaginations can generate trouble enough to throw our whole mental machinery off balance.

From the important field of psychosomatic medicine we learn that a large percentage of our stomach ulcers, nervous breakdowns, and heart diseases are caused by mental or emotional disturbances. The wrong kind of a spirit can readily break down our flesh. We get midget complexes in our minds, or bad attitudes in our emotions that can cause as much damage as any physical pain. And yet for one reason or another we allow this large group of phantoms to continually follow us around to eat away at our welfare and happiness.

For example, sin always produces phantoms. Frustrations produce phantoms, crooked thinking produces phantoms. The delirium tremens that can come out of a liquor bottle can cause us to be pursued by more terrifying imaginations than would be possible in reality. And the problems that come as a consequence of these phantoms range all the way from slight uneasiness to a poisoned misery that can actually cause physical death.

When our faith is destroyed by sin, or when our good works are cut off by our sloth, we can always depend upon having mysterious difficulties. When we lose our courage, or start rationalizing, or when we get mixed up about the real purposes and objectives of life, then these illusive specters begin haunting us with some measure of despair and unpleasantness.

Sometime ago a young woman who had just made an unsuccessful attempt to take her own life told of the severe mental and emotional depression that had held her in its power. But what was even worse, she said that she didn't know what was causing her trouble, even though she was committing some moral transgressions that were pouring spiritual poison into her blood stream. These foreign elements were producing enough distress in her soul to prompt her to commit suicide. Yet because of her need to keep on friendly terms with herself, she seemed unable to locate the source of the trouble or identify the pains that were causing her misery.

Most people have such a vast variety of good and bad experiences housed in their subconscious minds that the resulting pleasures and pains get so mixed up it becomes difficult to accurately pinpoint the origin of each. The dictionary says that a "pain" is a feeling that usually proceeds from some physical injury or derangement of bodily functions. However, one of our most distressing pains comes from a derangement in our conduct, or some faulty connections in our imaginations. Most of our physical pains can be corrected by medicine or surgery. Or sometimes with a little convalescence they will go away of their own accord. But the phantoms that get into our minds, corrupt our spirits, and break down our morale, are frequently much more difficult to reach with surgery or medicine.

Jesus was a great healer and yet in his greatest healing message he said, "Physician, heal thyself." Before we can practice this great art we need to know something about the particular disease causing our problem, and which part of us is being afflicted. Certainly our violations of the religious laws produce more pain than all of our bodily derangements put together.

No one can carry on a practice of alcoholism or dope addiction without causing some derangements that will always be accompanied by severe unpleasantness. Dishonesty causes pain, immorality causes pain, all kinds of failure cause pain. No one can inflict pain on someone else without himself suffering a disagreeable kind of misery and unhappiness. Then, when those pains get all mixed up in our lives, we may have some of the sensations of a lost foot.

We sometimes hear about some psychological problem when it is said that a particular person has his wires crossed. It is easily possible for some signal to get on the wrong wire and motivate the wrong responses. We can well imagine the confusion of a householder if the electrician improperly connected the wires. Then to turn the light switch in the bedroom might defrost the refrigerator in the kitchen, or to turn off the light in the garage might shut off the television in the living room. But think of the confusion when the personality wiring is operated by some irresponsible phantoms. Our anonymous messages from phantoms is like receiving harmful telephone calls without knowing who the caller is or where the message is coming from.

Sometime ago a young man with a whole bucketful of problems said, "I am all mixed up." Time after time he had violated his conscience and had shattered most of the Ten Commandments. He had made himself believe that all good people were stuffy and unhappy, and that in order to have any fun he must either be a criminal or a sinner. People show their defective educational wiring when they count it a burden to finish school, or believe that they must win a kind of endurance contest in misery in order to be decent or live the religion of Christ.

Some of our phantoms lead us to believe that everyone should endlessly do as he pleases, and that every kind of discipline is against his personal best interests. Dropouts from good are not wise people, and happiness does not come from indulgence in evil. As we get our wires crossed we begin producing a more abundant crop of vandals, delinquents, criminals and sinners. With enough time, our phantoms can get our wires so permanently crossed that we are always doing such unwise things as blaming the wrong causes, hating the wrong people and ending up at the wrong destinations. My friend lost his leg; how fortunate he is compared to those who lose their courage, their virtues, their good judgment, their righteous ambitions and then get their lives all mixed up with these phantom pains of evil. Most people have had the unpleasant sensation of being turned around in their directions. Then their best discernment tells them that north is south, and that the sun comes up in the west. Many travelers have lost their lives after they have lost their sense of direction.

In our journey through life we also need a North Star to serve us as a fixed point of reference. The gospel of Christ was intended to serve us as the fixed star in the sky of truth, and give us the most accurate sense of direction in guiding us to the proper objective.

I know a fine woman who married a man who has his wires crossed. All through their married lives he has so ridiculed her religion that she has abandoned her faith in God for the hope of having peace with a husband whose impulses have the wrong connections. He feels no obligation to obey the laws of morality involved in his marriage vows. Therefore his record now carries a large number of transgressions. He unlawfully indulges in liquor, which has placed his life under a heavy bondage to alcohol. These and other evil liberties have also been adopted by his children as they have followed him along the paths of unrighteousness. My friend lost a leg, but by getting his spiritual wires crossed this other man has lost his sobriety, his morals, his friends, and the best interests of his family. Now as he makes an uneasy approach to his grave, he blames everyone for his pains except himself. Because he has not been very good to life, life has responded in kind. And inasmuch as he has allowed evil delusions to rule his life he must now endure the misery of evil phantom pains.

One of the most important abilities of life is to learn that kind of housekeeping where we can clean out the phantoms, and stop the punishment that comes as a consequence. We need to make up our minds about where we want to go and have some better ideas about just how we are going to get there. Then we should put blinders on our eyes and allow no deviations from a straight course. For as we tolerate wrong, allow conflicts in our minds, and make exceptions in our judgment, our engine room receives the wrong signals and we end up with the wrong results.

According to God's immutable laws there must be conditions of reward in eternity as well as places of punishment, as evil always brings pain, and goodness always brings happiness. Certainly this law will not be done away with merely because we have passed the borders of this life. The scripture speaks as much of hell as it does of heaven. Satan and his followers will live in one place, whereas according to the natural law of consequences God and his followers dwell in another. It would be too bad if we got our wires crossed and ended up with the wrong crowd. It may be that we should first send our phantoms below and in imagination let them pre-live the pains of hell so that they will not want to suffer them actually.

Resentment

ONE OF THE BEST methods we have for judging another person is the way he handles his grievances. Before anyone goes very far in any undertaking in life, he usually meets some opposition and runs into the possibility of having his feelings hurt. He soon finds out that everyone does not think exactly as he does, and there is always the chance that some measure of friction may be developed. How one thinks and what he does under these circumstances will greatly influence his own success, as well as the service he may render to others.

One of the most commonly used methods of handling a grievance is for the aggrieved one to take offense or, as we sometimes say, we get "sore." We become resentful. The word "resent" is a very interesting word that represents a very dangerous trait. The word itself is derived from a Latin word meaning "to feel again." When our feelings get hurt we sometimes handle the situation by re-feeling the soreness over and over. When once we get the resentment habit, then we may suffer a thousand times for a single hurt. It is bad enough to be injured, but when we follow this destructive process of rerunning our injury, then we are really in trouble. There are some people who wake up in the middle of the night remembering the offenses that have been committed against them. They refeel their hurts, and each time the grievance is rerun the pain gets a little harder to bear. As this "refeeling" process is repeated, the grievance buries itself deeper and deeper into the personality. Soon the poisonous by-products overflow into the subconscious mind where they become a permanent part of our makeup. From this vantage point resentments often condition all future mental and personality responses. The slightest injury to a raw and festering personality can so multiply its importance as to keep one in constant pain. The consequences manifest themselves in many unpleasant ways, including peevish and touchy responses to life. This always reduces our happiness and success, and our mental, spiritual, and bodily health is adversely affected. When an offended person says, "That burns me up," he is making a fairly accurate statement of what is actually happening.

One of the synonyms of resentment listed in the dictionary is "ill will." The comparison is a good one, and when the will gets ill, the personality not only loses much of its health and strength but the other people involved are forced to suffer so many kinds of never-ending unpleasantness. It is certain that "ill will" has killed success in countless people, not only in their occupations but also in their social and spiritual relationships. The blessing of eternal life itself has often been lost because of resentment or ill will. And a new crop of these unfortunate victims is being cut down every day by this deadly disease.

As an example, here is an occupational case history of resentment. In 1937 a friend of mine had a job with a firm where he had wonderful opportunities. Everything was just fine until he became resentful over some small thing. No one intended to hurt him, but one's own imagination can often play the most grim tricks. The more my friend thought about the situation the worse he felt about it. As if to deliberately torture him, his imagination began picking up and magnifying every little bit of evidence to justify its position. And it was as though each additional bit of evidence was an individual poison that was being dumped into his ailing personality. As the resentment grew, his feelings began to swell up like a bucketful of bloated rice, and in their diseased state they continued to make his life unnatural and unhappy.

In the art of managing our own lives we should remember that if even a little resentment is given a free reign, it can sometimes grow to such proportions as to ruin our health and happiness, and even overcome our reason. If my friend had relied upon his reason instead of his feelings he would never have given this tiny offense a second thought. But, as he nourished his resentment by rerunning it, it soon developed to giant proportions. In justifying himself and trying to enlist the sympathy of his friends he further magnified the offense, and every time it was retold the soreness and ill will increased.

Pope described this damaging situation when he wrote:
> The flying rumor gathered as it rolled,
> And all who told it added something new,
> And all who heard it made enlargement too;
> In every ear it spread, on every tongue it grew.

We are great exaggerators of our own grievances. But my friend accepted his own prejudices at their face value. This simple delusion that he had been wronged made him feel so badly that he quit the best job he ever had, and thereby perpetrated a double injury upon himself. Even after many years he is still replaying this same old poisonous record of resentment. And each rerun is like thrusting a rusty dagger into his own vitals, where it twists and turns to cause him a maximum amount of pain. Each time he refeels this ancient hurt, additional damage is done to his personality, his spirituality and his mentality. Because of this weakness he naturally hasn't done very well in his occupation. His spiritual accomplishment has also suffered severely, and he has become old and sick and sour before his time.

Brigham Young once said that "He who takes offense where none is intended is a fool," but he is probably a fool who takes an offense into his heart even if it is intended.

Just suppose that someone *had* deliberately tried to hurt my friend and that a great injustice had really been done. Even then, what kind of logic could prompt him to *rerun* those poisonous feelings through the delicate tissues of his mind and heart to rehurt himself? We know what happens when somebody throws a handful of sand into the workings of delicate expensive machinery. But our personality machinery is even more sensitive to the gritty irritation of poisonous foreign matter. We may not be able to prevent an evil from coming our way, but we don't need to increase the damage by a daily rerun. More than most other things, we need to get the sand out of our machinery and the resentments out of our minds, and the hates out of our hearts. The greatest of all authorities on this subject said, "Love your enemies, do good to them that hate you, and pray for them that despitefully use you and persecute you." He meant that we should forget our grievances, and thereby keep all of the poison out of our lives. I am confident that Jesus was not thinking only of the welfare of the enemy. He was also thinking of the welfare of the one who was suffering from the offense. The hater always receives more damage than the hated. In one of his greatest Beatitudes, Jesus said, "Blessed is he, whosoever shall not be offended. . ." (Matt. 11:6.) To indicate that he was in dead earnest, he said, "And if thy right hand offend thee, cut it off, and cast it from thee: for it is more profitable for thee that one of thy members should perish, and not that thy whole body should be cast into hell." (Matt. 5:30.)

Someone has put this problem in a question form for us to answer. He said, "If you were bitten by a rattlesnake and had two choices: (1) you could chase and kill the rattlesnake, or (2) you could get the poison out of your system, which course would you take? You must choose only one or the other, because there is insufficient time to do both." In actual practice there are a great many people who answer that question by chasing the rattlesnake while they themselves are bloating up making ready to die. Very frequently we are more concerned with putting people in their places and getting even than we are in getting the poison out of our own blood streams. We have coined a phrase for one who has delirium tremens. We say he has snakes in his boots. Real snakes have hurt very few people, but these imaginary snakes do a lot of many kinds of damage. We should keep ourselves free of them by reducing our susceptibility to resentments. Resentments cause us nervous breakdowns and make us whiners and complainers, and give us a case of spiritual and social D.T.'s. With hearts full of vengeance we sometimes continue to *rerun* the poison and *resuffer* the slights and *refeel* the hurts.

This very bad habit causes us to fail in our occupations, and it also causes us to fail in our lives. Wouldn't it be interesting if we knew in advance how many of us will be sent to hell because of our resentments? Being sore and acting revengeful causes us to commit many sins. One of the most common reasons why we fail to go to church is because we don't like someone. Someone once justified himself in not going to church because he found too many hypocrites in the church. His friend said, "Don't let that keep you away, because we can always make room for one more." Think how many lives are ruined because we allow the jealousies and bitterness caused by someone else to break our spirit and bring this evil hate into our lives.

One very wise man, thinking of resentment, once said, "I will not let my enemy make me sin." One of the chief characteristics of Satan himself is that he is a hater, and he tries to fill everyone else with this same kind of evil. If he can get bitterness into our hearts and resentment into our minds, he pretty well has us in his power. There is an old axiom that whom God would destroy he first makes mad. Solomon said, "Keep thy heart with all thy diligence, for out of it are the issues of life." All of us know of the truth of these things as they apply to others, yet very few of us really practice these great Christian doctrines where we ourselves are concerned. We seem to love to talk and think about other people unfavorably, and we stir up hatred and resentment in our hearts until we finally puff up and die of our own poison.

We should make sure that no matter what happens we will never allow resentments to chew our vital organs to pieces. My friend mentioned above has needlessly and profitlessly filled his system with the cancer of failure and ill will. I suppose that the only way that he will ever be cured is by dying, and I doubt that even that will help him very much.

In our own interests we had better follow the counsel of Jesus and just forget our hates! Then it will be easier to love our enemies and to develop a more practical method for handling our grievances. Suppose that someone does step on our toes occasionally! Injured toes can be cured much more quickly than a bad case of ill will. For, once this damaging ill will has been aroused, who can tell where it will end? Most resentments can easily become malignant, and the mortality and the morbidity rates are always very high so far as resentments and hates are concerned.

Recently a man came to tell me what a terrible person his divorced wife was. He was putting on an organized campaign to hurt her. He was trying to get her fired from her job, and poison her friends against her. She had done nothing to hurt him. She had not asked the court for any alimony. During much of their married life she had worked to support him. She had no other heart interest. His trouble was that he had infected himself with ill will, which had made his whole mentality sick. In this condition he was now doing all these destructive, unchristian things with the zeal of one possessed of an evil spirit. The harder he worked at it the more sick he became. He seemed like one completely devoid of intelligence, reason or mercy. Every place he goes he reruns his bitterness under the pressure of the most intense emotion. There seems to be no cure in sight for him. I don't know how much harm he will be able to do to his divorced wife, but his ill will foretells social, mental and spiritual calamity for himself, either in or out of a mental hospital. In his frame of mind he cannot long escape failure in his occupation, nor can he long stand up physically with this much poison constantly running through his system. If he isn't already mentally unbalanced he probably soon will be.

We remember the experience of Shakespeare's Lady Macbeth, who helped to thrust a dagger into the heart of the sleeping King Duncan. Then she *reran* her feelings of guilt until it sent her insane. She washed her hands a thousand times, trying to get the blood off her hands, but the uncleanness was not on her hands, it was in her mind and heart, where it is a little harder to get at. Her husband finally sought medical help. He said to the doctor, "Canst thou not minister to a mind diseased? Pluck from a memory a rooted sorrow, raze out the written troubles of the brain and, with some sweet oblivious antidote, cleanse the stuffed bosom of that perilous stuff which weighs upon the heart?" But the doctor said, "Therein the patient must minister unto himself." And that is the way it is. There are times when we must be our own doctors, and getting and keeping the poison out of our own hearts is one of life's greatest abilities.

Jesus was called the "great physician." His ability was not curing just physical diseases. He was also an expert in curing people with sick souls. And with the thought of getting us well, he compounded those great prescriptions which said "Love your enemies," "Think no evil," "Learn how to handle your grievances," and "Get rid of your resentments and ill will." We hope that we may develop enough wisdom and love that we may also be great physicians, and at least that we may heal ourselves.

The Salt of the Earth

A LARGE PART OF our language is made up of symbols, word pictures and comparisons. The right illustrations can beautify our word meanings and help us to more clearly understand the ideas that are expressed. Jesus made his own speech picturesque and meaningful with many colorful parables. And while most of his discussions pertain to ordinary things that are easily understood, his parables illuminate his ideas and help to get his messages over with a maximum of effectiveness. His greatest discourse, known as the Sermon on the Mount, is made up of several of these interesting pictures and comparisons.

Immediately after Jesus had given the nine blessings called the "Beatitudes" or the "beautiful attitudes," he made two other comparisons trying to illustrate some of those qualities that should enrich human life. He said to his audience, "Ye are the salt of the earth." He wanted them to feel that they themselves were worthwhile. But one of the important teaching characteristics of Jesus was that he always let people see both sides of the possibility. And so in making them aware of what would happen if the prescribed requirements were not carried out he said, "But if the salt has lost its savor, wherewith shall it be salted? It is thenceforth good for nothing, but to be cast out, and to be trodden under foot of men." Then to add emphasis to this universal need for excellence he gave another illustration saying, "Ye are the light of the world. A city that is set on an hill cannot be hid. Neither do men light a candle, and put it under a bushel, but on a candlestick; and it giveth light unto all that are in the house. Let your light so shine before men, that they may see your good works, and glorify your Father which is in heaven." (Matt. 5:13-16) His listeners had a number of close-at-hand examples of the things he was talking about. For example, the area in which they lived contains an almost inexhaustible supply of salt. The Dead Sea is the saltiest body of water in the world. By weight it contains over 26% of salt and other substances suspended in its water. At the southern end of the Dead Sea there is a mountain of salt measuring seven miles long and

several hundred feet high. The "city set upon the hill" referred
to by Jesus might have been his own city of Nazareth. In the
days of Jesus this was a sizeable town with as many as fifteen
thousand inhabitants, although it has now dwindled to a small
village of only three or four thousand. It is located on the south
ridges of Lebanon above the plains of Esdraelon. We remember
Luke referring to the time when the people of Nazareth led
Jesus to the brow of the hill, intending to throw him down head-
long, (Luke 4:9) but he passed unseen out of their midst. This
city situated on the mountainside must have presented an impres-
sive night scene to those people who looked up to it from the
valley below. These substances of light and salt are very important for themselves alone, but they have also served as
important human symbols. Jesus was always trying to get this
quality of light shining as brightly as possible in human lives,
and also develop therein the genuineness of salt full of savor.
It would be very interesting if we could really picture the kind
of people that Jesus had in mind as he spoke of this "city upon
the hill," and pictured people as "the salt of the earth."

In addition to those interesting substances of air, water and
soil, salt and light are among our most important human resources.
Common salt or sodium chloride is a crystalline compound that
occurs in nature as a mineral. It is absolutely necessary to sus-
tain both plant and animal life, and yet it can destroy both if
applied in too large amounts. Salt is a preservative, and it is also
used for seasoning food. In countries where salt was less plentiful
it was occasionally used as the medium of exchange, and employees have sometimes taken their wages in salt. We still describe unprofitable employees as those who are not "worth their
salt." But certainly Jesus was thinking in very complimentary
terms when he said, "Ye are the salt of the earth." It is also
quite likely that he had someone in mind with seriously lessened
values when he spoke of those who had lost their savor. The
saltiness of life is provided by those traits that give life its
liveliness, genuineness and pungency. Interesting anecdotes and
illustrations are sometimes said to provide the salt to an interesting discussion. We represent another human trait when we
say that the words of some people should be taken with a grain
of salt. By this expression we are cautioning ourselves that care
should be exercised when one's genuineness is in question. Then
we hold reservations or make allowances in our acceptance. Any

lack of genuineness in us causes an attitude of skepticism. We can cure or preserve things with salt. Salt also means thrift. And when we want to save our money, we express our intentions by saying that we are going to salt it away for the future.

In addition to salt being one of our most essential articles of diet, it also symbolizes hospitality and faith. Under the old Mosaic law of sacrifice it was required that salt should always be included in the offering.

With all of these meanings it would probably be impossible to know exactly what Jesus had in mind when he said, "Ye are the salt of the earth." But then, as now, we can be sure that it was a very praiseworthy term. In both ages this expression represents high quality and genuineness, with a kind of purity that permits no adulterations. It signifies someone who can be trusted and believed in and followed. It means durability, fidelity and eternity. On several occasions the Old Testament refers to a "covenant of salt." (Num. 18:18, II Chron. 13:5, Lev. 2:13) It betokened an indissolvable alliance made between friends. This "covenant of salt" meant particularly that the people were bound by sacred obligations of fidelity to the king, and this gave added significance to the Israelite custom of including salt in their offerings to God. But about any way you look at it, to be "the salt of the earth" is a great idea.

As we think about this phrase, many people come to our own minds who seem to qualify under the Master's meaning. I always get a real thrill in remembering that great old prophet Job. The scriptures tell of a time when the Lord gave Job a very high compliment. While talking to Satan, God said, "Hast thou considered my servant Job, that there is none like him in the earth, a perfect and an upright man, one that feareth God and escheweth evil." Satan tried to belittle Job's virtues by saying that they came about because Job was so successful and had so many advantages; so God permitted Satan to subject Job to the most severe tests. In fact the Lord said, "All that he hath is in thy power, only upon himself put not thine hand." Then everything bad began happening to Job. But even though he lost his property and his family, Job still worshipped God. After being severely reduced in status, Job said, "Naked came I into the world and naked shall I return thither; the Lord gave and the Lord hath taken away; blessed be the name of the Lord." (Job. 1:21) Job was "the salt of the earth." But soon Job became the victim of another list of calamities. He lost his health, his body was afflicted with sores and he lost his friends. But Job's faith never wavered, and of God he said, "Though he slay me yet will I trust in him." (Job 13:15) And if you would like to hear an inspiring personal testimony, listen to Job as he says, "Oh that my words were now written! Oh that they were printed in a book! That they were graven with an iron pen and lead in the rock forever! For I know that my redeemer liveth, and that he shall stand at the latter day upon the earth: And though after my skin worms destroy this body, yet in my flesh shall I see God: Whom I shall see for myself, and mine eyes shall behold, and not another, though my reins be consumed within me."

Job was great because of the things that he considered important. He said, "While my breath is in me, and the spirit of God is in my nostrils; my lips shall not speak wickedness, nor my tongue utter deceit . . . till I die I will not remove mine integrity from me. My righteousness I hold fast, and will not let it go . . . so long as I live." (Job 27:3-6) What a great person! Job said, "There is a spirit in man: and the inspiration of the Almighty giveth them understanding." (Job 32:8) And what a wonderful spirit this great old prophet himself had! He was "the salt of the earth," and he lost none of his savor in being overwhelmed with troubles. His light that was placed high on the candlestick was never lowered. And he not only lighted the way for those of his own day but he still inspires us.

I often think of one of my own contemporaries who has greatly contributed to my personal welfare. The first time I ever met him I was greatly inspired with his friendly, pleasant cheerfulness. And in all the years since he has lost none of his savor. I have always known that I could trust him implicitly in every way, even to telling me some annoying truths about myself. Everyone needs a friend who is salty enough to point out his mistakes occasionally, and to talk to him frankly about those things that may be hidden by his own blind spots. My friend has always been very capable personally. He has a good character and high ideals. He adds up to be the "salt of the earth." He is a light set upon a candlestick, and from him I have received a great deal of personal illumination. I think Jesus had someone like him in mind when he made this statement in the first place.

And we are also all acquainted with the kind of people whom Jesus must have had in mind whose salt had lost its savor. So frequently some people disappoint us. When they lack this preserving quality, they often spoil too easily.

When the Lord selected Saul to be the king of Israel, he was a wonderful young man. But as soon as he got a little power in his hands his quality began to deteriorate. When he began making too many selfish decisions, his life began losing its value. He became disobedient, willful and moody. His bad traits and his evil spirit eventually made him useless as king, and the Lord finally had to get rid of him. It is a heartbreaking experience to see someone lose so much of his savor that no longer is he able to serve the constructive purpose for which his life was intended. When the light of the candlestick gets too dim, many people become dropouts from faith, or they let down in their industry or lose interest in their ideals. A workman loses his savor when he loafs on the job; a salesman loses his savor when he cheats his customer; a husband loses savor when he treats his wife with less respect than is her due; and a wife loses her savor when she allows a lessening in the love, honor and support given to her husband. Hitler killed millions of human beings because they were not members of his race, and he caused untold misery and heartache to many millions more. But on a smaller scale we sometimes exhibit similar tendencies when we resort to character assassinations, or allow any measure of bitterness or selfishness to get into our lives. Sometimes we are losing our savor and aren't aware of it. One of our greatest virtues is to be alert to any lessening that may be taking place in our salty activities or attitudes. There are so many processes by which we allow ourselves to become less than we should be. So frequently we resort to some kinds of wrong where the strong oppress the weak, the bellicose intimidates the peaceful, and we allow emotion to triumph over reason.

The famous psychologist Dr. Edward L. Thorndyke tells the story of some howler monkeys who used to have trouble in maintaining a peaceful coexistence with each other. When one group of monkeys trespassed on someone else's territory the invaders were immediately met with a vigorous chorus of howls. The intruders replied by howling back. The contest continued until one side was out-howled and decided to withdraw. We lose some savor when we attempt to control by an exercise of our howling instincts.

In saying, "Ye are the salt of the earth" the Master was probably trying to promote us to our highest denomination by reminding us that we were created in God's image and endowed with a set of God's attributes. If we lose our savor, the offspring of God may miss the goal of eventually becoming like God our eternal parent. We can only realize the image when we manifest God's greatness in what we do. God has given us a set of standards to live by, and only as we follow through can we qualify for that high title of "salt of the earth." How unfortunate if we should lose our savor and become something less than genuine! If we could not be trusted, even God would have to take our lives with a grain of salt or discard us altogether as he did King Saul. To be worth our salt in God's eyes is a very great accomplishment. Certainly our greatest opportunity is to be the right kind of people. Then not only are we a benefit to ourselves, but we may encourage others by bringing happiness and uplift to everyone. When our light is high enough on the candlestick that we may fill the house with light, God may compliment us as he did Job, and in addition we may hear the Master say, "Ye are the salt of the earth, ye are a city set upon a hill."

Satan

THERE IS ONE individual who is presently causing the people of our world a lot of difficulties. And we might help our personal situation somewhat if we knew more about him. He is called by several different names including Satan, Lucifer, the Devil, the Dragon, the Serpent, and some others. One of our difficulties comes from the fact that so many people don't believe that he exists. Others think of him only as some harmless figure of speech that has no reality and involves no actual danger. One minister said, "Of course I believe in the devil." He said, "I believe in many devils. I believe in the devil of fear, the devil of hate, the devil of lust, and the devil of discouragement." Others spread enough mystery about him to take away their fear. One minister said, "We don't know where he came from or what his purpose is. It is all very speculative. No one knows for sure." Probably the first step in solving our Satan problem is to believe that he exists. Of course, anyone who believes in the Bible must believe in Satan.

Jesus gives an account of his own encounter with Satan in the wilderness during his fast and trial. (Mark 1:13, Matt. 4) The scripture says that Satan entered into Judas Iscariot and caused him to betray Jesus. Satan helped to bring about the fall of Adam. Certainly there is no more speculation in the scripture about Satan than there is about God.

There are those who think that God is dead; but judging by the fruits of Satan's labors no one could very well make that claim about Satan, and in our own interests we should know something about him.

Abraham Lincoln once said that when he was preparing for a debate he spent one-fourth of his time deciding what he was going to say, and three-fourths thinking about what his opponent was going to say. There is a philosophy among salesmen that if you desire to be successful you must be well informed about your competition. Certainly if you want to win a football championship, you had better know something about your opposition so that you can successfully plan for a victory. It is very helpful for a country at war to have sources of information inside the enemy country to tell what its strengths and weaknesses are.

However, the greatest of all wars involve Satan. He is not only the cause but is usually the chief combatant. In our individual conflicts he is an expert in getting a hold upon the hearts of people. He is able to stir them up to do all kinds of harmful things. From the Bible, supplemented by latter-day revelation, we may learn a great deal about Satan. We do know who he is and how he got into his present situation. We know what his purposes are and what his final destiny will be.

To begin with, Satan and all of the legions that follow him are the spirit offspring of God. We first learned about Satan when we first learned about ourselves. Nothing is more clearly stated in the scripture than the fact that the life of Christ did not begin at Bethlehem. Neither did it end on Calvary. He said, "I came forth from the Father and am come into the world. Again I leave the world and go unto the Father." It is just as clear that our lives did not begin when we were born, neither will they end when we die. And Satan also lived for a long time before this earth was formed. The scripture tells us of a time when we were all assembled in the grand council of heaven. We were discussing the conditions that should obtain upon this earth when we would come to live here. We were to come here to be "added upon" with these beautiful, wonderful bodies without which we could never have a fullness of joy. This is where we would be given that great power of procreation, where we could have children and organize a family and have it sealed together under the power of the priesthood as the basic unit throughout eternity. Then we walked by sight. We have all seen God. He is our Father. But we were told that we must learn to walk a little way by faith. We had to be tested and proven and tried. God's plan was based on the individual free agency of man. Because it was known that with our free agency not everyone would be successful, a Savior was to be appointed to redeem us from death on condition of our repentance.

The prophet Isaiah gave a partial view of this proceeding when he said, "And I heard the voice of the Lord saying, 'Whom shall I send and who shall go for us?'" (Isaiah 6:8) Modern revelation tells us that there were two who responded. One was the first begotten Son of God in the spirit who was particularly qualified for this special mission. He answered and said, "Here am I, send me. Father, thy will be done, and the glory be thine forever." But another also spoke, and it was Lucifer, the brilliant son of the morning. He said, "Behold, here am I, send me. I will be thy son and I will redeem all mankind, that one soul shall not be lost and surely I will do it; wherefore give me thine honor." And the Father said, "I will send the first. And the second was angry, and kept not his first estate; And, at that day, many followed after him." (Abraham 3:27-28; Moses 4:1-4)

Using this free agency Lucifer rebelled against God, and sought to destroy the plan of God. As a consequence, John the Revelator says: "And there was war in heaven: Michael and his angels fought against the dragon; and the dragon fought and his angels, and prevailed not; neither was their place found any more in heaven. And the great dragon was cast out, that old serpent, called the Devil, and Satan, which deceiveth the whole world: he was cast out into the earth, and his angels were cast out with him." (Rev. 12:7-9)

About this same event Isaiah comments as follows: "How art thou fallen from heaven, oh Lucifer, son of the morning! How art thou cut down to the ground, which didst weaken the nations! For thou hast said in thine heart, I will ascend into heaven, I will sit also upon the mount of the congregation, in the sides of the north: I will ascend above the heights of the clouds; I will be like the most High. Yet thou shalt be brought down to hell, to the sides of the pit." (Isaiah 14:12-16) Satan drew away a third part of all of the hosts of heaven after him. (Rev. 12:4; D&C 29:36-38)

The magnitude of this event is a little staggering. Of the two-thirds that followed God, some 80 billion have already lived upon this earth since Father Adam. This would mean that the one-third that followed Satan, and were therefore deprived of a mortal body, would number at least 40 billion. It is also interesting to contemplate the kind of personage Lucifer must have been, to contend so successfully with God and influence such a vast number to prefer to follow him instead of God the Father and his pre-eminent first-born Son in the spirit. And what a tragedy for Satan to lead such a vast host to their eternal doom, and what a price he and they have had to pay!

The New Testament prophet Jude says, "And the angels which kept not their first estate, but left their own habitation, he hath reserved in everlasting chains under darkness unto the judgment of the great day." (Jude 6) In speaking of this event in our own day, the Lord said, "And they were thrust down, and thus came the devil and his angels; and, behold, there is a place prepared for them from the beginning, which place is hell." (D&C 29:37-38)

We know what great misfortunes have sometimes befallen men in this life when they have allowed their unrighteous ambitions to get so much out of control as to bring failure and unhappiness upon themselves and others. But here is the greatest of all disasters causing the maximum of eternal suffering. Lucifer's disobedience was greatly regretted in heaven, as the Lord says, "And he was called Perdition, for the heavens wept over him." (D&C 76:25-27)

Lucifer's proposal for using force to bring about the accomplishment is particularly interesting right now inasmuch as freedom and free agency are again being challenged. And again freedom and free agency are by far the most critical issues in the world. Lucifer had argued that he would save everyone. He had said, "Not one soul shall be lost." (Moses 1:4) But it would be done by compulsion. In that event human beings would be not much better than mere mechanical contrivances. For how could we ever gain any degree of merit without a chance to choose for ourselves? But the advantages of freedom were so tremendous in the minds of God and a majority of his children, that this most terrible of all wars was fought to preserve it. And Lucifer was expelled from heaven because he sought by force to deprive us of this great blessing. It is interesting to note that to this day Satan has not changed his opinion about the use of force. And many of those who fought against him in heaven have now in some degree gone over to his side.

Some of those who presently represent Satan in our world would, if they thought they could, deprive every human being of his God-given freedom without a moment's hesitation. And some important modern-day revelations make it clear that this great modern American nation has been set apart as the sanctuary of freedom with a mission to keep freedom and human dignity alive in the world. And God himself has ordained that

no dictators should prosper upon this land. It is our individual
mission, as it was in our ante-mortal existence, to safeguard
freedom against every evil power that would rob us of it.

As we know much about Lucifer's past, so we also know
quite a lot about his present and his future. He is still carrying
on his desperate rebellion against God. The scripture says that
he knows that his time is short and he is therefore raging furiously
to overthrow any and every part of the work of God, and to
destroy the success of all of those who opposed him in the council
of heaven. His influence will continue as long as he has this
freedom of action which he tried to take away from others by
force. He will continue to destroy until the glorious second coming of Christ to judge the world. When the millennium of peace
begins upon the earth, then for the ensuing thousand years Satan
will be bound and have no power.

John the Revelator says, "And I saw an angel come down
from heaven, having the key to the bottomless pit and a great
chain in his hand. And he laid hold on the dragon, that old
serpent, which is the Devil, and Satan, and bound him a thousand
years. And cast him into the bottomless pit, and shut him up,
and set a seal upon him, that he should deceive the nations
no more, till the thousand years should be fulfilled: And after
that he must be loosed a little season." But his own freedom
to do evil during this period will be short-lived, and when he
again begins causing bloodshed and trouble his end will come
speedily.

John the Revelator says, "And when the thousand years are
expired, Satan shall be loosed out of his prison, and shall go
out to deceive the nations which are in the four quarters of
the earth, Gog and Magog, to gather them together to battle: the
number of whom is as the sand of the sea." (Rev. 20:7-8) And
a modern-day revelation records the end of Satan's importance
by saying, "And then [after the thousand years are finished] he
shall be loosed for a little season, that he may gather together his
armies. And Michael, the seventh angel, even the archangel, shall
gather together his armies, even the hosts of heaven. And the
devil shall gather together his armies; even the hosts of hell, and
shall come up to battle against Michael and his armies. And
then cometh the battle of the great God; and the devil and his
armies shall be cast away into their own place, that they shall

not have power over the saints any more at all." (D&C 88:111-114)

We are greatly stimulated by thinking of the lives of some great men and contemplating the good that they have done in raising others to success and happiness. But what about the negative stimulation that we should get from thinking of the eternal misery and degradation of the billions caused by following the wrong influence? Or, think of the tragedy of those who have gone over to the side of Satan during their second estate, many of whom will share his fate in hell. In our own day the Lord has warned us of our own danger by saying, "And the righteous shall be gathered on my right hand unto eternal life; and the wicked on my left hand will I be ashamed to own before the Father; Wherefore I will say unto them — Depart from me, ye cursed, into everlasting fire, prepared for the devil and his angels." (D&C 29:27-28) As long as Satan is free in the world, we will have a powerful adversary to contend with. His ability comes largely as a result of his superior knowledge. And we can more intelligently combat him by increasing our own knowledge. He is presently able to deceive even some of God's very elect. And if one who was once designated as the light bearer has lost his exaltation, we should be warned of our own danger and leave all evil strictly alone. A great prophet once said that if we could look into heaven for five minutes we would learn more than by reading all that has ever been written on the subject. It naturally follows that if we could look into hell for five minutes and feel its suffering, we would never want to run the risk of ever being enticed to go there.

Scars

ONE OF THE questions usually asked during a life insurance examination is "Do you have any scars or marks of identification?" When an insurance company assumes a substantial financial responsibility in someone's life, it needs a dependable means of identification, but it also likes to know how these scars were obtained. If one's scars indicate that he has a proneness for accidents or that he is engaged in a highly hazardous occupation, the company may decline the application. Of course, interest in scars differs greatly with different people. Under the influence of the old German militarism, battle scars and sword wounds were often the most prized badges of honor and distinction. A soldier's cuts and gashes were a part of the evidence that long and difficult battles had been fought and won.

In our day, we put ribbons and medals on a soldier's chest and give him the "Purple Heart" if he is wounded in the line of duty. But all that the grizzled old warriors of former times had to show for their success was that they had survived the battle and had their distinctions cut into their faces. Before Horatio Nelson became the conqueror of Napoleon, he had lost one arm and one eye and had innumerable wounds. Some battle scars are badges of honor, and some are the marks of sin. The galley slave may not have been especially proud of the scars that were cut into his back, and a criminal may want to hide the marks of evil that he carries in his person. A few years ago the United States public enemy number one was a Chicago gangster named Scarface Al Capone. This man could be recognized by the many unsightly gashes that mutilated his features. His expression and his mental activities also indicated that some scars had been left upon his soul.

There is a great deal of evidence that this idea of scars will carry over with us after we have crossed the boundaries of mortality. And it may be that when our eternal status is being determined, God will also ask, "Do you have any scars or marks of identification?" It is one of life's most significant facts that all human beings are the self-registering instruments of their own lives. Psychologists tell us that every thought that passes through our minds makes a groove, or pathway, that remains there forever. Our toil and every other experience registers itself in our hands, our muscles, and our features. What we do always makes us what we are. Every emotion that penetrates our ambitions or settles in our hearts will alter our lives one way or the other.

If you take a photograph of someone at the instant he is possessed by an intense rage, the horrible disfigurement that shows in his face will be permanently retained in the picture. Then when his face is released from its passion it will tend to go back to its original form, but the recovery is never quite complete. As each recurrence takes place the permanent distortion of that particular evil is stamped a little deeper and tends to become a little more permanent. Soon the noble image of the Dr. Jekyll in our lives may be wearing the frightful visage of the depraved Mr. Hyde. Because we are self-registering instruments, we have little need of a recording angel to look over our shoulders and jot down our evil deeds in his book. When our records are complete, the evil will be clearly seen in our shifty eyes, our sinful faces, and those mental distortions that we ourselves have brought about. Our wrongs will also show up as defects in our personalities and as damaging scars upon our souls. Of course, the most ugly human blotches are never physical; they are always spiritual and moral.

The dictionary describes a scar as the mark that is left upon the body after the wound or sore has healed. Given a little time the injury itself may no longer concern us; but it is frequently much more difficult to get rid of the scars. Sometimes the sore itself never really heals. But the ugly patchwork of gashes that may be cut into one's face are not as unsightly as those that disfigure his reputation, or mutilate his spirituality and prevent it from performing its normal life's functions. Sometime ago a friend showed me a scar on his hand. The former injury was evidenced only by a thin, white, calloused line, but my friend said, "That scar never sweats." To at least that extent the past injury was still preventing a normal body function. Many people have had serious internal operations, and sometimes their systems get so filled with adhesions and scar tissues that effective natural responses become difficult for the future.

We might make a helpful comparison by understanding the phenomenon that takes place when one scars or disfigures the green rind of a sapling quaking aspen. The effect of the injury can never be erased. Instead of eliminating the scar, the mutilation in the bark will actually get worse. Then, in place of a pretty, smooth surface as seen in the uninjured trees, this particular quaking aspen will keep enlarging its injuries as it develops its dark, rough, growing disfigurement.

Humans are also more or less like that. A few little friendly drinks of liquor to begin with may eventually produce all of the scars of alcoholism. The scars of nicotine and immorality also have their own way of increasing in importance. There are other kinds of scars that are difficult to get rid of. For example, if you twist a young oak, a scarred and crooked tree will advertise your deed for centuries to come. The Japanese capitalize on this idea by producing ornamental midget oak trees. They wrap a copper wire tightly around the root of a young oak tree shoot just below the surface of the ground. This stunts its growth so that the young tree may produce all of the appearances of maturity without growing more than fifteen or eighteen inches tall.

Human lives are also stunted, twisted, and perverted by those sinful pressures that we impose upon ourselves. In the process enough scar tissue and rough bark is developed to prevent a normal happy functioning in their souls. Other kinds of injuries may also be very serious. A poet gave us something to think about along this line when he said:

> I walked through the woodland meadows
> Where sweet the thrushes sing,
> And I found on a bed of mosses
> A bird with a broken wing.
>
> I healed his wound, and each morning
> He sang his old sweet strain;
> But the bird with the broken pinion
> Never soared as high again.
>
> I found a young life stricken
> By sin's seductive art;
> And, touched by a Christ-like pity,
> I took him to my heart.
>
> He lived with a noble purpose,
> And he struggled not in vain,
> But the life that sin had stricken
> Never soared as high again.

Each loss has its compensation —
There is healing in every pain.
But the bird with the broken pinion
Never soars as high again.

In many situations and on every side, we see this philosophy repeating itself. Thousands of beautiful young people and thousands of wonderful older people each day are being slashed and cut and gouged and twisted in such ways that they may later be knotted and crooked and stunted. Many scars are made as we rationalize to each other that "everybody's doing it," or we minimize the evil in ourselves by saying, "This is such a little sin that it couldn't hurt us very much." But it doesn't take a very big wrong to seriously jeopardize one's chances to live at his maximum.

The other evening the newspaper told the story of a heartbroken mother who had just discovered that her young son was a dope addict. At first she just couldn't believe it; she had had such confidence in her manly son. His splendid young life had previously held such promise, but now it is completely at the mercy of this dreadful substance called dope. It seems absolutely incredible that intelligent people, knowing the evil powers and heart-rending terrors concealed in narcotics, would deliberately take up a habit that produces such tortures. We wouldn't deliberately allow a rattlesnake to occupy the bed in which we expected to sleep. Then why do we tamper with immorality, dishonesty, alcohol, and those other instruments of evil that can so quickly destroy the utility and beauty of our lives? Most of us have a tendency to try to lock the barn door only after the horse has gone. It is a wasteful process to spend part of our time downgrading our lives, and then spend the balance in a state of useless regret. It is strange that so many people can see no harm in their present sins and have so much confidence in their ability to heal up the wounds after they have been made. It would be difficult for a quaking aspen to smooth over the rough spot growing in its green rind, or for an oak tree to straighten out its crooked, twisted trunk. It is even more difficult to erase the scars or untwist the distortions we frequently cause in the lives of other people.

A few years ago a beautiful young woman who had just come home from the hospital with her third child was out for an evening's automobile ride with her husband and their family. Without warning, a drunken driver crashed into them head-on. Her husband was killed, and she will be a hopeless cripple throughout the remainder of her life. She will be forever tortured by her continual pain and hopelessness. One moment she was strong, proud, and happy about life's prospects, and the next moment she lay paralyzed and bleeding, doomed to weary years of suffering and a hundred blighted hopes. She is now completely unable to provide either for her children or for herself. Her husband had just finished his college work and had obtained a promising job. They were buying an attractive home, and the children had every hope of going to school and growing into strong manhood and womanhood under the most favorable conditions. But in one second a little alcohol in the wrong place had changed everything. Their attractive home had to be sold to someone else, and a deep, dark shadow has settled over the children's future. This wonderful young mother who was so ambitious to do great things for others will now be confined to her bed forever.

Another bird poem with its human life angle may help us to understand this idea. It is entitled "The Wounded Curlew":

> By yonder sandy cove,
> Where every day the tide flows in and and out,
> A lonely bird of sombre brown and grey
> Limps patiently about,
>
> And around the basin's edge, o'er stone and sand
> And many a fringing weed,
> He steals upon the rocky ledge, doth stand
> Crying with none to heed.
>
> But sometimes from the distance
> He can hear a comrade's swift reply;
> Sometimes the air rings with their music clear
> Sounding from sea to sky.
>
> And then, oh then, his tender voice so sweet
> Is shaken with its pain;
> For broken are his pinions strong and fleet
> Never to soar again.
>
> Wounded and lame and languishing, he lives
> Once glad and blithe and free,
> And in his prison limits frets and strives
> His ancient self to be.

The little sandpipers around him play.
The shining waves they skim
Around his feet, they seek their food and stay
As if to comfort him.

My pity cannot help him,
Though his pain brings tears of wistfulness.
Still must he grieve and mourn, forlorn and faint —
None may his wrong redress.

Oh you bright-eyed boy, was there no better way
A moment's joy to gain
Than to bring sorrow that must mar the day
With such despairing pain?

Oh children, drop your guns, your cruel stones,
And listen to my words:
Here with me the wounded curlew moans;
Have mercy on the birds.

It is also very important that we learn to be kind to ourselves. God desires that we should all be well and happy. He
wants us to have a real part in his program of endless progress.
Hudson incites our imagination when he says, "This morning
before dawn, I ascended a hill, and looked into the crowded
heavens, and I said to my spirit: When *we* shall become the
enfolders of those orbs and the pleasure and knowledge of everything in them, even then our unfinished lives will continue on."

And when the time comes for us to inherit our eternal destiny
as the children of an all-powerful and all-knowing God, we will
then not want any unsightly blemishes growing in our minds or
on our souls. As wise men, we should protect our attitudes and
our spirits from everything that could do them harm. Our minds
are the guardians as well as the stimulators of our souls, and
ignorance is a form of self-inflicted injury that always leaves its
gloomy marks upon us. Just a little spiritual decay can destroy
a great potentiality and leave us too weak to fly and too lame
to run, whereas the man whose heart is pure is invincible. He
has integrity as his shield and virtue as his sword, and if he
is always seeking wisdom and righteousness with a faith-hungry
heart and a godly ambition, he will be impervious to the scars
of error, hatred, and failure, and may this be our own happy
accomplishment.

Solomon

ONE OF THE MOST famous men who ever lived upon the earth was Solomon, the third and last king of the united nation of ancient Israel. The history of this unusual nation began with Abraham, who was called the father of the faithful, and it ended with Solomon. Abraham had a son whose name was Isaac. Isaac had a son named Jacob. Jacob, whose name was later changed to Israel, became the father of the twelve sons who were the leaders of the twelve tribes.

God himself had called this nation "the chosen people." And it was his plan to make it into a kingdom of priests, a holy nation to be a peculiar example of excellence. He desired that their lives would not only please God, but also inspire all other nations.

Solomon was born about a thousand years after Abraham, and Israel had already had a long and eventful history. During this period the people had been blessed when they had done well, and they had been punished when their lives had turned to evil. Just as this group was out-growing its family status and emerging into a nation, it had gone into Egypt to protect itself from the famine that was ravishing its homeland. Then had followed many years of backbreaking, heartbreaking slavery to the Egyptians. Finally, amid the terror of the plagues, they were delivered by God through the leadership of Moses. Then, after a tremendous experience with God at Mount Sinai, they were preparing to enter their promised land when disobedience and rebellion broke out among them. This brought upon them a forty-year sentence of wandering in the Arabian wilderness. Finally they were led by Joshua into the land set aside for their inheritance, and for over 300 years after Joshua's death they lived under the direction of the judges, the last of whom was the Prophet Samuel.

At this point in their history they demanded a king, that they might be like other nations. Through Samuel the Lord had tried to dissuade them from making this error, but they were insistent and so the Lord selected Saul from the tribe of Ben-

jamin to be their king. Saul was a fine young man, but he didn't
work out very well as king. He was ineffective, disobedient to
God, and afraid of the pagan Philistines whom he had been
appointed to drive out of the land. Because of his evil he developed a severe melancholia and depression and finally he committed suicide by falling on his own sword. Saul was followed
upon the throne by David.

David was characterized by great courage, industry and
righteousness. The Lord referred to him as a man after God's
own heart. David finished Saul's assignment of driving out the
Philistines and destroying their influence. He moved the capital
of Israel from Hebron to Jerusalem, and so greatly built up
the strength of the people that Israel became one of the world's
great nations.

When David knew that he was about to die he delivered his
famous charge to his son, who was to succeed him upon the
throne. He said to Solomon "I go the way of all the earth: be
thou strong therefore, and show thyself a man; and keep the
charge of the Lord thy God, to walk in his ways, to keep his statutes, and his commandments, and his judgments, and his testimonies, as it is written in the law of Moses, that thou mayest
prosper in all that thou doest . . . That the Lord may continue
his word which he spake concerning me, saying, If thy children
take heed to their way, to walk before me in truth with all their
heart . . . there shall not fail thee (said he) a man on the throne
of Israel."

We usually think of people in terms of their outstanding
characteristics. And probably the chief characteristic of Solomon's life was its contradictions. On the one hand Solomon was
noted for his wisdom. His reign was characterized by the greatest
national wealth and elegance ever known. Because of the excellent work done by his father, there was continual peace and
friendliness with other nations during the forty years that Solomon sat upon the throne. And yet Solomon is charged with
his nation's rebellion and final downfall. In one sense he brought
to an end God's great attempt to build up a holy nation among
the Israelites. And Solomon himself died an idolator, very much
out of favor with God.

When Solomon ascended the throne, it was customary to
erect altars on high hilltops, and the people went there to offer
sacrifice. These were called "high places" and served as centers

of worship. The *great* "high place" was at Gibeon located some five miles north of Jerusalem, on one of the hilltops of Benjamin. Soon after he had been crowned, Solomon went to Gibeon and offered a sacrifice of a thousand burnt offerings. Here the Lord appeared to Solomon in a dream and said, "Ask what I shall give thee." And Solomon said, "Thou hast shewed unto thy servant David, my father, great mercy, according as he walked before thee in truth, and righteousness, and . . . thou hast given him a son to sit on his throne . . . But I am but a little child: I know not how to go out or come in . . . Therefore give thy servant an understanding heart to judge thy people, that I may discern between good and bad." Solomon's speech greatly pleased the Lord, and he said, "Because thou hast asked this thing, I have done according to thy words: lo, I have given thee a wise and understanding heart; . . . and I have also given thee that for which thou hast not asked, both riches, and honour: so that there shall not be any among the kings like unto thee all thy days. And if thou wilt walk in my ways, to keep my statutes and my commandments, as did thy father David, then I will lengthen thy days." (I Kings 3:5-15)

This important event started one of the most notable periods of history. The reign of Solomon has been called "the Golden Age of Israel." Solomon ruled with undisputed power all of the kingdoms from the river Euphrates to the land of the Philistines and to the borders of Egypt. His 40-year reign was blessed with unheard of prosperity. He made many beneficial alliances with other nations, and he himself enjoyed the greatest personal prestige and popularity of anyone in the world. The record says that "God gave Solomon a largeness of heart . . . His wisdom excelled the wisdom of all the children of the east . . . and all the wisdom of Egypt. For he was wiser than all men . . . and his fame was in all nations round about. . . . And all people came to hear his wisdom." (I Kings 4:29-34)

The record says, "The Lord magnified Solomon exceedingly and bestowed upon him such royal majesty as had not been in any king before him in Israel." He was permitted to build a magnificent temple from the most costly, imported woods, ornamented with precious stones and overlaid with millions of dollars worth of pure gold. It was richly furnished with the most costly material in the most attractive colors. The finished temple was the greatest wonder of the ancient world. It required seven years to build and then for the next thirteen years Solomon used this great labor force and its facilities to build a much larger palace for himself.

But as always the Lord had qualified his promise of success; he had said to Solomon, "If thou wilt walk before me as did David thy father, and do as . . . I have commanded thee and observe my statutes . . . then will I establish the throne of thy kingdom forever. But if ye turn away and forsake my statutes and my commandments and serve other gods, then will I pluck thee up by the roots out of the land which I have given thee, and this house which I have sanctified for my name, will I cast out of my sight, and will make it to be a proverb and a byword among all nations." That is, all blessings are based upon the continuing worthiness of the receiver.

But so far as worthiness is concerned, Solomon failed miserably. In order to cement his alliances with other nations, and to consolidate his control over subjugated provinces, Solomon married many foreign wives from among the people with whom intermarriage had been specifically and strictly forbidden. Solomon not only married these foreign women, but he allowed them to practice their idol worship in Jerusalem, and to some extent he himself participated with them. The record says, "Then did Solomon build an high place for Chemosh, the abomination of Moab, in the hill that is before Jerusalem, and for Molech, the abomination of the children of Ammon, and likewise did he for *all* his strange wives which burnt incense and sacrificed unto their gods." (I Kings 11:7-8.) The idol-worshipping Ammonite princess, Naamah, became the mother of his son, Rehoboam, who succeeded his father upon the throne. (I Kings 14:21-31)

The scripture says, "And King Solomon loved many strange women together with the daughter of Pharaoh, women of the Moabites, Ammonites, Edomites, Zidonians, and Hittites, and all the nations concerning which the Lord had said unto the children of Israel, "Ye shall not go in to them, neither shall they come in unto you: for surely they will turn away your heart after their gods." But "Solomon clave unto these in love, and . . . it came to pass . . . that his wives turned away his heart after other gods: and his heart was not perfect with the Lord his God, as was the heart of David his father. For Solomon went after Ashtoreth the goddess of the Zidonians, and after Milcom the abomination of the Ammonites, and Solomon did evil in the sight of the Lord, and went not fully after the Lord, as did his father." Many men and women have allowed the disbelief of a spouse to turn their hearts away from God. This is always a tragedy.

Here we see the world's wisest man make such serious mistakes that his bad example led a whole nation of his own people away from the God who had given him these great blessings. No wonder the record says that "the Lord was angry with Solomon, because his heart was turned from the Lord God of Israel, which had appeared unto him twice, . . . wherefore the Lord said unto Solomon, Forasmuch as this is done of thee, and thou hast not kept my covenant and my statutes, which I have commanded thee, I will surely rend the kingdom from thee.

"Nothwithstanding in thy days I will not do it for David thy father's sake: but I will rend it out of the hand of thy son." (I Kings 11:1-13)

Solomon had several other very serious problems. His great glory and luxury had been very expensive and he had reduced many of his people almost to a condition of slave labor in order to support it. With his large peace-time army, Solomon could easily enforce his will upon the people, but as these unrighteous interests absorbed more and more of his life, his grip upon the empire gradually became more feeble.

When Solomon died in 930 B.C. his kingdom was still peaceful on the surface and his son, Rehoboam, succeeded to the throne without dispute. However, to renew the covenant made by the Israelite tribes with David, the new king went to Shechem to have his succession publicly acclaimed there. There he was met with a plea for the abolition of some of the forced labor and a request that the taxes be lightened. The counselors of his father advised him to heed the request. They said, "If thou wilt be a servant unto this people and will serve them and answer them and speak good words to them, then they will be thy servants forever."

But after consulting with his own young advisors, he said to his people, "My father made your yoke heavy; I will make it heavier. My father chastized you with whips, but I will chastize you with scorpions." And when the people saw that Rehoboam would not listen, the northern section of the kingdom made up of the ten tribes rebelled. Thus the united nation was split in two: the people of the northern kingdom would soon be taken as captives into Assyria, and those in the south would become slaves to Babylon. So once more they were back to about where they were a thousand years earlier when they had served as slaves in Egypt. The Lord's great program had been scuttled by the very man he had selected to promote it. Solomon had destroyed the Jehovah worship of many people and the intended glory of Israel was ended forever by the world's wisest man.

The shortcoming of Solomon points out one of our own greatest failings. Frequently, we also allow a discord to develop between our wisdom and our righteousness. We allow an unbeliever to turn us away from God. Solomon knew what was right, but he allowed his own selfish interests and disobedience to destroy his people and the favor in which he was held by God himself. Solomon was an expert in making proverbs, and signing commercial treaties with foreign nations. He was popular with the dignitaries of other lands. He knew how to display his wealth most advantageously, but he turned out to be a failure so far as the people he had been called to serve were concerned, and he also fell down with Deity himself.

Solomon failed, but we ourselves may succeed by living the important charge given by his great father, David, and thus reap the corresponding reward that it promised.

The Tower of Babel

ONE OF THE VERY interesting work projects mentioned in the scriptures is the building of the Tower of Babel. In ancient times towers were very common and served the people in many ways. Military towers were numerous. These were usually fortified posts for the protection of those living on the frontiers or otherwise exposed to the attack of enemies.

The Bible describes one of Gideon's military campaigns by saying, "And he beat down the tower of Penuel and slew the men of the city." (Judges 8:17) The scriptures also tell about the attack of the warrior Abimelech on the City of Thebez. The record says, "But there was a strong tower within the city, and thither fled all the men and women, and all they of the city, and shut it up to them, and gat them up to the top of the tower. And Abimelech came unto the tower, and fought against it, and went hard unto the door of the tower to burn it with fire." (Judges 9:50-53) Then a woman in the tower threw down a rock and hit Abimelech on the head, breaking his skull and ending the siege.

Dozens of these towers are mentioned in the scriptures. There was the tower of Edar, the tower of Syene, (Ezekiel 29:10) the tower of Shechem, the tower of Hananeel. (Zech. 14:10) A tower gave the people a better visual command of the surrounding territory and also provided greater safety during an attack. Towers were also commonly built in vineyards as a necessary part of that particular agricultural operation. (Isa. 5:2) Some towers were built as a place to speak from when large groups of people were present.

The prophets also used these fortified places as symbols with religious significance. The scriptures refer to God as a "tower of protection." The writer of Proverbs says, "The name of the Lord is a strong tower and the righteous runneth into it and are safe." (Prov. 18:10) The Lord showed great honor to Jeremiah by calling him a tower. God said, "I have set thee for a tower and fortress among my people that thou mayest know and try their way." (Jer. 6:27) But of all of these various towers the most famous of them all was the Tower of Babel. We may not understand exactly what the builders of Babel had in mind. It seems that there was some kind of antagonism for God among them, and they may have been trying to protect themselves against another flood or some other divine interference with their lives. They seemed to know some of the things that God wanted them to do that they were not doing. The memory of the flood itself was not very old when the people decided to build this great tower, and their specifications prescribed that its top should reach to heaven. This designation of the tower's height may have had some figurative meaning, as I suppose they didn't actually plan to get into heaven by this means. The scriptures give us an interesting setting for this unusual experience by saying, "And the whole earth was of one language, and of one speech. And it came to pass, as they journeyed from the east, they found a plain in the land of Shinar; and they dwelt there. And they said one to another, Go to, let us make brick and burn them thoroughly. And they had brick for stone, and slime had they for mortar.

"And they said, Go to, let us build us as city and a tower, whose top may reach unto heaven; and let us make us a name, lest we be scattered abroad upon the face of the whole earth." The inference is that they had some instruction that they were not obeying, and their consciences may have been bothering them a little. Then the scripture says, "And the Lord came down to see the city and the tower, which the children of men builded. And the Lord said, Behold, the people is one, and they have all one language; and this they begin to do: and now nothing will be restrained from them, which they have imagined to do. Go to, let us go down, and there confound their language, that they may not understand one another's speech. So the Lord scattered them abroad from thence upon the face of all the earth: and they left off to build the city." (Gen. 11:1-8)

The record says that they wanted to make a name lest they be scattered abroad. And the divine action taken against them seems to indicate that they had seriously displeased God. However, we are impressed with what seems to be the very real respect that the Lord had for their ability to accomplish what they had set out to do. God said to his heavenly associates, "Behold, the people is one, and they have all one language; and this they begin to do; and now nothing will be restrained from them, which they have imagined to do." When any group act as "one" and when they all speak the same language and have a common determination in their hearts, they become almost all-powerful. And it is significant that the best way that the Lord knew to stop them was to confound their speech. If he had taken away their tools, undoubtedly they would have made some more; if he had deprived them of their skills, they would have relearned them; if he had taken away their bricks, they would have built their tower from other materials. But when he confounded their speech and left them with no means of communication, all the building stopped and the project had to be abandoned.

As I read this interesting account pointing out the limitations involved in this confusion of tongues, I find myself making some comparisons with our own lives. In the first place we wonder to what extent our own projects have incited the disapproval of God, and have caused the confusion that is presently holding us back. In one way or another all of us are builders, working on some project for our own benefit. And whether we are building a tower, or a business, or a family, or a life, we must work in teams where close cooperation and a good communication with others is always of primary importance. As long as the members of the team are "one" and speak the same language, we can accomplish about anything that we set our hearts on.

In fact in one of the greatest scriptures, Jesus indicated the importance of team work when he said, "If ye are not one, ye are not mine." He was trying to make the point that in unity, harmony, understanding with a communication that is free and effective, we can reach about any objective. But when communication breaks down, or when we begin speaking a language that is not accepted or not understood, then the results of our efforts begin to deteriorate and progress quickly slows down to a standstill.

Sometime ago in counseling with a wife about some of her family problems, I said, "What does your husband think about this?" She said, "I don't know; I never talk to my husband about these things." For her to attempt to communicate with her husband even on their family problems, would be like speaking to someone in a foreign tongue about a strange business which he didn't understand. The previous disagreements of this man and his wife, plus their lack of appreciation for each other, had confounded their language as surely as if they had been laying bricks at Babel. And as I go about a little bit I am impressed that in most of the things that we attempt, we spend far too much time reenacting this ancient confusion scene at the tower of Babel, and in the presence of too much confounding of language parents don't understand their children and the children don't understand their parents.

Our major racial and national groupings had their beginnings at Babel, and we have not made much progress in becoming unconfused. The difficulty involved in lack of cooperation is still one of our biggest problems. Instead of all being united, nations are taking up swords against other nations, and they are now doing about all they can to tear down and destroy each other. With our modern technical "know-how," if we were all of one heart and of one language we could build such a world of unity and such a tower of civilization that its top would reach to heaven — or come very close to it. And most of our problems still come because of our inability to communicate. It doesn't seem to matter much whether the area needing our cooperation is in business, or government, or education, or religion. And we are presently even having trouble communicating with ourselves, and with God.

Think of the confusion caused in our own lives by the discord existing between our deeds and our creeds. And because we are always working against our own best interests, our towers of accomplishment never rise very high before the confusion cuts off our growth.

However, the Bible tells us that many years after Babel, an interesting ability called "the gift of tongues" was announced to our world at Jerusalem, as a remedy for our confusion. In one way this gift was the exact opposite of what happened at Babel. This important event took place at the Feast of Pentecost, which was the Jewish feast of the harvest. At this feast following the resurrection, certain people were given the ability to understand those who spoke with strange tongues and in foreign languages. Luke describes what happened as follows:

"And when the day of Pentecost was fully come, they were all with one accord in one place. And suddenly there came a sound from heaven as of a rushing mighty wind, and it filled all the house where they were sitting. And there appeared unto them cloven tongues like as of fire, and it sat upon each of them. And they were all filled with the Holy Ghost, and began to speak with other tongues, as the Spirit gave them utterance. And there were dwelling at Jerusalem, Jews, devout men, out of every nation under heaven. Now when this was noised abroad, the multitude came together, and were confounded, because that every man heard them speak in his own language. And they were all amazed and marvelled, saying one to another, Behold, are not all these which speak Galileans? And how hear we every man in our own tongues, wherein we were born? Parthians, and Medes, and Elamites, and dwellers in Mesopotamia, and in Judea, Cappadocia, in Pontus, and Asia, Phrygia, and Pamphylia, in Egypt, and in parts of Libya about Cyrene, and strangers of Rome, Jews and proselytes, Cretes and Arabians, we do hear them speak in our tongues the wonderful works of God." (Acts 2:1-11)

At Babel they couldn't understand each other even though they had all spoken the same language all of their lives, but at Pentecost they could understand even those laguages that they had never heard before. The confusion at Babel caused all building to stop, and the people were scattered abroad. But because of the unity at Pentecost the people came closer together, and began the most constructive period of their lives. They had the Holy Ghost in their hearts. They had all things in common. They received God's message through the apostles and three thousand people joined the Church at once. Then the record says that they continued with one accord and "added to the Church daily such as should be saved." (Acts 2:47)

Isn't it interesting how in some degree these opposite traits still manifest themselves in us? Some of us seem to exercise a kind of gift for confusion and misunderstanding about everything that happens. On the other hand, if we have the Holy Ghost and have a little love and a little appreciation in our hearts, we can even learn to understand our wives and our children. When confusion is excluded from our lives then we can build up those great towers of success, faith and righteousness that will not only reach up to heaven, but they will also enable us to climb up to God upon them.

Before Jesus ascended into heaven, he said, "And I will pray the Father, and he shall give you another Comforter, that he may abide with you forever. . . . He shall teach you all things, and bring all things to your remembrance, whatsoever I have said unto you." (John 14:16, 26) God is not dead and the Holy Ghost did not close his career after his performance at Pentecost. Jesus said that if we would qualify ourselves, the Holy Ghost would abide with us forever and teach us all things. And that includes how to build our own towers of safety and accomplishment. The Holy Ghost is the third member of the Godhead, and with the Father and the Son he serves in the Presidency of heaven. With our consent and cooperation he can bring great benefits in our lives.

When John Milton was preparing to write his great narrative poems entitled *Paradise Lost* and its sequel *Paradise Regained*, he didn't contemplate an ordinary effort. He planned a poetic flight of great ideas that he thought would reach from heaven to hell, and from hell to heaven. And that is about the kind of building that we are all personally doing with our deeds. If we follow the examples of confusion set by our forefathers at Babel we will go down to failure just as they did. But if we get the spirit of Pentecost in our hearts we may go up so far that our towers of accomplishment will reach unto heaven.

The Israelites were commanded to seek the Lord, obey his laws and keep his commandments. And one of their most righteous kings said to them, "let us build our cities and make about them walls and towers and gates while the land is yet before us." And then the record says, "so they built and prospered."

With the right spirit this may also be said about our towers of righteousness, our towers of safety, and our towers of faith, which we may build and which will reach up to God.

The Trial

THERE IS A VERY meaningful word called "trial" that
plays several significant roles in our general success.
The dictionary says that a trial is an examination. It is an opportunity for submitting proof. Ideas, things and people are frequently placed on trial as a means of testing them and finding
their values. Many controversies have been settled and many
objectives have been established by means of a trial. We speak
of a "trial run" as a kind of experiment to test either the practi-
cality, efficiency, or worth of some particular thing. By the
examination and demonstration involved in a trial we can go
on all sides of any particular idea, either on its inside or its outside. We thereby get meanings that were not evident on the
surface. Frequently a salesman asks for a trial for his product.
By this means he seeks to encourage a more open-minded inquiry
and a more intelligent investigation of its values. And one of
the best ways to establish a value is by a period of actual use.
We use political campaigns as a kind of "trial run" in which our
candidates may be tested and proven before they are elected.

In a legal sense a trial is a means of going before an unbiased
tribunal and resolving the differences between disagreeing contestants. A competent court of law is able to make a formal
examination where unknown facts may be discovered, and claims
may be verified, in order that a just decision can be reached.

In Europe in earlier times some disputed issues were often
settled in a trial by combat. On such an occasion the people
attempted to determine right and wrong by an official appeal to
force. This form of trial was a legal procedure in England from
the time of William the Conqueror until it was abolished in the
year 1818. However, we have never gotten completely away from
this idea of appealing to force. And as late as World War I
the Kaiser of Germany publicly and soberly proclaimed his philosophy that "might makes right." Present-day Communist dictators are currently conducting some underground trials by hate,
falsehood and trouble-making. As a close companion for the

old British law of a trial by combat there was another law governing a trial by ordeal. This was a trial in which the innocence
or guilt of an accused person was determined by the manner
in which he sustained some form of ordeal. For example, if
someone was accused of practicing witchcraft, she might be thrown
into the river as a means of testing her guilt. If she were drowned
she might be declared innocent, but if she were able to save
herself that might be interpreted as a sign of her supernatural
powers and consequently she would be punished accordingly.

We still practice many of these subreasonable means of solving problems. We have a kind of trial by lot, where we determine
issues by flipping coins, or drawing straws, or looking for omens,
or indulging in some pet superstition. Many people are greatly
influenced by a fickle popular opinion. Often we follow the
example of those earlier weather experts who used to send up
trial balloons as a means of testing air currents, wind velocity,
etc. This is also a device used by politicians and others where
they may make some statement or tentatively announce some
project as a means of testing public reaction or determining
popular opinion.

In our individual programs we sometimes launch a trial
by gossip, or we attempt to produce the necessary guilt in those
we wish to see condemned by a smear campaign. Guilt or innocence is also frequently determined by resorting to bribery, or
by inciting fear. Closely related to these subreasonable activities
there are many people who operate their lives by a system of
trial and error. This is a program used by those who feel it
necessary for them to make all of the mistakes personally. But
probably one of the most important of all ideas is that life itself
is the biggest, most important and most long-drawn-out trial.
The entire period of our mortality is spent in being tested and
proven and tried. We were born into a world of opposites and
everyone is continuously on trial, and his employer, his family,
society and God himself are acting as his judges. Each one of us
also has the responsibility for judging himself.

Recently a couple of young students came in to talk about
some of the problems that had developed as a result of their
use of the drug L.S.D. Among other things they were suffering
from a considerable amount of guilt reaction. They seemed to be
about 60% decided to give up this evil association. But their
indefinite and unstable 60% verdict was subject to a 40% minor-

ity objection that kept the trial going on underneath the surface of their minds. They didn't like some parts of this drug program, and yet they couldn't completely give up the idea behind it. Their taste for it had not yet been fully developed, yet it did give considerable support to the 40% minority dissent. They had enlarged the subreasonable areas of their thinking and were wondering if there weren't some advantages to drug addiction. To help them make up their minds I explained to them Benjamin Franklin's procedure for trying a controversial idea. He would draw a line down through the middle of a piece of paper and make up a balance sheet of pros and cons by listing all of the reasons against it on the debit side, and all of the reasons in its favor on the credit side. Then when all of the facts were in and their importance weighed, a more intelligent and a more firm decision could be arrived at.

Frequently we fail in our decision-making because we don't get all of the facts out on the table in recognizable form. So many of us are surprisingly unskilled in the use of reason, and even the use of light, in solving problems. Consequently, when we are required to act in a combination capacity of judge, jury, counselor and witness for both sides, an intelligent trial becomes pretty nearly impossible. These students with 40% of themselves in the hands of L.S.D. kept referring to "their search for happiness." They had been favorably impressed with the feelings they had had during these excursions in the enhancing world of drugs. Their delusions of grandeur, their illusions of ease, and their feelings of imagined well-being were accepted at full face value as evidence in favor of drug addiction. More than anything known to them L.S.D. was able to push all of their problems out of the way, at least temporarily. They also went to great lengths in praising the sincerity and friendliness of their hippie friends who were also seeking happiness through their love-ins, their irresponsibility and the intense pleasures of their dreams. And while they had cast a 60% vote against L.S.D., they wanted the seeming advantages of both good and bad, and in a subversive, underground kind of a way they subconsciously hoped to find some way to justify this evil and fantastic way of life. One of their problems was that when they returned from this land of make-believe they were confronted with the need of making a living. They also had an uncomfortable feeling that they were not highly approved by the world's non-hippie population. They also felt that they should be carrying on their share of the necessary work of the world. They were bothered by a guilt complex and the recollection of their irresponsible sins. Yet it was difficult for them to give up easily this project of unearned pleasure and false peace that the drugs were capable of giving them.

I tried to help them understand the idea that life at its best is much more than a mere pleasure trip into a land of make-believe that doesn't exist. Life is real, and to make the most of it demands that moral characters must be built, industry must be learned, and minds must be disciplined and trained to think and reason clearly. Minds and bodies should also be taught to work and made capable of difficult accomplishment. At least we should build a more solid foundation for happiness than mere dreams, delusions, and idleness. Even fatigue, hunger, self-discipline, difficult problem solving and disappointments add something to life. There may be some lemonade drinkers who would not like to include anything but sugar in their lemonade. But the best lemonade also requires some lemon. And even though the lemon, if taken by itself, is very sour, lemon is the basic ingredient in lemonade and might properly be the first to go into the mixture.

Employers sometimes have an interesting custom of expecting employees to do a little work before they present themselves at the pay window. And the Lord seems to have some similar ideas. He says, "Ye receive no witness until after the trial of your faith." (Ether 12:6) If there are no thorns, there can be no crowns. There are many people who criticize God for the way he runs our world. One man pointed out recently how much easier it would be for everyone if all evil temptations, as well as mental and physical suffering, could be done away with. He also thought that it would be a good idea if all of the work could be done for him. He felt that if God surrounded everyone with nothing but good, it would be easier for him and his family to be decent. And yet even the Son of God "learned obedience by the things that he suffered." Adversity has many uses. Suffering sometimes adds as much to life as the sour lemon does to lemonade. If all of our prayers were answered no one would ever die, no one would ever be sick, we would always get our own way and there would be no strength.

Oscar Wilde once said that if God wished to punish us, all he would need to do would be to answer our prayers; for if hardship, suffering, disappointment, and work should be done away with, we might find our world full of hothouse plants without characters, backbones, muscles, brains, understanding or personality. Just in case we don't think God is doing a very good job, who would we like to nominate to take his place in running the world? There aren't very many good prospective substitutes for God. In the past even some of the most religious men have been some of the most tyrannical. It was supposedly good men who instituted the holy wars, fought progress, and burned good people at the stake. Even our own Pilgrims who came here seeking religious freedom did not always grant to others the freedoms that they so much craved for themselves. Someone has written:

> The Pilgrims landed — worthy men
> And saved from the wrath of stormy seas,
> They fell upon their knees — and then —
> They fell upon the Aborigines.

We need some suffering as well as some opposition, and a little struggle in our life's lemonade. It takes hard pounding to make good steel, and it is a well known fact that the pursuit of easy things makes men weak. We grow by exercise, and we develop strength by struggle and by overcoming hardships. We also need to know how to conduct a trial so as to make up our minds between right and wrong. It would be pretty difficult to develop virtue if we had no choices. Isn't it interesting that even Satan is permitted in this world for our benefit. That is, God could destroy Satan at any instant that he desired. And we might ask ourselves, then why doesn't he? God himself has given us the answer. He has said, "And it must needs be that the devil should tempt the children of men, or they could not be agents unto themselves, for if they never should have the bitter they could not know the sweet." (D&C 29:30) However, some even base their claim that God is dead on the fact that he does not prevent suffering and evil and labor by force.

But in the very beginning God made an undeviating and everlasting commitment to freedom. In the Council in Heaven when plans were being made by which this earth should be governed, the free agency of man was the basic principle underlying all other considerations. The rebellion of Lucifer took place over this point. Satan was a believer in force and he tried to get control over the people who would live upon our earth. If Lucifer's plan had been adopted, everyone would have obeyed all of the laws, everyone would have gone to Church, everyone would have paid his tithing, etc., etc., so that not one soul would have been lost. But everything would have been done by compulsion.

A slave never rises because he acts under the lash. And how much credit is anyone entitled to who does things because he is forced to do them? With force as the ruling principle, human beings would be no better than a lot of mechanical contrivances, for no one could act for himself. Then no one could properly receive any reward for meritorious conduct and there would be little purpose in life. What a thrilling moment when God said to his children, "Thou mayest choose for thyself!" Of course the problem arises for the disobedient in that everyone must be held strictly accountable for his deeds. The hippies are now engaged in a very serious trial of themselves; and so are we. Our faith must be tried, our industry must be tried, our ability must be successfully tested and proven. We must learn how to use suffering and hardship in order to develop the greatest strength in us.

Through the poet, God said:

> When through fiery trials thy pathways may lie,
> My grace all sufficient shall be thy supply.
> The flames shall not hurt thee, I only design
> Thy dross to consume and thy gold to refine.

In our own interests we need to wholeheartedly accept God as the ruler of life and always remember that we are a part of the most important trial in the universe in which we are to show and prove that we can effectively govern our own lives.

Think and Grow Rich

NAPOLEON HILL once wrote an important book entitled *Think and Grow Rich.* He presents some excellent ideas that take a firm hold on our interest, inasmuch as everyone wants to be rich. Our problem comes from the fact that so many people don't want to do the necessary thinking. This defect in us is even more serious because of the fact that in addition to being rich in material things, we also want to be rich in cultural attainments, spiritual power and social graces. Mr. Hill effectively points out that the secret of our success in all of these fields is to obtain a good mastery over our thinking processes. God must also have had this in mind when he equipped us with our miraculous mental machinery. The greatest invention that has ever been perfected even by God himself is the human mind. If we can learn to operate it successfully it can make us rich in every resource. The key to every part of everyone's success is in his own thoughts. What we are and what we will become will be determined by what and how we think. Happiness is developed in our minds. The field of psychosomatic medicine has taught us that health also originates and is destroyed in our thoughts. We can change our circumstances by changing our thinking. Yet most of us never learn to think very well or very much. Some minds live to be a hundred years old without having the thrilling experience of ever being effectively used.

Mr. Hill attempts to help us over our thinking difficulties by analyzing and discussing them under several interesting subheadings. He has such important chapter titles as faith, desire, mental discipline, the power of suggestion, specialized knowledge, initiative, organized planning, firm decision-making, persistent study, and how to develop the subconscious mind. Mr. Hill contends that everyone has six senses, rather than just five. As the Sense Number Six he lists "Creative Imagination." This is thinking with power to a purpose. By creative imagination our thoughts can be effectively harnessed to bring about any desired accomplishment. However, too often we keep this sixth sense in a very poor state of development. But that is also frequently true of the other five senses. Jesus himself pointed out the fact that we have eyes that don't see, and ears that don't hear, and hearts that fail to understand.

Someone once wrote a fantasy about an imaginary invasion of our earth by a group of men from space who had seventy-two senses instead of five. I suppose that all of us actually have a great number of senses, at least in their rudimentary form, and we should take time to properly develop them. God gave us a valuable sense of discernment. We have a sense of right and wrong to serve us as a life's compass. We have a sense of humor to keep the personality oiled and running smoothly. We have a sense of fairness, and a sense of direction, and a sense of dependability, and a sense of responsibility. We have a natural instinct to worship God. In large part all of these are controlled and directed by the brain, which is the presiding officer of the entire personality. Some of the functions of the mind are to make plans, form images, paint pictures, mold ambitions and motivate activities. The mind sets up our expectations and supervises the fulfillment of our dreams. The mind is the headquarters of hope, and the home office of our life's purposes. At its best the mind sees, hears, thinks and understands. It may produce the finest fruits of reason, straight thinking, sound judgment and high accomplishment. A good mind is free to speculate. It is able to meditate, reflect, resolve and create. How our minds look at things is called attitude. And most of us are not happy or unhappy because of our circumstances, but because of what we think about our circumstances. Someone once asked Caesar what he thought of conditions, and he replied, "I make conditions." So do we all.

Abraham Lincoln once pointed out that most people are about as happy as they make up their minds to be; and we are also about as successful, and as faithful, and as industrious as we make up our minds to be. Plato described "thinking" as the soul talking to itself. And the kind of thing that our soul talks about has the greatest possible importance to us. As Herder lay in the parched weariness of his last illness he said to his son, "Give me a great thought that I may quicken myself with it." One of our finest accomplishments would be to have enough great thoughts to quicken our whole lives.

"Thoughts rule the world." They also rule our success and happiness. Our most worthwhile treasures are pleasant thoughts.

The richest life is the one with the greatest number of the right kind of thoughts. Spurgeon said that good thoughts are blessed guests and should be sought after, welcomed, well fed and then strengthened by use. Like rose leaves, pleasant thoughts give out a sweet smell when they are properly laid up in the jar of our minds. And when our lives are finally reviewed, we will probably find that our worst fault will be that we have thought too little and too late about too many important things. Jesus said, "The Kingdom of God is within you." However, that is also where the kingdom of hell is. And very few physical tortures ever equal the suffering of a mind filled with damned thoughts.

But the mind is also the center of our joys. It is the operator of our picturing power and the architect of our growth. To understand the advantages of straight thinking, we need the contrast of coming in contact with the thinking of a warped, distorted mind. Good minds can build fortunes, whereas fortunes cannot build good minds. Therefore good minds are greater than fortunes.

And just as we can think and grow rich, so we can also think and grow wise. We can think and grow powerful. We can think and grow righteous; and we can think and grow faithful. The lack of faith in most people is not that they particularly disbelieve in God, but rather they just haven't thought about him one way or another. The problem is not so much that people don't believe in immortality as that they just don't care about it. Jesus severely rebuked the unprofitable servant because he hid his talent in the ground. But our greatest talents are our religious talents. The right kind of religious talents can make us happy, give us control of our minds and save our souls. Recently in talking with a friend of mine about his church activities, he shrugged his shoulders and said, "But I am just not religious," the shrug meaning, "There is nothing that I can do about it." In trying to help him I said, "Bill, I am sure that what you say is true, that you are not religious, but have you ever thought about the circumstances that brought that situation about? How could you ever hope to be religious? You don't study, you don't go to church. You don't read the scriptures, you don't pray to God. Actually what right do you have to be religious?" One can't just snap his fingers and get a great spirituality any more than he can snap his fingers and get great musical ability. Talents must be earned. And no religious talents grow very fast while buried in the ground.

Sir Isaac Newton said that he discovered the law of gravity by thinking about it all of the time. And that is the way we discover faith, and success, and God, and ourselves.

The psychologists say that each of us has two minds. One is the conscious mind, which may resemble a machine shop or a power plant. The other is a miraculous God-given creation which more resembles a great underground success reservoir. We don't know very much about the subconscious mind because we see only the surface. In this wonderful reservoir we may store all of the greatest ideas and ambitions that have ever been devised in the history of the world. But the subconscious mind also has some hidden springs that flow into it from the universal intelligence. No one can fathom his own mind. It is a well of thought that has no bottom. The more you draw from it the more clear and fruitful it will be. Many people get discouraged because at first their ideas are shapeless and homely. But everything is imperfect at birth. But with time, perseverance and thought our ideas can be polished, strengthened and beautified. The great orators, writers and inventors have often expressed their amazement at the ability of their subconscious minds to furnish them with a steady flow of great thoughts.

> Mind is the master power that builds and molds;
> And mind is man.
> And ever more he takes the tools of thought and
> Fashions what he wills,
> Bringing forth a thousand joys — a thousand ills.
> We think in secret, and it comes to pass.
> Environment is but our looking glass.

Someone has asked this question, "How would you like to create your own mind?" But isn't that exactly what we all do. William James said, "The mind is made up by what it feeds upon." We may feed our minds on the richest diet, build up its mental powers and stock it with the finest literature including the words of God himself. "The mind, like the dyers hand, is colored by what it holds." If I hold in my hand a sponge full of purple dye my hand becomes purple. But if I hold in my mind the great ideas of faith, righteousness, and success, my whole personality is colored accordingly. The mind can become the greatest of all creators. Out of the brain of Thomas A. Edison came a whole string of electric lights, refrigerators, phonographs, television sets and hundreds of other things that no one had ever thought about before. And someone has said that if *we* ever want to hatch out something all we need to do is just to set our minds on it.

A prominent British neuro-physicist once said that you could not construct an electronic computer for 3 billion dollars that would be the equivalent of the human brain. The brain is made up of some fourteen billion cells. It can contain more information and programs of accomplishment than could be loaded into ten truckloads of books. Every day millions of our brain cells are dying, and millions of new ones are being formed to take their places. As we sluff off our worn-out cells, we can also sluff off our inferior attitudes and our ideas of weakness and install new ones in their places. As these new cells are being formed, they are stamped with the imprint of the particular ideal that is dominant in the mind at that time. As our new brain cells come into being they can be stamped with health, impregnated with faith, endowed with loyalty and given the characteristics of the most worthwhile spirituality.

Jesus said that everyone ought to be born again. We can be reborn spiritually. But we can also come forth in a newness of mental life. As our new cells are being formed we are actually being reborn a little at a time. And all of our cells are completely changed at least once each seven years. Therefore in seven years each of us will be a brand new person. Our job is to make sure that these new cells are stamped with superior characteristics, as the mind can be thrown into a partial deadlock by a damaging neutrality if we stamp too many brain cells with negative ideas. The Republicans in Congress think they can do a better job in carrying out their programs if they have a full majority in all branches of the government. Our success can also do better this way.

The scripture says that no one can be saved in ignorance. But no one can be saved in indifference or indecision. If too many of our cells are voting negatively we can't get a very strong majority for righteousness. And there is nothing more miserable than to be all mixed up where we can't make up our minds. When we stamp too many cells with ideas of atheism and sin we are heading away from success. It's good to keep in mind that we can go backward through wrong thinking just as fast as we can go forward through right thinking. It is reverse thinking in individuals and groups that brings on our material and spiritual depressions and causes our apostasies from God. Good thoughts and feelings of love have more power to eradicate disease than does medicine. Some good doses of right thinking will produce emotions that give us longer life, greater health and more peace of mind, whereas with the wrong thoughts we burn out our faith and give ourselves stomach ulcers, heart attacks, nervous breakdowns and spiritual deaths. Our thoughts are heard in heaven. Therefore, we should nurture our minds with goodly thoughts. An arrow may fly through the air and leave no trace, but every thought cuts a permanent path through the brain and stamps its image upon each cell as it is being born. It is said that our good thoughts never expire, and our great dreams live on forever. Nothing is more practical nor more valuable than a good thought. It molds our lives and gives us a clearer, richer world in which to live. As to believe in the heroic makes men heroes, so to believe in God makes men godly. We won't need to think all original thoughts, as we can memorize and run through our minds the greatest ideas of others until they become as much a part of us as if we ourselves had been the first to think them. We can think and grow rich and we can think and grow faithful. We can think and grow righteous, and may God help us so to do.

Under Bond

THERE IS A procedure in the business world where the parties to some important transaction are placed under bond. Those concerned are required to put up securities to guarantee that their obligations will be fully and faithfully met. When one doesn't have enough assets of his own he may hire a bonding company to back up his responsibility for him. If he should fall down in his performance the posted values are forfeited. But life has a very similar operating procedure.

We begin this life with a tremendous responsibility and very few assets. The Son of God put up his own life to redeem us from death. As a consequence the Apostle Paul says, "Ye are not your own. For ye are bought with a price, therefore glorify God in your body and in your spirit which are God's." (I Cor. 6: 19-20) God started us out by creating us in his image and endowing us with a set of his own attributes and potentialities. And each of us is held fully accountable that that image does not become marred by our weaknesses or corroded by our sins.

For a long ante-mortal existence we lived with God in heaven in what has been called "the childhood of our immortality." But as we now approach the maturity of our mortality we must be tried, tested and proven. And if we show ourselves irresponsible we forfeit the most priceless benefits. We did not come to this earth accidentally. It was the program of God ratified by us in our pre-existence. God had said, "They who keep their first estate shall be added upon and they who . . . keep their second estate shall have glory added upon their heads forever and ever." Covenants between God and us were made and mutually accepted in our ante-mortal lives. As we were added upon with these beautiful, wonderful bodies, these magnificent minds, these marvelous personalities with their Godlike possibilities, our bonds were increased. Mortality is the period when we build up our life's estate by forming our families, developing our friendships, and learning to love righteousness. Before our mortality began we were only spirits. But we had come to a place where young people always come when it is desirable for them to move away from the homes of their parents.

God wanted us to move away from him, where we could see good and evil side by side, and where we could develop the ability to choose the good and reject the evil. This is the process by which we lay a proper foundation of character, righteousness and happiness, and eventually become even as God is. Limited as we were as spirits we could never have had a fullness of joy. Therefore God created this valuable earth exactly suited for this next phase in our eternal progress.

God made this investment for us with the understanding that we would do all things whatsoever the Lord God should command us. And so delighted were we that this great program was brought into fruition that the scripture says that all of the spirit children of God shouted for joy. But we do not live under a "profit system" as has sometimes been suggested. Actually we live under a "profit and *loss*" system. In honoring the image in which we were made, we were given an unlimited freedom for improving our intelligence, perfecting our righteousness and multiplying our happiness. But unless our life account shows a profit it is possible for us to lose everything, and of some who failed it was said it would have been better for them if they had never been born.

Because Jesus was the eldest and most valiant son of God, he was chosen, with our concurrence, to be the Savior of the world. But many others were among the noble and great spirits who stood with God, and because "where much is given much will be required" all of us who were permitted to take this next step in our eternal progression were put under bond.

Because God is firmly committed to the freedom of his children, we were given a part in approving everything that was done, even in heaven. We were members of the forces that fought against the rebellion of Lucifer, and according to the law of responsibility our possible failure made all of our assets subject to loss. If we fail we may lose our invested capital as well as our invested capacity. The Creator set up these great capital assets of life, brains, physical powers, personality qualities, and mental abilities for us. But they were not given to us as free gifts. They must be earned before they can belong to us permanently. We are able to keep our abilities only as long as we make satisfactory use of them and to the extent that they are wasted we must pay the forfeit.

Sometime ago a stranger came in to talk about his problems. He said he thought most of his difficulties came because he lacked capital in his business. After visiting with him I was impressed that the reason he lacked capital in his business was because he was wasting the capital which God had invested in him. I told him the story of Fred Douglas, the negro journalist and statesman of American slave days, who six months before his birth was pledged by his white master to a creditor in payment of a debt, and until Fred Douglas was 25 years old he didn't own even his own body. Then some friends of his took up a collection of $720 and purchased Fred Douglas and made him a present of himself. I suggested to my friend that he go into the library and get some good books on physiology and psychology and religion, and read what great assets God had invested in his hands, his eyes, his brain, his reason, his voice, his personality, and his immortal spirit. The poorest among us is equipped as only the great God of heaven and earth could equip him, and we are bonded for the development and full use of every faculty.

No banker would loan us money and allow us to waste it without paying a penalty. And neither does God permit us to waste his precious resources without suffering a loss. We remember the action taken in the case of the unprofitable servant who said, "I was afraid, so I hid my talent in the ground." Because his talent was not improved Jesus said, "Take the talent from him and give it unto him who has ten talents, and cast ye the unprofitable servant into outer darkness, where there shall be weeping and wailing and gnashing of teeth." God can forgive us our sins, but who can forgive us our fear or our sloth or our ignorance?

The story is told of a horse that once ran away from its master. After a period the horse repented and returned to his master, and said, "I have come back." The master said, "Yes, you have come back, but the field is unplowed." It is pretty hard to repent of unplowed ground or unimproved talents.

Everyone is charged by the Creator for the maximum employment of this capital. Under our agreement of trusteeship, when each ability was given us, a performance bond was attached. Disuse of our talents is as mortal a sin as actual abuse, as in either case when the talent is lost the forfeit must be paid.

When we withdraw our works our faith dies; if we don't practice the God-given gift of integrity, we soon find ourselves without integrity; and if enough of our other assets go unused our entire personality department may be thrown into bankruptcy, with forfeits corresponding to the losses. And only after our mortality has been finished will these assets belong to us permanently. Only then will glory be added upon our heads forever and ever.

When God came down onto the top of Mount Sinai he offered to make a covenant with the children of Israel in which they were granted the greatest possible blessings based on their obedience to those laws on which blessings must always be predicated. The people responded by saying, "All that the Lord hath said, we will do." And when they kept their covenants they prospered, but as they failed, frightful penalties were imposed. It is a terrible experience when badly needed capital is lost or withdrawn, or when securities must be forfeited. Of course, values are not always completely destroyed. Bankruptcies are not always total losses. An individual or a business may be 10% or 20% or 90% insolvent. On the other hand, everyone is rewarded according to his works. And one with a 90% devotion is entitled to a greater reward than one with a 50% or a 10% devotion. Paul explained to the Corinthians that there were three main degrees of glory. Then he said, "for as one star differeth from another star in glory, so also is the resurrection of the dead." (I Cor. 15:40-42) The glories of heaven have been designed to match the merit in our individual lives, and as the blaze of the noonday sun is above the twinkle of a tiny star, so is the glory and desirability of the Celestial glory above that of the Telestial. Then, of course, there is another kingdom that is not a kingdom of glory. That is a place called hell, provided as a permanent abode for Satan and his angels, and those others whose lives most nearly approach complete bankruptcy.

The Celestial is the highest glory and that is the order to which God himself belongs. And each grade below the Celestial will be minus those benefits that have been forfeited by the inferior behavior of the one concerned. All who live in mortality have passed the requirements of their first estate. Now the only condition standing between us and eternal glory is to honor our covenants in these few short years yet remaining in our mortality. Then if we have fulfilled our responsibilities, our blessings will become permanent, and we will have the promised glory added upon our heads forever and ever.

In the meantime we should keep in mind that we are under bond in both big and little things. And for every infraction of the laws of our eternal success a toll is being exacted, and sometime if we finally discover that our securities are badly impaired, then we will surely feel that our forfeits have been of frightful size. All penalties must be paid out of the most valuable of all resources, which is life itself. We cannot be too careful, as even a little wasted time may drop us into a lower kingdom. One meaningful line in the scriptures says, "Woe unto him that wasteth the days of his probation, for awful is his state."

To make the most and the best of our own lives we should be sure that every occasion of life is a great occasion. We should be greater than our calling, and stronger than any evil that can happen to us. Faithfulness is our most profitable endeavor, because every unrepented sin and every uncorrected failure causes the bonding company to say, "Take the talent from him and give it to him who has ten talents." Our forfeitures may be imperceptible at first, but the scales are so accurately adjusted that the slightest letdown causes a corresponding forfeiture of our all-important God-given capital.

It is significant that this process of increasing our talents is the original do-it-yourself project. And everyone must do his own growing. We are not only the architects of our own fate, but we must also lay the bricks ourselves. Carlyle said, "Know thy work and do it like a Hercules."

Emerson has pointed out that every man's task is his life preserver. Every man's task is also his greatest opportunity. It is his road to happiness. It is his means of becoming like God. It has been said that triumph is just a little umph added to try. And those people who some day wake up to find themselves famous will be those who have never been asleep. When we learn to work effectively at the right things, most other benefits

to me the kind of God that you don't believe in." The younger man then detailed the attributes of the kind of God taught by some so-called Christian creeds. Some think that God is a shapeless mass, filling the universe, and yet he is so small that he can dwell in a human heart. Some claim to believe in a God who is permanently invisible, without a body, or parts, or passions. They believe that in some mysterious way the Father, Son and Holy Ghost have all been joined into one being. After listening to the young man's recital the older man said, "If that is anywhere near an accurate description of God, then I myself am also an atheist." Then the older man tried to do for his friend what Paul tried to do for the Greeks on Mars Hill when he said to them, "He whom ye ignorantly worship, him declare I unto you."

God is clearly described in the scriptures, but we have so spiritualized him and made him into so many mere figures of speech, that the great God in whose image man was created has largely been erased from some understandings. Sometime ago one of the prominent ministers of the world wrote a book in which he compared several of the important Christian doctrines as taught in the Bible with the doctrines taught by some of the popular ministers of the present day. Then in making a comparison between the two he said, "The God of the Bible is a personal God, there can be no question about that." But he said, "We don't believe that any more." Then to make the contrast clear he quoted from the answers he had received from the present-day teachers of religion, explaining what they believed God to be. One said that he was like a giant electronic brain. One said that God was "anything that you couldn't explain." He said that "God was atheism to the atheist." Another minister said that "God was a mobile cosmic ether." The one making the survey said, "Imagine Jesus praying to a mobile cosmic ether." Jesus prayed, "Our Father, which art in heaven." We might ask what did he mean? We would not dare to accuse him of double talk or of an attempt to deceive people. When Jesus said to Mary, "I ascend unto my Father and to your Father, and to my God and to your God," he certainly did not have in mind that he was going to meet some incomprehensible, shapeless, invisible influence without body, parts or passions of which he himself was an undivided part. Because of the close relationship existing between God and man they can best be studied together.

It has not only been said that God has no body, but some say that we will also lose our bodies. This in spite of the fact that the human body is the greatest and most useful of all of God's creations. What would you suggest as a substitute for your body? If in God's opinion a body had not been necessary, it never would have been created in the first place. If it were not necessary for eternity the resurrection never would have been instituted. If a body were not necessary for God the Father, then God the Son would never have been resurrected. None of God's works are temporary or whimsical. If God had had something better than a body he would have put it into operation. But if there is nothing better, why should what we have be discarded? It must offend God when some so-called ministers of religion say that we will be well rid of this great creation of the body. Jesus did not lose his own body after his resurrection. It did not evaporate. It did not expand to fill the immensity of space. It does not change its shape or size. A resurrected being does not discard his body or pick it up at will. In the resurrection the spirit and body are inseparably joined together, never again to be separated.

When Jesus ascended up into heaven he had his body, and the angels who stood at his side said, "This same Jesus which is taken up from you into heaven shall so come again, in like manner, as ye have seen him go into heaven." The Father who begot Jesus Christ was a person. And he has a body of flesh and bones as tangible as that possessed by Jesus, and it is in the same shape and form. The Apostle Paul says that "Jesus was in the express image of his Father's person," and the Father and Son are no more merged together than are you and I. The angels who stood by Jesus as he ascended were men high in authority in heaven. Jesus said to the Pharisees, "Ye do err, not knowing the scriptures." (Matt. 22:29) So frequently men make very serious mistakes for this same reason. For example John says, "No man hath seen God at any time." (John 1:18) And yet Moses saw God face to face. When Moses was with God in the Mount, God's glory rested upon him so that he could endure his presence. A great modern-day scripture says, "For no man has seen God at any time in the flesh, except quickened by the spirit of God. either can any natural man abide the presence of God." And the Lord has said, "Ye are not able to abide the presence of God now, neither the ministering of angels; wherefore, continue in patience until ye are perfected." (D&C 67:11-13) Even during his earth life Jesus said, "The Father is in me and I in him." (John 10:38) He said, "The Father and I are one." Both before and after mortality Jesus ruled and reigned with his Father as separate individual beings. It would be ridiculous to suppose that Jesus actually lived physically in the bosom of the Father. They were one in mind, and one in purpose. Certainly they were not merely one being.

Because God is not always visible to human eyes doesn't mean that he lacks substance. Or because God is all-knowing and because his influence and knowledge reach throughout all space doesn't mean that he himself has been diffused throughout space. God is not a "thing," nor an influence, nor an "it;" he is a "thou." He is the Father of the spirits of all men, and he is also the literal earthly Father of Jesus Christ. A modern revelation says, "The Father has a body of flesh and bones as tangible as man's; the Son also; but the Holy Ghost has not a body of flesh and bones, but is a personage of Spirit." (D&C 130:22)

The most authoritative knowledge of the Father and Son has come to the earth in our own dispensation, as both of them have reappeared upon the earth in our day. In recounting this appearance the Prophet Joseph Smith said, "When the light rested upon me I saw two Personages, whose brightness and glory defy all description, standing above me in the air. One of them spake unto me, calling me by name and said, pointing to the other — 'This is My Beloved Son. Hear Him!' " Joseph said, "My object in going to inquire of the Lord was to know which of all the sects was right, that I might know which to join. No sooner, therefore, did I get possession of myself, so as to be able to speak, than I asked the Personages who stood above me in the light, which of all the sects was right — and which I should join.

"I was answered that I must join none of them, for they were all wrong; and the Personage who addressed me said that all their creeds were an abomination in his sight; that those professors were all corrupt; that 'they draw near to me with their lips, but their hearts are far from me, they teach for doctrines the commandments of men, having a form of godliness, but they deny the power thereof.' " (Jos. Smith 2:17-19)

In commenting on the persecution that followed, the Prophet said: "I had actually seen a light, and in the midst of that light

I saw two Personages, and they did in reality speak to me; and though I was hated and persecuted for saying that I had seen a vision, yet it was true; and while they were persecuting me, reviling me, and speaking all manner of evil against me falsely for so saying, I was led to say in my heart: Why persecute me for telling the truth? I have actually seen a vision; and who am I that I can withstand God, or why does the world think to make me deny what I have actually seen? For I had seen a vision; I knew it, and I knew that God knew it, and I could not deny it, neither dared I do it; at least I knew that by so doing I would offend God, and come under condemnation." (Jos. Smith 2:25)

So much misinformation has been disseminated about God that it is sometimes difficult for some people to think of him as a glorified, all-knowing, all-powerful personal being as he has revealed himself to be, who is our eternal Heavenly Father, in whose image we were created. The dictionary says that the word "anthropomorphic" stands for the conception of God with a human form, and with human attributes and affections. It could more accurately be said that the word anthropomorphic describes the man who was created in God's image and endowed with his attributes and potentialities.

It might help us to understand God if we think of the progress that a man makes within the narrow limits of this life. From a helpless baby may come one like unto Demosthenes or Moses, Michelangelo, Caesar, Washington, or the Apostle Paul. If in a few years a man can rise up out of infancy to become a great scientist, or artist, or orator, or prophet, what may we not hope to accomplish in a few hundreds of thousands or millions of years? With eternal life granted to a man, and God for his guide, why should any limitations be thought of? God is perfect in knowledge, power, love and righteousness, and said to us, "Be ye therefore perfect, even as your Father which is in heaven is perfect." One of our most unfortunate situations is that man has always so strenuously resisted this glorious conception of his own destiny.

God has told us over and over again that he is our Father, and we ought to try to understand that greatest of all truths, and believe in him and in our own future and our own possibilities.

Someone has said, "I don't know what the future holds, but I do know who holds the future." We may not even understand very much about ourselves, but based on our obedience God has promised the greatest possible destiny to the members of his family. And as Emerson has said, "All that I have seen teaches me to trust in God for those things that I have not seen." And so we might say again, "We believe in God." We trust him and will follow him, and try to be worthy of his blessings.

We Would See Jesus

I WOULD LIKE TO recall to your minds one of the great scenes of the Holy Scriptures. It has been referred to as the Lord's Triumphal Entry into Jerusalem. After a long absence, Jesus and his disciples were making their way toward the temple for what was to be the last three days of the Lord's public ministry. As he came near the historic city, he wept because of the wickedness of its people.

The Feast of the Passover was at hand, and as he approached the city, other travelers, Jerusalem bound, merged with his party at the crossroads. Soon there was an imposing procession, with Jesus, as the central figure, riding upon a colt in fulfillment of an ancient prophecy. As they entered the Holy City, the people cast branches of Palm trees in his path, thus carpeting his way as for the passage of a king. And for the time being he was their king, and the voices of the multitude sounded in reverberating harmony saying, "Hosanna to the Son of David: Blessed is he that cometh in the name of the Lord." (Matt. 21:9)

This picturesque scene might well symbolize another coming, as the scripture projects our minds ahead to that time when, with holy angels, he will appear in flaming fire to cleanse the earth of sin, and to inaugurate the millennial era of a thousand years of peace during which Christ will reign personally as King of kings.

Among those attending this particular passover were certain Greeks who sought a conference with the Master. In making their request through Philip they said, "Sir, we would see Jesus." (John 12:21) In these five words they were also voicing an idea that has the greatest significance for every age. That is, what could be more helpful in our own days of miracles, atheism and crime, than for everyone to have an unshakable testimony of, and an inspiring personal relationship with, the divine ruler of this earth.

Since that long-ago day, some nineteen wide centuries have come and gone. And we now have the judgment of time shining upon the life of Christ, enabling us to see it in clearer perspective.

We are now aware that he is much more than a prophet from Nazareth. He is also the Son of God, the Savior of the world, the author of life, the Redeemer of men, and the giver of all good things. By absorbing the spirit of his life, understanding his doctrines, and following his example, we might hope that this ancient Grecian request to see Jesus would be granted in our own behalf. Certainly this request should represent the universal desire of all people. For as the sun is the center of the solar system, so is the Redeemer the center of our lives. Without the sun our solar system would fly apart, and without God the greatest values in our lives would be lost. As the Apostle Peter said, "Neither is there salvation in any other, for there is none other name under heaven given among men whereby we must be saved."

The prophets have looked forward to his coming since time began, and even as Jesus was being born wise men from the east were asking "Where is he that is born King of the Jews? for we have seen his star in the east, and are come to worship him." (Matt. 2:2) And that is what wise men have been asking and doing ever since. The Master himself said, "This is life eternal, that they might know thee, the only true God, and Jesus Christ whom thou hast sent."

After the people had listened to the preaching of the gospel at Pentecost, they were pricked in their hearts and, desiring the better way of life that had been recommended, they cried out to the apostles, "Men and brethren, what shall we do?" And Peter answered, "Repent and be baptized every one of you, in the name of Jesus Christ, for the remission of sins, and ye shall receive the gift of the Holy Ghost." (Acts 2:37-40)

People have found Jesus in different ways. The Greeks found him through Philip; the wise men from the east were led to Bethlehem by his star; Peter was taken to Jesus by his brother, Andrew; and Paul found him through a miracle on the Damascus road. Jesus gave his own formula for discovery when he said, "If any man will do [God's] will he shall know of the doctrine." (John 7:17) He also said, "Seek me diligently and ye shall find me." (D&C 88:63) However, the greatest tragedy of our world remains the fact that so many never attain this all-important objective. And yet only he who fails to seek fails to find.

Emerson pointed out the consequences of failure in this important quest when he said, "On the brink of an ocean of life and truth we are miserably dying. Sometimes we are furtherest away when we are closest by." So frequently that is true. Think how near they were who lived contemporaneously with Jesus. He walked among them, they heard him speak, they knew of his miracles and yet they were so far away that they said, "His blood be upon us and our children." And so it has been, and so it may be with us. We are so near, and yet we may be so far away. We are standing on the brink of an eternal life, and yet each must take the steps that will bring him there.

Jesus gave us the best approach for this accomplishment when, on the last day of the Passover Feast, he stood up and cried, "If any man thirst, let him come unto me and drink, and out of the belly of him . . . that believeth in me shall flow rivers of living water." (John 7:37-38) That is, our eternal success is not like pouring water into a cistern, rather it is like opening a living spring within ourselves. Through the Prophet Jeremiah the Lord said, "For my people have committed two evils, — they have forsaken me, the fountain of living waters, and have hewed them out . . . broken cisterns that can hold no water." (Jer. 2:13) And Jesus elaborated upon this idea by saying, "Unto him that keepeth my commandments I will give the mysteries of my kingdom, and the same shall be in him a well of living water, springing up unto everlasting life." (D&C 63:23) What a tremendous possibility for us!

As Jesus was passing through Samaria on his way to Jerusalem, he stopped to rest at Jacob's well near the ancient city of Shechem, and requested a drink from the woman of Sychar. He said to her, "If thou knewest the gift of God, and who it is that saith to thee, Give me to drink; thou wouldest have asked of him, and he would have given thee living water. . . . But whosoever drinketh of the water that I shall give him shall never thirst; but [it] shall be in him a well of water springing up into everlasting life." (John 4:10-14) Water is the universal element, and it is the symbol of life. Jesus used it to describe a personal testimony of his divinity. Pure water will also be one of the secrets of the earth's regeneration in preparation for its millennium. The Lord said, "And the parched ground shall no longer be a thirsty land." (D&C 133:29) However, the richest treasures do not come from water breaking forth in the wastelands of the desert.

The greatest enrichment comes when we acquire a personal testimony of the divine mission of the Savior of the world, and a firm determination to make our lives productive in godliness. Dr. Henry C. Link once said that nothing puts so much order into human life as to live by a good set of sound principles. And the soundest principles are the principles of the gospel of Jesus Christ. Water is also a symbol of cleanliness, and Jesus indicated that after cleansing ourselves with the soap and water of repentance we should be baptized and have our sins washed away by his atoning sacrifice.

Five days after the Greeks sought their interview, Jesus was crucified. In the following years his apostles were slain, his doctrines were changed, and the long black night of apostasy settled upon the world. In foretelling this event the Lord again used water as a figure of speech about obtaining the word of the Lord. Through the Prophet Amos he said, "Behold, the days come, saith the Lord God, that I will send a famine in the land, not a famine of bread, nor a thirst for water, but of hearing the word of the Lord; and (men) shall wander from sea to sea, and from the north even to the east, they shall run to and fro to seek the word of the Lord, and shall not find it." And the Lord added, "And in that day (they shall) faint for thirst." (Amos 8:11-13) But God always provides the remedy before the plague. On the Tuesday before his crucifixion on Friday, the Lord sat on the Mount of Olives and foretold the wars and troubles that would immediately precede his glorious second coming to the earth. And he himself made a solemn promise saying, "And this gospel of the kingdom shall be preached in all the world for a witness unto all nations; and then shall the end come." (Matt. 24:14)

In the early spring of 1820 in upper New York State in fulfillment of this promise, God the Father and his Son, Jesus Christ, reappeared upon this earth to reestablish among men a belief in the God of Genesis, the God of Calvary, and the God of the latter days. The eternal springs were reopened, divine revelation was again established from heaven. And the gospel of Jesus Christ was restored to the earth in a fullness never known before in the world. The universal thirst is now being relieved for all of those who effectively seek their Redeemer. By divine order the world has now been given three great volumes of new scripture, outlining in every detail those simple principles on which the exaltation and eternal happiness of every human life depends. On every fundamental point of doctrine we again have an authoritative "Thus Saith the Lord." We also have the testimony of many new witnesses supporting those of old that God lives, that the gospel is true, and that many of the great events spoken of in the scriptures are about to be fulfilled.

In our own day another prophet has known God as Moses did, face to face, and in bearing his certain witness he has said to us, "And now, after the many testimonies that have been given of him, this is the testimony, last of all, which we give of him: that he lives! For we saw him, even on the right hand of God; and we heard the voice bearing record that he is the Only Begotten of the Father — that by him, and through him, and of him, the worlds are and were created, and the inhabitants thereof are begotten sons and daughters unto God." (D&C 76:22-24)

The greatest opportunity of our lives is found in following the spirit of this ancient Grecian request saying, "Sir, we would see Jesus," and in consequence of our faithful, righteous search we may have an inspiring personal testimony of his divinity springing up in our own hearts.

Modern travelers to that ancient city of Shechem near the site of Jacob's well tell us that there are rivers of water flowing beneath the streets. During the daylight hours they cannot be heard. But when evening comes, and the clamor dies out of the streets, when kindly sleep rests upon the city, quite audibly in the hush of the night you can hear the music of these buried streams.

God has provided our earth with great underground reservoirs and buried rivers that may be brought to the surface to keep our earth productive and beautiful. Likewise there are some great unseen spiritual powers that can be used to vitalize our spirits and make our lives beautiful and happy. And in the quiet obedience of our faith and love of righteousness, God may touch those hidden abilities implanted in the depths of our souls and release great spiritual strength to purify our lives and bring about our eternal exaltation in his presence.

As someone has said, "What cool sparkling pure water is to the welfare of the rose, so is the spirit of Christ to my life." And may God help us to drink freely from those living waters that even now are springing up unto eternal life.

X the Unknown

MANY YEARS AGO in a beginning Algebra class, I was impressed with the use made by the teacher of the letter "X." It was a symbol standing for something else, and often representing the unknown answer. Then, by a little effective reasoning and a series of calculations, the scholar could solve the problem and discover the value of the "X." Since that time I have been impressed how we sometimes carry our algebra over into life. There are many things that we represent with an "X" because we don't know the answer. We sometimes even use an "X" to stand for the divine. Some people spell Christmas "X-M-A-S." The word Christmas was originally made up of two words meaning Christ's Mass. These words had a specific reference to a church festival held on December 25 in memory of the birth of Christ. But for many present-day people Christ has been taken out of Christmas, and all that is left centers around an unknown "X." There is also a group of people who have taken Christ out of their lives, and in many cases the purpose of life itself is unknown to them.

There are people who have been trying to get rid of God since time began. During the short life of Jesus, many references are made to those who were continually scheming about putting him to death. Sometimes when a writer wants to strike out his written ideas, he merely takes his pen and draws lines diagonally through the page. He makes a large "X" marking out what he doesn't want. But this is just about what some people have been doing to their Redeemer. They first killed his physical body, then in addition they have been trying to destroy his influence and kill any belief in him. God is dead in the lives of some, only because they have first reduced him to a nothing. It has always seemed a little astounding to me that some people have been so insistent about depriving God of his body, taking away his personality and denying his attributes, so that in some minds the once all-powerful Creator has become merely an "influence" or an "essence," or an "X" that no one can understand or be very interested in. After this downgrading of God goes on for a while he becomes so weak and unrecognizable in the minds of some that it is a short easy step to spreading the rumor that he is dead. God's death leaves many people free to go on making greater records in various kinds of crime, drunkenness, indecency and sin. We frequently operate a kind of reverse piety, where we merely "X" out the divine to relieve an uneasy conscience. The death of God would naturally leave a great void that would be quickly filled with evil. To some people God never lived in the first place, and to others he is only a misty fraction of reality. Many people, who think of him as some impotent unknown "X" that has no real significance, fill in the vacancy with profane oaths and other evidences of their disbelief. As the Lord was preparing to restore the gospel, he himself described our situation by saying, "They draw near to me with their lips but their hearts are far from me. They teach for doctrine the commandments of men, having a form of godliness, but they deny the power thereof." (Pearl of Great Price, Joseph Smith 2:19)

This attitude has been more or less characteristic of the men and women who have been trying to get rid of God. Because they lacked understanding the ancient Athenians had erected a monument on Mars Hill to the *unknown* God. Trying to help them fill in their spiritual vacuum, Paul said to them, "Whom therefore ye ignorantly worship, him declare I unto you." (Acts 17:22) Then Paul tried to explain to them about that great being who had created the heavens and the earth, who is our own eternal Heavenly Father. He quoted a statement of one of their poets saying that they were the offspring of God. Paul explained to these folks about the literal bodily resurrection promised to every child of God in the process of his eternal progression. In the resurrection the eternal spirits of the righteous will be inseparably connected with a resurrected, glorified, immortal, physical body. This is a part of the program to become like the resurrected Son of God and his and our Eternal Father. But instead of being willing to learn so that they might find out about God and do his will, the Athenians made the usual mistake of "X-ing" him out of their minds. They also "X-ed" out the teachings of Paul. The record says that when Paul mentioned the resurrection of the dead, some mocked and others crossed the whole idea off by saying "we will hear thee again on this matter." That is, the Athenians used the two most common methods of crossing God off their list. One was outright rejection, and the other was by indefinitely postponing any investigation. Consequently, when Paul left their city their chances of finding God went with him, and so to this day many of these good people are yet living in uncertainty and are still worshiping at the feet of the unknown God.

But many people besides the Athenians handle this important matter of religion in a peculiar manner. One of the most important events that ever took place upon this earth was the birth and ministry of Jesus Christ. He came to redeem us from sin and help us obtain eternal life and happiness. Like every other child of God, Jesus had a long ante-mortal existence in God's presence in heaven. The scriptures tell us clearly that he was the first begotten child of God in the spirit, and the Only Begotten in the flesh. In his long pre-mortal existence he had proven himself to be the most capable and worthy of God's spirit children. And he was one of those three individual beings who served in the presidency in heaven. Jesus, then known as Jehovah, was included in God's plural pronoun when, in referring to the mortal creation, Elohim the Eternal Father said, "Let *us* make man in *our* image, after *our* likeness." (Gen. 1:26)

In referring to Jesus, the Apostle John also makes clear that Jesus was in the beginning with God. He says, "all things were made by him and without him was not anything made that was made." (John 1:3) In a revelation to Moses, and revealed again in our day, God said, "And worlds without number have I created; and . . . by the Son I created them, which is mine Only Begotten." (Moses 1:33) Because he was the one best qualified to redeem man from his fallen state, he temporarily vacated his part of the presidency of the universe. He left his Father in heaven, and came to earth to perform the great service leading to our redemption.

We can only wonder at the treatment he was given. In spite of the fact that all of the details of his coming had been foretold, he was not treated kindly by the people. There was no room for him to be born in the inn. But this idea of "no room" became the continuing cry throughout his life. He was not very many days old before the fierce antagonism of Herod was turned against him. Herod sent soldiers to Bethlehem to kill the infants, to make sure that this new king would not remain alive. Because there was no room for him in the realm of Herod, Joseph and Mary were warned in a dream to flee with him into Egypt. As soon as his active ministry began, the unjust persecution greatly increased. Because his doctrines were incompatible with those of the religious leaders, there was no room for his teachings in their spheres of influence. After his shameful trial and condemnation, he was hung upon a Roman cross and had a Roman spear thrust into his side. But even after he had initiated the universal resurrection benefiting everyone who ever had or ever would live upon the earth — even then the world found no room for him. There was no room for his teachings, no room for his doctrines, no room for his religion. One by one his chosen apostles were eliminated by a violent death, and many of those who professed to follow him had soon fulfilled the prophecy of Isaiah which had said, "The earth also is defiled under the inhabitants thereof, because they have transgressed the laws, changed the ordinances, broken the everlasting covenant. Therefore hath the curse devoured the earth, and they that dwell therein are desolate." (Isaiah 24:5-6) In this universal apostasy from God the people had "X-ed" him and his doctrines out of their lives, and the long night of the dark ages settled upon the world to fill the void.

The present sad state of our affairs did not occur by an all-at-once kind of blow-out in our faith. Our loss of God could more properly be described as a series of slow leaks. By just a little disbelief and a little disobedience, a little sin, the people lost God. They first worked up enough antagonism to kill him physically. Then by rationalizing, doubting, belittling, and making allegories they killed the belief in his doctrines. They also "X-ed" out his personality traits, his abilities and his reality.

A great modern minister recently said "God is absolutely unknowable, indiscernible and undiscoverable. He is not limited to boundaries and we can be certain that he has no body or shape." This would make salvation impossible, as Jesus said, "This is life eternal, that they might know thee, the only true God, and Jesus Christ whom thou hast sent." But what kind of a father could be conceived that had no body, boundaries or shape? Certainly such a description would not apply to him who begot Jesus Christ and to whom Jesus directed his love and prayers. Or if God is undiscoverable, how did this great minister discover that God has no body?

The universal resurrection is one of the most important parts of God's program for our salvation. Jesus was not resurrected merely to suit some temporary convenience. At the resurrection his spirit and body were inseparably joined together. He took his body with him into heaven, and with it he again took up his position of presidency at the side of his Eternal Father. Jesus did not lose his identity, nor his memory, nor his personality, after his resurrection. He is still the resurrected son of God, and he is still in the express image of his Father's person, as under his Father he rules the universe. Both are individual, personal beings; both have bodies of flesh and bones. What a thrilling idea that God is God, that we can know him, and that he is actually the literal Father of our spirits; that we were created in his physical and spiritual image; and that we have been endowed with a set of his potentialities! How unfortunate are they who have tried to "X" out God's body, or his personality, or his identity, or his doctrine! There are too many people like the ancient Athenians who are still worshiping at the feet of an unknown and an unreal God, who never was. With many people, it is not only God who is unknown; his doctrines and his inspiration are also unknown. His personality is unknown, his modern-day revelations are unknown, and his future program for our eternal exaltation is unknown, and even his righteousness is unknown. The great minister referred to above, may not know — but I know, and many others know, that God is alive, that he has a body, and boundaries, and a personality. That he is our Eternal Father, that his laws are still in force, and the tremendous events that are in the immediate future of our world may make us very unhappy that we did not take time to get more accurate information so that faith and righteousness would not be "X-ed" out of our lives. It is not God who is dead, we are the ones who are dead and we, not God, are the ones who are also in danger of that more terrible second death.

This term "X" is a very interesting one. It is not only the 24th letter of the English alphabet, but also represents ten among the Roman numerals. It also has an interesting ability for effecting the value of the number next to it. When an "X" is placed in front of some other Roman numeral, it indicates that ten points must be subtracted from that number's value. When the "X" is placed behind some other number it means that ten points should be added. In Roman numerals "L" stands for fifty. But if you put the "X" behind the "L" its value is raised to 60. But if you put an "X" in front of the "L" it is reduced to a forty. Therefore, if "X" stands for the divine, we had better not be found on his wrong side with our lives filled with unrighteousness and sin. For the Lord said, "And the righteous shall be gathered on my right hand unto eternal life; and the wicked on my left hand will I be ashamed to own before the Father; Wherefore I will say unto them — Depart from me, ye cursed, into everlasting fire, prepared for the devil and his angels." (D&C 29:27-28)

The first and greatest commandment is that we should love God, and love truth, and love righteousness; and may God help us to get all of our X's behind us, in such a way that our scores with God may be increased.

You Were There

A NUMBER OF YEARS ago there was a very popular radio program going out over the airwaves entitled "You Were There." Each week the sponsor selected some important historical event with a common interest, and then with a group of competent actors the various scenes were dramatized as though they were actually taking place. Alert reporters assumed to conduct live interviews with the real people involved. And they supplied the listeners with hundreds of interesting details that would not ordinarily find their way into the history books or newspaper accounts. In "You Were There" one could go onto the battlefield while a decisive battle was being waged. Or he could sit at the table in the General's tent or assume any other vantage point in order to watch history in the making. Through a "you were there" experience one could become a part of the greatest events of any age and be an eye, ear, and soul witness of destiny being fulfilled. With this technique impressions were sharper and the effects in the listener were greatly increased. And while this radio program itself was only a fantasy, each of us have been personally equipped with the greatest "you were there" possibilities.

We frequently talk about the desirability of developing those important traits of sympathy, empathy, and understanding. We can actually learn to put ourselves in someone else's shoes, see things through their eyes and understand from their point of view. We can also learn to effectively transport ourselves across time to any given point in history. Under ordinary circumstances ideas usually don't get through to us with sufficient power. A deeper impression would be made if we had actually starved with Washington at Valley Forge, or suffered the pressures of discouragement and rebellion with Christopher Columbus. By making the great experiences more real we can multiply their effectiveness for our own benefit. About such an experience Frank Crane said, "My soul is a Columbus and no watery wastes nor gloomy fears shall ever turn me back, or make me cry enough."

We come fairly close to understanding this more intense kind of experience when we have a realistic dream. It may be a beautiful vision or some terrible nightmare, but it has more than ordinary power because "You were there." There is an old Spanish proverb that says, "He who would bring home the wealth of the Indies must carry the wealth of the Indies with him." That is, the experience itself must become a part of us.

The story is told of Gene Tunney training to win his championship fight with Jack Dempsey. Tunney internalized his training and increased his power by imagining that his sparring partner was Dempsey. As he took his running exercises he chanted slogans of victory. When playing golf it was always Dempsey that he was driving before his club. By actually living his ambition he got the fight into himself by a kind of "you were there" process. On a comparable basis we can also make a more effective reaction to our physical, mental, spiritual, or social environment. Our mental associations actually have some advantages over the physical. If one desires the surroundings of Waikiki Beach, or the atmosphere of St. Paul's Cathedral, or wishes to freshen his memory of what happened in the stable at Bethlehem, a physical journey may completely miss the desired emotion because the beach may be cold and stormy, or the cathedral may be closed up for repairs, and the ancient scene at Bethlehem may no longer be the same. But in our own "you were there" experiences we have much greater latitude, as we can more or less make our own environment. John Milton said, "The mind in its own place and of itself can make a heaven of hell or a hell of heaven." If we have a "you are there" ability we can hear the angels sing on the hills of Judea, or lay our own treasures at the feet of the newborn king under circumstances of our own choosing. We can also get more from reliving an original experience when we ourselves can set the stage. An actual experience also has the limitation that it usually takes place only once, whereas in our minds we can duplicate the original stage settings and then rerun the greatest of experiences again and again.

Someone has said that about the only thing that we ever learn from history is that we never learn very much. But that is not necessarily so. We can actually learn many things from the past if we see them clearly enough. There is a helpful learning technique in the movies that is called a flashback. With a flashback the producer can leave the present, and have his audience relive the past to better teach them how to cope with the present. We remember that in Charles Dickens *Christmas Carol*, a kind of flashback transported Scrooge back into his own past. Then, when he re-attained his own childhood, he was better able to recapture his more favorable Christmas experiences and reteach himself how to properly celebrate the Christmases of the present. When Scrooge had finished the experience he said, "I am not the man I was." Our memories of former events can be powerful instruments in molding our lives. Memories are such awful or such wonderful possessions, depending upon which kind they are.

The flashback is also the main tool of the psychiatrist. The secrets of our present frequently exist in the past, and in attempting to undo any past damage hiding in us the psychiatrist must go back to the time when the damage was being done. And he must then do a "you were there" for his patient. Then by eliminating the past injury he is often able to cure the present problem. God also uses this technique of a flashback into the past, in order to strengthen our present and our future. The Lord instituted the Passover among the children of Israel, and for hundreds of years he regularly reminded them of their deliverance from bondage. God took Abraham back into his own antemortal existence and let him relive some of those important events before the earth itself was organized. To let Abraham stand again in memory among the noble and great wonderfully increased his future power. The sacrament of the Lord's Supper is also a kind of flashback. Once each week with a "you were there" reality we partake of the emblems of his sacrifice for us and the atonement that he made for our sins.

Many years ago Mr. H. G. Wells wrote an interesting fantasy about a man who invented a time machine. In this machine he could travel through time much as an airplane could take him through space. By pressing a lever he could go thousands of years back into history. Being a historian himself, Mr. Wells took great delight in witnessing the important events of the past as they were actually taking place. He could personally verify the account of the Battle of Hastings by going back to the year 1066, or by going still farther back he could visit the golden age of Greece and personally discuss government with Pericles and philosophy with Socrates 400 years B.C. When the time traveler pushed the lever in the other direction he could go up into the future much as the prophets have done while receiving their visions. Many prophets have lived through important events thousands of years before they actually took place. We can now read John the Revelator's eye-witness account of the final judgment, which is even yet in the future.

In this idea we have the seeds of some of our greatest possibilities, as our minds have been divinely equipped with some interesting time machine functions. It has been said that this "mental maneuverability" is one of the greatest gifts that God has ever given to man. It makes it possible for our thoughts to travel backward or forward across time, and bring to us the greatest advantages from both directions. In processes called retrospection and meditation we can relive the past, and by this reflection we can re-absorb the original good from every past situation. Then, by pushing our mental lever forward, we can use our picturing power, our knowledge and our faith, to pre-live every important situation. With enough understanding and insight we can rerun the visions of the prophets with a "you were there" clarity. These great mental abilities were given to us for a good purpose, and it was God's intention that they be used. When he said, "Where there is no vision the people perish," he was trying to encourage us to develop the ability to look ahead. There is an important time-machine line in the Old Testament where it said, "Remember thy last end, and thou shalt never sin." (Eccl. 7:40) The Creator is saying that if we would pre-live the end of our lives before we get there, and then keep in mind the consequences of good and bad and what we would like the end of our lives to be, we would be so attracted by good and so repelled by evil that we would never sin. Certainly we can get great resolution and great faith from pre-living future events, as well as from reabsorbing the original good by reliving the past.

Because I have a special admiration for my pioneering great grandmother, I like to get into my time machine and go back to 1847 and walk with her across the plains while she was seeking a new home for her future family in the valleys of the Rocky Mountains. Her husband had been called to march to San Diego with the Mormon Battalion, and she brought their 8-year-old daughter and their scanty earthly possessions across the plains in a wagon drawn by an ox and a cow. On the plains the ox died. But my great grandmother lifted the yoke of the fallen animal onto her own shoulders and continued the journey.

Many times in my mind I have retraced her steps, and relived her struggles and hardships. In my imagination I get great pleasure from associating with her and trying to take some of the burden from her frail shoulders. I am also uplifted by sharing her courage and the faith that kept her going toward her destiny. My problems are very different from hers, but I like to hope that I have some of her kind of faith flowing in my veins. And I expect that my time machine will actually bring us together in the future life for some very pleasant associations.

One of the best ways to get the most good out of this "you were there" time travel is through the use of great books. There is a certain uplifting magic about books. When one becomes absorbed in a good book he may travel thousands of miles in any direction in just a few minutes. When you go to see someone at his home you may be told that he is in the library and you may see him sitting there with his back toward you, and yet the indicator of his time machine may tell you he is half way in his climb up Mount Everest, or before your presence recalls him to the library he may be sailing under the Polar Ice Cap, or marching with Jesus on his triumphal entry into Jerusalem. With all of our miraculous possibilities, how tragic when we waste our precious hours of life reliving the cheap stories of crime, violence and sin that we get in some movies and magazines! One time traveler said, "I prefer Goldsmith to golf, and Plutarch to a cocktail party." Guided by good books we can please any mood or build up any capacity or mount any summit of accomplishment.

Choosing to think in a little lighter vein, John A. Holmes writes:

> Every day in books
> Rip Van Winkle lies asleep,
> Moby Dick patrols the deep,
> Every day in books.
>
> Tall windmills turn in Spain,
> Where across the empty plain
> Rides the rusty knight in vain,
> Every day in books.
>
> Falstaff laughs, and Hamlet dreams,
> Camelot is all it seems.
> Kublai Khan in Zanadu
> Hears the rivers running thru.

And Marco Polo sails away,
Mr. Pickwick has his say,
Troy is falling every day,
Every day in books.

You can pass, and I can pass
Toward them, through the looking glass
Every day in books.

The most important experiences of life are stored away for our benefit in these wonderful instruments of our welfare called books. The Holy Scriptures themselves present one of the most amazing of our great opportunities. In the very beginning God instructed Adam. And to many of the great prophets since Adam, God has given a preview of the earth's history to the very end of time and beyond. Through the scriptures we may pre-live the resurrection, and the final judgment, and we may contemplate the wonders of the Celestial Kingdom, or through the scriptures we may go back into the past and absorb its every benefit. And we may go back and live in Jesus' day. Each year in our minds we may go back to Bethlehem to renew and strengthen the good in those events surrounding his birth. We also go with him into the temple in Jerusalem. We may visit his hometown of Nazareth, or sit with him at the last supper in the upper room. As we reread his sermons and think of what he did for us we may sing his praises, ask for his blessings and worship at his feet. With our time-machine ability we sing many songs wherein we go back some nineteen hundred years. In one we say:

I think when I read that sweet story of old,
When Jesus was here among men,
How he called little children as lambs to his fold;
I would like to have been with him then.

And whether child or adult, we can also be with him now. We can reread his words, rememorize his ideas, refeel his spirit, relive his religion and repractice his philosophy of life. Phillips Brooks said, "Be such a man and live such a life, that if every man were such as you, and every life a life like yours, then this earth would be God's paradise." And in this greatest experience may it be said of us "you were there."

Your Book of Proverbs

ONE OF THE IMPORTANT books in the Bible is the Book of Proverbs. It is a collection of profound truths, and thought-provoking maxims, intended to bring about a betterment in human conduct. It includes some the most pungent statements in the scriptures with many motivating ideas from the wisest men. Under the title of the Book of Proverbs has been assembled several thousand of the most noble axioms and finest adages that have ever come from human minds.

It is an interesting thought that all important things are made up of parts. A molecule is composed of atoms. An atom is a collection of electrons and protons. Books are made up of chapters. Chapters are assembled from paragraphs, and paragraphs are constructed from sentences, words, and letters.

Our greatest building responsibility is that of putting together our own personalities in such a way as to make the best and the most of our own possibilities. The wise man Solomon gave us the key to this success when he said, "As a man thinketh, . . . so is he." That is, we build our lives with ideas, and the quality of the individual thoughts that make up our philosophies, attitudes and ambitions will determine what we ourselves will become. Bible wisdom reminds us that we always get out of life about what we put into it. And when we get good ideas into our minds, they soon start operating in our hearts, activities, and accomplishments. Of course, there are many excellent proverbs that may be had from sources outside of the Bible.

The claim has been made that Benjamin Franklin was the wisest man ever produced in America. And he is remembered primarily for his proverbs. He made his living as a printer, and sent out in his newspaper short pithy statements to enlarge the minds of people. And as Oliver Wendell Holmes once said, "A mind once stretched by a new idea never returns to its original dimensions."

Because of the proverbial truth, that "the teacher always learns more than the student," it is suggested that each of us should write down some proverbs of his own. Solomon and Franklin prepared these capsules of wisdom to benefit other people, but their proverbs reacted inwardly to make their authors the wisest men of their time. We may also literally lift ourselves up by the bootstraps of our own wisdom after it has been made a part of us.

This principle of learning by teaching was once illustrated by a nationally famous life insurance salesman. Someone asked him how he got out of a sales slump. He replied that he usually took three or four of his fellow salesmen friends out to lunch. Then he gave them an enthusiastic discussion about how to sell life insurance. He didn't say what the discussion did to his friends, but after he had finished instructing them he had so greatly enlightened and motivated himself that thereafter any accomplishment seemed easy. Most worthwhile success begins with us. Success does not so much resemble pouring water into a cistern, it is more like opening a spring. When we give an idea its life and charge it with power, it always cuts a deeper pathway through our minds and makes a greater alteration in our personalities than those ideas do that we get from others.

Solomon prayed for wisdom to more effectively lead his people. Then by going to work thinking up and writing down his wisest thoughts, he helped to answer his own prayers. Just suppose that you undertook a similar project of writing down over three thousand proverbs, covering every subject, to be loved, memorized and lived by thousands of people in all future generations. If we prayed for wisdom and then worked as hard and as long as Solomon did in thinking, composing, testing, discarding, improving and memorizing, we would also be wise men.

Of course, we do not need to invent every good idea personally. There are thousands of old ideas of excellent quality that we haven't yet used. These can be memorized, practiced and made an integral part of us. If we effectively used each Bible proverb and each of those that made Benjamin Franklin great, our lives would also blossom with the same kind of success that distinguished theirs.

What an exciting thought that everything that has been well said belongs to us personally! The Apostle Paul said, "Whatsoever things are true, whatsoever things are honest, whatsoever things are just, whatsoever things are pure, whatsoever things are lovely, whatsoever things are of good report: . . . think on these things." (Phil. 4:8) In this thinking process we may even use the ideas of God himself in making our mental grooves so broad and deep that all future ideas will want to follow them.

Proverbs may also be used to correct our faults. If this seems too difficult we might try to find proverbs to correct the faults of other people. Then it is comparatively easy to incorporate our ready-made solutions into our own program. Or when we see someone else demonstrating some special virtues or helpful abilities, we may adopt them for our own use. Any abilities may be made to grow in our lives by filling our minds with their particular thought seeds. Even by helping others, we help ourselves. One proverb says, "Tow your brother's boat across and lo, your own has reached the shore." As soon as Solomon and Benjamin Franklin set out to solve the problems of others, they began solving their own more or less automatically. All great events first take place as thoughts in the mind. The problems of idleness, fear, immorality, and dishonesty that we can definitely solve in our minds even for other people can then be more easily solved in our own lives.

And many millions of people have changed their lives for good by reading, loving, and memorizing the great Bible proverbs. Just think how we might tone up our own lives by living the following. In the first chapter of the Book of Proverbs, it is written, "The fear of the Lord is the beginning of knowledge: but fools despise wisdom and instruction." The second chapter says "Walk in the way of good men, and keep the paths of the righteous." Here are some others. "My son, despise not the chastening of the Lord; neither be weary of his correction." 3:11. "Keep thy heart with all diligence; for out of it are the issues of life." 4:23. "A wise son maketh a glad father; but a foolish son is the heaviness of his mother." 10:1. "The way of transgressors is hard." 13:15. These lessons are all less expensive when learned from the book rather than from actual experience. "He that walketh with wise men shall be wise: but a companion of fools shall be destroyed." 13:20. "A soft answer turneth away wrath: but grievous words stir up anger." 15:1. "He that refuseth instruction despiseth his own soul: but he that heareth reproof getteth understanding." 15:32. "Pride goeth before destruction, and an haughty spirit before a fall." 16:18. "He that answereth a matter before he heareth it, it is folly and a shame unto him."

18:13. "A good name is rather to be chosen than great riches, and loving favor rather than silver and gold." 22:1. "Train up a child in the way he should go: and when he is old, he will not depart from it." 22:6. "A man that flattereth his neighbor spreadeth a net for his feet." 29:5. Of course, we are not limited to those proverbs recorded in the Bible. Some of the proverbs best suited to our need will frequently come either out of our own experience or from the experiences of others near to us. But they need to be given definiteness and importance by writing them down and memorizing them.

Suppose therefore that we make up our own collection of those well expressed principles that we expect to govern our lives. Every day most people meet up with enough good ideas to completely transform their success, but if these ideas are not impounded most of them will get away. If we wrote all of our own best ideas down, we would soon have a good answer for every need. Then they could be sharpened, polished and given power through activity. Jesus himself made great use of proverbs, many of which he took out of the Old Testament, and some he distilled from his own experience. He illustrated the greatest truths with everyday experiences and taught people wisdom from the things that they already understood.

In building our great, modern freeways, we have found it profitable to protect them with fences and illuminated markers. Delays and accidents are prevented by having some underpasses, overpasses, and interchanges. We no longer permit stray horses or other animals to wander across our highways to slow down our speed or cause us damage. But we should also create some spiritual safeguards to make that straight and narrow highway leading to eternal life safe for our souls to travel. Our lives can be guarded against evil and failure by erecting some good strong mental and moral fences out of those great ideas that we have memorized and made commitments to live by. When we are in danger of being injured by pride, we may flash upon the screen of our minds that great truth that says, "Pride goeth before a fall." When the foolishness of others attracts us, we can recite to ourselves the proverb that says, "The companion of fools shall be destroyed." In hundreds of great Bible proverbs we are urged to seek knowledge," "develop wisdom," "love righteousness" and "fear God." These should be made as solid as reinforcing steel in our souls. Our daily activities are made up of hundreds of problems, and we need hundreds of firmly-made ready-to-use answers. It is not always easy to do accurate, safe and original on-the-spot thinking; therefore, we frequently let our problems go unresolved unless we have on hand some prefabricated, pre-tested solutions ready for immediate use. For this purpose we may use the best thinking already done by the wisest men, the greatest prophets, and even God himself.

Our own book of proverbs will also serve us as a book of inspiration. Most of the problems of our lives can be anticipated. We can tell in advance that sometimes we will meet with discouragement. We know that there will be moments of weakness and temptation, hours of fear, and days of loneliness. To have our fortifications already erected and the solution previously worked out is the most valuable kind of wisdom. There are certain ideas that, if used, never fail to cheer us up. By proper preparation we may flood our minds with courage and infuse strength into our hearts at a moment's notice. We may develop some ready-made antidotes for loneliness, and provide such a reserve supply of virtues that we will never be at the mercy of temptation or fall to defeat's most dangerous ally, which is known as surprise.

Abraham Lincoln once said that when he was preparing for a debate he spent three-fourths of his time thinking about what his opponent was going to say, and one-fourth thinking of what he was going to say. Good hindsight is a common quality, but by thoroughly exploring all of the possibilities in advance, Lincoln was able to develop a foresight nearly comparable to his hindsight. By advance planning and advance organizing, Lincoln could plug up every loophole and stop every possibility of his opponent's escape. We can also greatly reduce the chances of our own failure by having a sufficient supply of these proverbial success elements readily at hand. Almost always we lose our contests with evil because we are not prepared. But we can inoculate ourselves against weakness and error by the use of these powerful little maxims just as a good doctor can immunize us against the measles. Properly used, good proverbs may guide our success and enable us to score a victory in every play of life.

Each member of a great football team is drilled in advance so that he knows what he should do in any given situation, without taking the day off to figure it out at the time it occurs. Even the substitute sitting on the bench is never idle. In his imagination he is always in the game. He knows that the same situations that are calling for answers now will be coming up again when he is carrying the responsibility for victory. If he can develop the strategy to solve the problems while he is sitting on the bench, he will be able to solve them more or less automatically when he is in the spotlight. It is the same in life. History repeats itself, and no one is allowed time out to solve his problems after the play has been called.

However, if solutions are worked out in advance, we may develop enough foresight to handle the hardest problems with ease and assurance, and thereby we may help God to answer some of our own prayers for wisdom. And that will help us and greatly please him.

Index